KARMA
Rhythmic Return to Harmony

Cover design by Carol W. Wells
COVER PHOTO BY MOLLY DEAN

KARMA
Rhythmic Return to Harmony

Edited by V. Hanson, R. Stewart & S. Nicholson

*This publication is made possible with
the assistance of the Kern Foundation*

The Theosophical Publishing House
Wheaton, Ill. U.S.A.
Madras, India/London, England

A publication of the Theosophical Publishing House,
a department of the Theosophical Society in America.

Library of Congress Cataloging-in-Publication Data

Karma, rhythmic return to harmony / edited by Virginia Hanson,
Shirley Nicholson, Rosemarie Stewart. -- 3rd ed.
  p.cm.
  Rev. and enl. ed. of: Karma, the universal law of harmony. 1981.
  "This publication is made possible with the assistance of the Kern
Foundation."
  Includes bibliographical references.
  ISBN 0-8356-0663-5
  1. Karma.   I. Hanson, Virginia.   II. Nicholson, Shirley J.
III. Stewart, Rosemarie, 1925- .   IV. Title: Karma, the universal
law of harmony.
BP573.K3K37 1990
291.2'2 -- dc20   90-50200
                                                              CIP

Printed in the United States of America

 recycled paper

A stone falls into the water and
creates disturbing waves. These
waves oscillate backward and forward
till at last . . . the water returns
to its condition of calm tranquility.
Similarly *all* action, on every plane,
produces disturbance in the balanced
harmony of the universe, and the
vibrations so produced will continue
to roll backward and forward . . .
till equilibrium is restored.

H.P. Blavatsky

Contents

Preface

In 1975 when Quest Books first published an anthology on karma, the concept was already becoming familiar in mainstream America. Introduced in the mid-1800s by Emerson and others who were studying Eastern thought, it was expounded in great detail in the late 1800s by H. P. Blavatsky, one of the founders of the Theosophical Society and author of the volumes of *The Secret Doctrine*, a major source book of modern esoteric studies. Those in the Theosophical movement and similar groups for long were the main custodians of ideas of the Ancient Wisdom such as karma.

Today the picture has changed. The word "karma" shows up in films, comic strips, conversations among ordinary people. Eastern and Western scholars, psychologists, astrologers, health practitioners, even students of society and economy have written about karma. This kind of literature had begun to appear in 1981 when the second and expanded edition of the Quest anthology came out. By now there is a wealth of material on the subject of karma that has originated outside of esoteric circles. The term is even included in English dictionaries.

The present volume includes fourteen articles that were not in the earlier editions, by such authors as Joseph Goldstein and Ananda Coomaraswamy, who write from the Buddhist position, Christopher Chapple, scholar who specializes in yoga philosophy, Alfred Taylor, research scientist, Liz Greene and Stephen Arroyo, psychologist/ astrologers, Roger Woolger and Harold Coward, Jungians.

Obviously, many points of view are covered, but they all contain, either explicitly or implicitly, the concept of karma as the harmonizer that restores balance, as the facilitator of a "rhythmic return to harmony." As Joy Mills said in the foreword to the earlier editions:

> The Sanskrit term, *karma*, has been adopted in English dictionaries as the all-embracing term for that universal law, the harmonic law of adjustment, of compensation, action-reaction, to which all natural processes are subject. The ramifications of the law must be endless and complex as those processes; yet in its ultimate simplicity, the law is harmony, the perfect relationship which obtains between all things everywhere.

It has become increasingly clear in recent years that we live in an interconnected, holistic universe in which "all things everywhere" are interdependent. In this context it is more evident than it was in the nineteenth century, when karma was introduced in the West, that past and future are connected, that events flow in the Whole where movement at any level of life affects all other levels. This current view of holism, which is held by many scientists, ecologists, philosophers, as well as esotericists, can easily accommodate the concept of karma. In the words of Prem and Ashish, who wrote from the point of view of *The Secret Doctrine*, (*Man, the Measure of All Things*, p. 210):

> Particular events take place . . . because of an organic linking of the whole of cosmic experience, a linkage which is such that all events in the Cosmos are bound together in one harmonious correlation.

In the overview of life implicit in much of modern thought, the concept of karma seems almost inevitable. Moreover, considering karma as it relates to such areas as Western psychology, social problems, spiritual growth, even economics throws new light on this ancient concept. The articles which follow should enrich our understanding of this simple yet complex law that operates continually in our lives and in the world.

Acknowledgments

This anthology is based on *Karma: The Universal Law of Harmony*, edited by Virginia Hanson and Rosemarie Stewart, Wheaton, IL: Theosophical Publishing House, Quest Books, 1981. The following articles are from that collection: Geddes MacGregor, "The Christening of Karma"; Dane Rudhyar, "The Transmutation of Karma into Dharma"; L. H. Leslie-Smith, "Karma and Reincarnation"; Clarence Pedersen, "The Source of Becauses"; Laurence Bendit, "Karma and Cosmos"; Felix Layton, "Karma in Motion"; Haridas Chaudhuri, "The Meaning of Karma in Integral Philosophy"; George E. Linton, "The Side Blows of Karma"; Virginia Hanson, "The Other Face of Karma."

"Karma as Organic Process" by Shirley Nicholson is a chapter called "Karma" in the author's book *Ancient Wisdom—Modern Insight,* Wheaton, IL: Theosophical Publishing House, Quest Books, 1985.

The compilers wish to thank the following publishers for permission to reprint their material:

"God Is Not Mocked" is an excerpt from *The Perennial Philosophy* by Aldous Huxley. © 1944, 1945 by Aldous Huxley. Reprinted by permission of Harper & Row, Publishers, Inc.

"A Buddhist View of Karma" is a chapter called "Understanding Karma: Cause and Effect" from *Seeking the Heart of Wisdom* by Joseph Goldstein and Jack Kornfield, © 1987. Reprinted by arrangement with Shambhala Publications, Inc., 300 Massachusetts Ave., Boston, MA 02115.

"Karma, the Link Between Lives" appeared on pp. 106-109 in *Buddha and the Gospel of Buddhism* by Ananda Coomaraswamy, D.Sc., New York: Putnam's Sons, 1916.

"Karma, Jung and Transpersonal Psychology" is an

article by Harold Coward titled "Karma and Rebirth in Western Psychology" in *Karma and Rebirth: Post Classical Developments* edited by Ronald W. Neufeldt, © 1986, Albany, NY: State University of New York Press.

"Psychic Scars" is excerpted from pp. 147-151 from *Other Lives, Other Selves* by Roger Woolger, copyright © 1987 by Roger Woolger, Ph.D. Used by permission of Doubleday, a division of Bantam, Doubleday, Dell Publishing Group, Inc.

"The Ancient Shape of Fate" is the Introduction in Liz Greene, *The Astrology of Fate*, 1984 (York Beach, ME: Samuel Weiser, 1984) pp. 1-14. Used by permission.

"Can We Avoid Karmic Debts?" is Chapter VII, slightly edited, from *The Secret Doctrine—Commentaries and Analogies*, Series I, by Alfred Taylor, Ph.D. Ojai, CA: The Krotona School of Theosophy Publications, No. 1, 1970.

Contributing Authors

Stephen Arroyo, M.A., is a marriage and family counselor. He has lectured at numerous international conferences and taught astrology and various healing arts at three colleges in California. A pioneer of person-centered astrology, he is author of many books including *Astrology, Karma and Transformation; Astrology, Psychology and the Four Elements;* and *Relationships—and the Life Cycles.* His writings have been translated into nine languages.

Laurence J. Bendit, M.D., was a psychiatrist, lecturer and author who held degrees of M.A., M.D., and B. Chir. (surgeon) from Cambridge University, as well as other medical diplomas. Among his best known works are *Self-Knowledge: A Yoga for the West, The Mirror of Life and Death, The Transforming Mind,* and with his late wife, Phoebe D. Bendit, *The Psychic Sense.*

Christopher Chapple, Ph.D., is Associate Professor of Theology at Loyola Marymount University in Los Angeles. He is author of *Karma and Creativity* and co-translator with Yogi Anand Viraj of *The Yoga Sutras of Patanjali.* Additionally, he edited *Samkhya Yoga Proceedings* and *Religious Experience and Scientific Paradigms,* both published by the Institute for Advanced Studies in World Religions. Dr. Chapple studied classical yoga for twelve years under the tutelage of Gurani Anjali, Founder and Director of Yoga Anand Ashram in Amityville, New York.

Diana Dunningham Chapotin was for many years on the the faculty of the Krotona Institute of Theosophy in Ojai, California. Originally from New Zealand, she teaches and lectures there, in Paris where she resides with her husband, at Krotona and elsewhere in the United States.

Haridas Chaudhuri, Ph.D., was President and Founder and Professor of Philosophy of The California Institute of Asian Studies (now California Institute of Integral Studies) in San Francisco. He served as President of the Cultural Integration Fellowship, dedicated to the promotion of cultural understanding between East and West. After receiving his doctorate from the University of Calcutta, he was a member of the educational service of the government of West Bengal and Chairman of the Department of Philosophy at Krishnagar College. He was a disciple of Sri Aurobindo. Among his books are *Integral Yoga; Being, Evolution and Immortality;* and *The Evolution of Integral Consciousness.*

Ananda K. Coomaraswamy (1877-1947) was Curator in the Department of Asiatic Art at the Boston Museum of Fine Arts, where he built the first large collection of Indian art in this country. He was a cardinal figure in twentieth-century art history and in the cultural confrontation between East and West. His writings, about a thousand items, range over the visual arts, aesthetics, literature, religion, metaphysics, and sociology.

Harold C. Coward, Ph.D., is Professor of Religious Studies and Director of the Humanities Institute at the University of Calgary in Alberta, Canada. Among his numerous articles and books are *Religious Pluralism and the World Religions, Sphota Theory of Language,* and *Jung and Eastern Thought.*

Ralph Waldo Emerson (1803-1882) attended Harvard and became a prominent Unitarian minister, but left the ministry to devote himself to writing and lecturing, through which he awakened a sense of spiritual seeking and intellectual independence in the young American nation. At his Concord, Massachusetts, home he gathered New England's finest philosophical minds (Hawthorne, Thoreau, Margaret Fuller, et al), and they brought into being the transcendentalist movement, encouraging a vision of broader spiritual values based on universal principles of wisdom and harmony. Among his essays, some of the best known are "Nature," "The American Scholar," and "Self-Reliance." His poetry was also published.

Joseph Goldstein has taught numerous meditation classes, workshops, and retreats and is one of the founders and primary teachers of the Insight Meditation Society in Barre, Massachusetts. He studied for many years in India and with the renowned Buddhist meditation master Anagarika Sri Munindra. He is author of *The Experience of Insight* and with Jack Kornfield of *Seeking the Heart of Wisdom.*

Ray Grasse, an artist, teacher and writer, is a long-time student of comparative religious traditions. He has published numerous articles in various journals and is presently working on two books concerning synchronicity and symbolism. He studied for fifteen years under two teachers in the Kriya Yoga lineage, Goswami Kriyananda (of Chicago) and Sri Shelly Trimmer, a direct disciple of Paramahansa Yogananda.

Liz Greene is an astrologer, artist, student of mythology, and a practicing Jungian analyst. She is author of several books including *Saturn: A New Look at an Old Devil, The Astrology of Fate, The Outer Planets and their Cycles,* plus children's books and a novel.

Virginia Hanson was Senior Editor for the Theosophical Publishing House and Editor of *The American Theosophist* from 1962 to 1975. Before retiring from the United States Government service, she was Publications Editor in the U.S. Department of Justice. She is author of a historical novel, *Masters and Men*, as well as other works of fiction, and of numerous articles. She is the original compiler of the anthology *Karma: Universal Law of Harmony*, on which this present work is based.

Edward Hoffman, Ph.D., is a licensed psychologist in the New York City area. He is author of several books on Jewish mysticism and spirituality, including *The Way of Splendor, Sparks of Light,* and *The Heavenly Ladder*. Dr. Hoffman's most recent project has been to coproduce a video entitled *A Mystical Journey Through the Hebrew Alphabet*.

Aldous Huxley is considered one of the greatest of modern English prose writers. Among his many novels are *Point Counter Point, Brave New World, Eyeless in Gaza,* and *After Many a Summer Dies the Swan*. He was interested in the spiritual world and the potentials of the human mind and was an early experimenter with psychedelics. His anthology, *The Perennial Philosophy*, documents the essential unity of religions.

Felix Layton, M.A., was educated in England, Canada, and the United States. For a number of years he was active in educational work at the international headquarters of the Theosophical Society at Adyar, Madras, India, serving as Principal of the Besant Theosophical School and, at a later period, as Principal of the Olcott Harijan Free Schools. He has traveled and lectured widely throughout India and other Asian countries, New Zealand, Australia, and Europe. He is presently Director of the Krotona Institute of Theosophy in Ojai, California. He is author of *Einstein's Theory in the Light of Theosophy* and with his wife Eunice Layton of *Life: Your Great Adventure*.

Anna Freifeld Lemkow, a Canadian of Russian birth, lives in New York City. From 1946 to 1975 she worked in the United Nations Secretariat as an economist in the area of economic and social development of developing countries. In 1981 and 1982 she submitted, on behalf of the Theosophical Society (Adyar), a series of papers on peace education curriculum to the U.N.-sponsored University for Peace, Costa Rica. These papers later led her to develop her book *The Wholeness Principle: Dynamics of Unity within Science, Religion and Society.*

L. H. Leslie-Smith, M.C., M.A., a graduate of Oxford, served for thirty-eight years on the editorial staff of *The Times,* London. He was General Secretary (President) of the Theosophical Society in England from 1965 to 1969 and also Chairman of the Theosophical Publishing House in London.

George E. Linton, a civil engineer, was on the staff for a number of years at the international headquarters of the Theosophical Society at Adyar, Madras, India, where he supervised the construction of a new building for the Adyar Library and Research Centre. He is a life-long student of Theosophy and the Ancient Wisdom.

Geddes MacGregor, Docteur-es-lettres, (Sorbonne), D.Phil., D.D. (Oxford), LL.B., F.R.S.L., L.H.D., is Emeritus Distinguished Professor of Philosophy and former Dean of the Graduate School of Religion, University of Southern California. He held the first Rufus Jones Chair of Philosophy and Religion. Recipient of the California Literature Award, he is author of twenty-four books including his well known *Philosophical Issues in Religious Thought,* as well as *Reincarnation in Christianity* and *The Christening of Karma.* He has lectured widely in American and other universities and, as an Anglican priest, has given more than forty years of ordained service to the Church. He is listed in *Who's Who in America, Who's Who in Europe,* and *Who's Who* (London).

William Metzger, D.Min., is Editor of *The Quest*, a quarterly journal of philosophy, science, religion, and the arts. He has been a journalist and an adult educator and is an ordained Unitarian Universalist minister. He holds the M.A. from the University of Chicago and D.Min. from Meadville/Lombard Theological School.

Shirley Nicholson is Senior Editor for the Theosophical Publishing House and the Quest Book imprint. She is author of *Ancient Wisdom—Modern Insight* and a study guide called *A Program for Living the Spiritual Life*, and has compiled two anthologies, *Shamanism* and *The Goddess Reawakening: The Feminine Principle Today*. Mrs. Nicholson was a teacher and counselor for some years and wrote a children's book, *Nature's Merry-Go-Round*.

Clarence R. Pedersen served as Publications and Marketing Manager for the Theosophical Publishing House from 1971 to 1987, after a business career. He served for two terms on the Board of Directors of the Theosophical Society in America.

Dane Rudhyar (1895-1986) for over sixty years attempted to transform the character of the assumptions and patterns of thinking that structure Western culture and way of life. He is perhaps best known for his pioneering work in reformulating astrology along contemporary psychospiritual lines. He was also a composer of avant-guarde music, a writer of musical and social criticism, poetry, and two published novels. In his eighty-fifth year he received honorary degrees from John F. Kennedy University and the California Institute of Transpersonal Psychology. He is author of over a thousand articles and more than thirty-five books, including *The Astrology of Personality, Astrological Mandala,* and *The Astrology of Transformation*.

Alfred Taylor, Ph.D. earned his doctorate in physiology at Oregon State College where he taught before becoming a research scientist in oncology at the Clayton Foundation

Biochemical Institute of the University of Texas. His original biological research resulted in nearly a hundred papers in scientific journals and included pioneer work in the field of viral etiology of cancer and other investigations in cancer chemotherapy and nutrition. Dr. Taylor served for some years as Director of Studies at the Krotona School of Theosophy, Ojai, California. His book *A Human Heritage* is an early endeavor to harmonize science and spirituality.

Roger J. Woolger, Ph.D., is a graduate of Oxford and a Jungian analyst. He is author of *Other Lives, Other Selves*, a definitive account of past-life therapy, and with his wife Jennifer Barker Woolger of *The Goddess Within: A Guide to Eternal Myths that Shape Women's Lives*. The Woolgers conduct Goddess workshops throughout the United States.

I

Understanding Karma

To the Western mind the Sanskrit term karma *may have an alien, at times even forbidding quality about it. For many it may conjure up images of fatalistic impersonality, of cold determinism, retribution, punishment. But is karma a cold, mechanistic principle? Is it punishment? And if it exists, how do we explain the fact that many seemingly good people suffer, while criminals often live comfortable lives? These are some of the basic questions addressed by authors in this section. They approach the meaning of karma from a variety of viewpoints, showing that it is both simple and complex, with many subtleties that are frequently overlooked by the casual observer of Eastern thought.*

Felix Layton begins by examining the most fundamental aspects of this principle and its balancing role in the lawful order of nature. Drawing upon the frequently made comparison with Newton's Third Law of Motion, he shows how karma is likewise a natural law with its own subtle "physics" that we can understand and consciously work with. Shirley Nicholson points out the less deterministic, more organic side of the law, drawing on analogies from nature that illustrate how karma is subject to the modification of newly emerging influences, and that it is multidimensional in nature, rather than purely linear and rigid. Emerson, in his classic essay, addresses the subtle qualities of karma-like compensation seen throughout nature in the interrelation of creatures and elemental forces. Especially in the lives of humans we see a sense of lawfulness in which every excess causes a defect, every defect an excess, and all seems governed by the "deep remedial force that underlies all facts." Leslie-Smith considers some facets of karma in the context of reincarnation, as causes develop over successive lives. Aldous Huxley portrays the concept of karma through the eyes of a twentieth-century intellectual. He reminds us that the process of karma cannot by itself deliver us from the bonds of time, that this can be achieved only through our own efforts and right conduct. Clarence Pedersen concludes with a look at karma in the larger context of creation, ethics, and mystical union.

1

Karma in Motion

FELIX LAYTON

Isaac Newton's Third Law of Motion states: "To every action there is an equal and opposite reaction." This is sometimes thought to be a statement of the Law of Karma. But Newton's three laws of motion consider only physical force, matter, and motion. Karma includes life, consciousness, and motive as well as physical force and matter. This article considers analogies between the limited laws of motion in the physical world and the all-inclusive principle of karma. It seeks by considering the laws of physical motion to gain increased understanding of the universal principle.

Imagine a large, heavy, steel ball at rest on a perfectly level plane. Imagine further that there is no friction between the ball and the plane. The ball will remain at rest until some force makes it move, but if it has once started to move it will continue to move indefinitely until something stops it. So said Sir Isaac Newton in his first Law of Motion, sometimes called the Law of Inertia, a law which has been verified countless times and seems to be common sense.

Now let a man somehow exert a force on this ball to push it in a certain direction. Let him continue to push the ball in the same direction for a long time. As long as he keeps pushing, the ball will move faster and faster. How fast it will finally move depends on how hard and how long the man pushes. This is according to Newton's second Law of Motion. Since this system is frictionless, when the man stops pushing, the ball continues to move in that direction.

Now suppose that the man who worked and pushed so hard, finds that he made a mistake and pushed the wrong way, and really wants the ball to go in the opposite direction! The ball now has "within it" the momentum which it stored when the man first pushed, and this momentum carries it steadily on in the direction of that first pushing in exact proportion to how hard and how long the man pushed—and if he pushed hard and long he will have to push exactly that amount in the opposite direction before he can stop the ball.

It all works out with absolute exactness. Knowledge of these laws is the basis for the calculations of forces to send space capsules on their way. Knowledge of the same laws enables us to calculate exactly what length of burn, generating a certain force, will slow, accelerate, or change direction a certain amount. One astronaut in flight remarked that we owe it all to Isaac Newton.

The laws seem to be absolute, and they apply not only to a single object and force but to any system of many masses and forces. Although first stated by Sir Isaac Newton they have been realities from the beginning of creation. They are part of the nature of things—or at least of the nature of force and matter.

Many people believe that there are correspondences between physical and spiritual laws. Let us first consider correspondences between these first two laws and wider fields.

The law of karma is often compared to Newton's third Law: "To every action there is an equal and opposite reaction," but perhaps even more interesting correspondences exist with the first two laws, and often those who quote the third law as an illustration of karma misunderstand Newton's meaning.

In laboratory experiments, and in the steel ball illustration two factors are involved: *force*, in the example, applied by the man pushing, and *matter*, in this case a steel ball. Let these two correspond to life and form or spirit and matter, or, in our illustration, to the unit of life or consciousness called a man linked to his bodies or personality represented by the steel ball. Let us assume that this life or consciousness functions *within* the body, or the steel ball, and not externally in the same way that the engine functions inside a car.

When such a unit of life, or consciousness, is starting its series of incarnations, it is attached to a body which as yet is at rest, like the ball, for no force has yet acted through it. The boundless level plane on which the ball can be pushed in any direction corresponds to nature, which will allow us to move in any direction we want—if we work hard enough. As astronaut Eugene Cernan said, "Things may come with difficulty but nothing is impossible to man."

The unit of life, the human being, looking out through the senses of the body, sees things he or she desires. This causes a person to work, to strive to obtain them—to move toward them. Suppose he or she is attracted to wealth. He wants it. He works for it. He struggles and pushes toward it. Perhaps he does this for many lives. In doing so he is building an ever greater momentum in the direction of wealth, for nature gives to man that for which he works. When he obtains it however, he may find that it does not give him the happiness for which he had hoped. He ceases to push and strive toward the goal of wealth. He may continue to coast effortlessly, carried along by his past efforts, but his desires will soon be attracted to another goal and he will begin to try to move in a new direction. However, all his past effort over a long time has built a momentum in the direction of wealth and this keeps him moving in that direction until, after long struggle and pushing against circumstances which seem to frustrate his every effort to move in the new direction, he eventually stops the movement and is free to move in another direction. If this analogy holds, these forces are not merely equal to, they actually are the forces he himself has generated and is now opposing. The more strongly he struggles to stop the ball and move toward the new goal, the more violent will be his conflict with these forces of the past, but the sooner they will be overcome. A believer in karma would say that he is working out his karma.

The shifting of the individual's goal in life usually is

toward a nobler goal and comes after some sort of "revelation" or expansion of consciousness. In the nature of things
it is then that one tries to move in a new direction and meets
the forces generated earlier, which might be called one's
karma. Perhaps in this lies an explanation of the phrase,
"Whom the Lord loveth he chasteneth." We consider one
whom the Lord loveth to be one who has seen a great goal,
such as the service of humankind, and is struggling toward
that. Such a person is therefore probably facing momentum
and forces he or she created when moving in other directions
and struggling toward less noble goals. The struggle to
overcome this momentum would be the chastening.

When individuals perform "wrong" acts, which cause pain
to another, they do it only because they know no better. It
is not wrong for them. They are ignorant, as yet. If the karmic
consequence of pain returned to them immediately they
would probably resent it, fight against it, consider the world
unfair. They would learn nothing and would probably make
the same mistake again. If however, the Lords of Karma
defer payment, so to speak, until they "change direction"
and then allow them to meet the consequences of their acts,
they may then be in a condition of mind which will enable
them to learn from the experience of pain and replace the
ignorance, which made them perform the wrong act, which
with wisdom will prevent them from making that mistake again.

When a cannonball is shot from a cannon, the explosion
causes a force to act on the ball and shoot it from the cannon's
mouth. If this is the action, then the reaction of which
Newton spoke is the force which pushes back on the cannon
and causes it to recoil. His third law, applied to this case
would mean that the force acting on the cannonball is equal
to the force reacting on the cannon, and that they act in
exactly opposite directions. This has an interesting correspondence, for just as the action of firing the shot cannot
be performed without reaction on the cannon, so individuals
in this world cannot perform actions which do not react
on others. They must create karma with one or many others,
or with the whole world, on whom their actions produce

an equal and opposite reaction. As with the gun, someone has to absorb the recoil. Acts may be of hate, of love, or mixtures of the two, but whatever they are they act and react, and these actions and reactions are always equal and opposite. In this example, action which shoots the ball in one direction makes the gun recoil, and this reaction or recoil is absorbed into the great mass of the earth, disturbing the whole earth's motion and equilibrium. The shock wave of big guns being fired can be felt to shake the ground at considerable distances, as the earth patiently absorbs the shocks. When the action has been performed, the earth's motion has been altered; it may have been accelerated, reduced, or pushed sideways. This alteration to the earth will be too small to measure but the motion of the ball may be very fast. Eventually the ball will hit the earth again and stop. When this happens it returns its energy to the earth; equilibrium is restored, for it exactly neutralizes the disturbance to the earth's motion, made when the gun was fired. The ball may be in the air for a relatively long or short time before it hits the ground, but eventually the disturbance to the earth's motion will be neutralized.

There are correspondences between this example and the law of karma that emphasize the reality of the unity of humanity for, whether we like it or not, everyone in the world is affected by every individual action, as the whole world is affected by the firing of every gun. Let the firing of the cannon in the example correspond to an act performed by an individual. This greatly affects that person as the explosion greatly affects the cannon ball, and it slightly affects the whole world. The condition of imbalance exists between the individual and the world until the karmic consequences are met, just as the ball hits the earth and equilibrium is restored.

The timing of the reaction is of crucial importance. When does this karmic reaction which restores equilibrium occur? There are references which suggest that at great sacrifice to those who perform the work, karmic consequences may be held back. The moment of impact of the cannon ball, which could be devastating to the individual, may be delayed until the individual is strong enough and in a condition to profit by facing such shocks. One such reference in *Light on the Path* says:

> ... try to lift a little of the heavy karma of the world; give your aid to the few strong hands that hold back the powers of darkness from obtaining complete victory.[1]

It may well be that in the early stages of human evolution, and probably today also, people are creating more karma of a destructive, painful type than of a constructive, helpful type. Perhaps in some way, at the cost of untold sacrifice, great Intelligences, Lords of Karma, take some of these ugly, painful forces and store them in their own consciousnesses until humanity and its individuals are ready and able to face them. When that time comes, their sacrifice will be over, and the world, which could be overwhelmed if karmic settlements were promptly and automatically made, will literally have been saved. Perhaps such are the Lords of Karma and this is part of their function.

A later reference in *Light on the Path* describes a time when the individuals reach a stage where they can force the karmic consequences of their earlier selfish acts and take back the load which the Lords of Karma have been carrying for them. It suggests that there will now come a great clearing up and an opportunity for learning from this karma of the past as we do our part "to lift a little of the heavy karma of the world." Henceforth we will not be shielded but must face the full karmic consequences of our acts. The passage is an interesting reversal of the way the law of karma is usually stated:

> Out of the silence that is peace a resonant voice shall arise. And this voice will say: It is not well: thou hast reaped, now thou must sow. And knowing this voice to be the silence itself thou wilt obey.[2]

It is said that when individuals complete their human pilgrimage they are no longer the slaves of karma; they reach a state of karma-less-ness. This happens, it is said, when their actions are completely selfless and their wills (sublimated desires) are one with the One Will. Ordinary actions are self-centered and may be compared to the cannon ball flying within the earth's gravitational field. It is the self-centeredness which eventually draws the reaction back to the doer, just as it is the earth's gravitational field which eventually draws the cannon ball back to earth. The completely unselfish action of the Adept, however, is not drawn back and neutralized. It might correspond to shooting a capsule into space which does not return and neutralize itself in earth impact. The laws, possibilities, and limitations of such selfless acts may correspond to completely different phenomena as the weightless world of space travel is completely different from our gravity-bound life on earth.

This article has considered only some details of karma. It has made no attempt to cover the whole sweep of the great law. The examples have been extremely simplified in order to make principles stand out. Only closed systems with two or three factors have been considered. Such simplification is used in early experiments in laboratories where students are learning to understand basic laws. The problems of engineering and physics, which they will study later, involve using these laws in complex open systems with many bodies, forces, actions and reactions, all interacting on one another. The painstaking application of the simple law to one part after another of the complex gives one the capacity to understand, balance, and control the resultants of such interconnected factors. Similarly, there may be principles considered in this article which can be used first to understand, and then partially to control the enormously complicated interacting systems of life which surround us with countless individuals, forces, actions, and reactions. Perhaps this article may suggest further correspondences. It seems a fruitful field. The correspondences have not been suggested as mere intellectual games but as ideas with practical yet spiritual significance.

References

1. Collins, Mabel, *Light on the Path*, Part I, Note to Rule 20.
2. Ibid., Part II, opening lines.

2
Karma as Organic Process

SHIRLEY NICHOLSON

*As no cause remains without its due effect from
greatest to least, from a cosmic disturbance down to
the movement of your hand, and as like produces
like, Karma is that unseen and unknown law which
adjusts wisely, intelligently, and equitably each
effect to its cause, tracing the latter back to its producer.*

The Secret Doctrine

Karma, the concept of cause and effect from Buddhism
and Hinduism, has become widely known in the West, as it
has always been in the Orient. The word has found its way
into conversations among people at all levels of Western
society and has even shown up in popular music. However,
most people familiar with the idea think of it as shaping
our personal lives, as "paying us back" for our actions,
good and bad. This perhaps is the realm in which karma
seems closest to us. Yet karma is a universal law inherent
in the One and encompasses all of manifestation, all kingdoms of nature, from atoms to galaxies, from rocks to human
beings. H. P. Blavatsky, who introduced esoteric studies in
the West in the 19th century, assures us "every creature is
subject to Karma,"[1] "no spot in the manifested universe is
exempt from its sway."[2]

She states that "the One Life is closely related to the One
Law which governs the world of Being—Karma,"[3] and that
this is "the *Ultimate Law* of the Universe." She says that it
"exists from and in eternity, truly, for it is eternity itself."[4]
Its reaches are far greater than our human affairs. Like all

10

the principles outlined in esoteric philosophy, karma is an aspect of the one nonmaterial Reality that comes into play as manifestation proceeds. Karma as the law of cause and effect is involved in all differentiation and all relationships, spiritual as well as physical. Therefore, it must have become active at the awakening of the universe with the polarization of consciousness and matter. The first manifestation of cause and effect occurred when consciousness as Divine Mind began to create a world by impressing organization on precosmic matter. This, presumably, is the beginning of karmic action, which continues on every level of being throughout the entire cycle of manifestation.

> At the first flutter of renascent life . . . 'the Mutable Radiance of the Immutable Darkness unconscious in Eternity' passes, at every new birth of Kosmos, from an inactive state into one of intense activity . . . it differentiates, and then begins its work through that differentiation. This work is Karma.[5]

H.P.B. defines karma as "the unerring law which adjusts effect to cause on the physical, mental, and spiritual planes of being."[6] She depicts it as a law of harmony that continually restores the naturally harmonious state of the cosmos whenever it becomes disturbed. "The only decree of Karma —an eternal and immutable decree—is absolute harmony in the world of Matter as it is in the world of Spirit."[7] Karma "restores disturbed equilibrium in the physical and broken harmony in the moral world."[8] She compares it to a bough which "bent down too forcibly, rebounds with corresponding vigor."[9] Thus karma appears not as an external law acting from the outside but as an elastic quality of the cosmos itself, which causes it to spring back into harmony when distorted.

The Secret Doctrine does not depict karma mechanically or as "an eye for an eye" doctrine as some later writers have interpreted it. H.P.B. does not predict a one-to-one relationship between cause and effect—a predetermined course in which certain types of actions always have the same karmic consequences. In her view karma is not a mechanical system in which engaging a gear moves a cam, that in turn eventually turns a wheel, in a prescribed, linear, cause-and-effect manner. This kind of causality implies a rigid determinism—an unalterable sequence of events—which is not in keeping with theosophical philosophy. Rather, karma is fluid and flexible, as outcomes are continually shaped by the input of new factors. "Karma does not act in this or that particular way always."[10] Rather it works in an interconnected system in which everything affects everything else.

The workings of karma might be compared to the complexities of weather patterns. Huge areas of high and low pressure swirl through the atmosphere replacing one another, causing winds and many atmospheric conditions. Moisture from the earth rises and forms clouds, which may blow hundreds of miles before releasing their moisture as rain or snow. The jet stream high above the earth has an effect, as do deserts created centuries ago by nomadic peoples who overgrazed their herds. Seas of blacktop and concrete in modern cities play a part. The weather at a given place on a given day results from a combination of innumerable factors, past and present, local and distant, and new influences keep entering the system to change the outcome. Karma, too, is multidimensional, not linear. It is affected by and works on physical, mental, and spiritual levels, on all the planes and fields of nature. It brings into play influences from the distant past as well as those of the moment. Though determined by the past, the future is far from set. It is the result of countless causes. Prem and Ashish bring out the wholeness within which karma works:

> No *thing* causes any other thing, for causality resides not in things but in the whole. Particular events take place not because of any power in some other events which are said to be their causes, but because of an organic linking of the whole of cosmic experience, a linkage which is such that all events in the Cosmos are bound together in one harmonious correlation. Movement of any one "part" or element of the Cosmos necessitates movements of all the other elements, not because of any direct "causal power" exerted by the first but because all exist together in one seamless garment that is the Whole.[11]

Karma is involved in the vast sweeps of cyclic life that wheel behind evolution, which are "pre-ordained, so to say, by Karmic law."[12] While the law of cycles sets manifestation going in recurrent patterns, it is karma that fashions the specific events within the cycles.

[It is] the mysterious guiding intelligent power, which gives the impulse to and regulates the impetus of cycles and universal events.... Karma's visible adjuster on a grand scale.[13]

Karma connects each cycle of manifestation to all the previous ones, as "the working of Karma [is] in the periodical renovations of the universe."[14] The geological ages, the birth and death of species and kinds of plants and animal life, the coming and going of great races of men, the rise and fall of civilizations are all involved in karmic continuity. "There is a predestination in the geological life of our globe, as in the history, past and future, of races and nations. This is closely connected with what we call Karma."[15] It embodies what might be called a law of universal conservation—ensuring that nothing is lost, that the fruits of one cycle are passed on to the next.

Individual Karma

Karma also acts intimately and precisely in the affairs of individuals. While cosmic karma rolls on in grand cycles, individual karma gathers together tendencies and discharges them as events in our lives and evokes our inherent characteristics, whether physical, emotional, or intellectual. We all receive the repercussions of our own acts and thoughts, our personal karma. Just as each person has an individual scent which can be detected by a dog, it seems that each individual can be "sniffed out" by forces of karma. In the unimaginably complex karmic currents set up by humanity, in some mysterious way our own waves ripple out and return precisely to us. H.P.B. likens the process to the effects created by a stone falling into a pond and setting up waves which roll back and forth until equilibrium is restored, and the pond is again quiet. All action, no matter on what level, produces such disturbances.

But since each disturbance starts from some particular point, it is clear that equilibrium and harmony can only be restored by the reconverging *to that same point* of all the forces which were set in motion from it. And here you have proof that the consequences of a man's deeds, thoughts, etc., must all react upon *himself* with the same force with which they were set in motion.[16]

According to esoteric philosophy, as humanity won through to the higher levels of mind and became capable of choice, individuals became responsible for their actions in a way not possible among lower animals. With this responsibility came personal karma. According to this doctrine, we ourselves are responsible for our lives, for our circumstances, our pain and joy, our opportunities and limitations, even our character traits, talents, neuroses and personality blockages. Everything about us is the outcome of forces we ourselves have set in motion, either in this life or in some distant past. We are "under the empire of [our] self-made destiny."[17] Karma has given us back the actual consequences of our own actions. The way we live, our actions and thoughts, enter a continuous stream of causes that determine our lives. Nothing is lost. All the thoughts, motives, emotions which we generated in the past have gone into the complex strains that make us what we are today. "It is not . . . karma that rewards or punishes us, but it is we who reward and punish ourselves."[18]

However, as karma works with cycles and evolution on the grand scale, so does it work with evolution to promote growth in our individual lives. It "adjusts wisely, intelligently, and equitably each effect to its cause,"[19] reflecting our past actions in our outer lives and in our inner make-up. Thus our lives give us feedback, if we know how to read it, showing us a record of how we are doing, what is going well, where we have erred and failed. Because of karma we can learn from life.

It must be stressed, however, that karma is not fatalism or determinism. Prem and Ashish point out that our lives are neither absolutely determined nor absolutely free. We live according to "a determined track within whose unformed potentiality lies the opportunity for change and growth."[20] We cannot erase influences we generated in the past, but we can influence the course of our lives at any time by pouring in new energies in new directions. We may not see the results immediately, but karma assures that they will come, as any energy we generate must have its effect. Scanning our lives for recurrent patterns can reveal the areas in which we need to work. If we repress harmful tendencies, try to eliminate defects, and counteract negative elements within us, we set up new causes which alter the karmic outcome of past actions. Any help we offer others, any service we perform for worthwhile causes, any helpful, positive thoughts and emotions we send out will affect the karmic balance. In this realm right motives, feelings, and thoughts are more important even than right action, for energies from higher planes or fields are more powerful than physical energies. According to H.P.B.:

> It is a law of occult dynamics that a given amount of energy expended on the spiritual or astral plane is productive of far greater results than the same amount expended on the physical objective plane of existence.[21]

Thus love and hate are powerful factors in fashioning our karma.

Karmic Interconnections

H.P.B.'s exposition of karma also includes group and national karma. The strands of our individual karma are interwoven with those of our nation and other groups with which we have strong ties. All social evils are karmic, as are social opportunities. We each participate karmically in the actions of our nation, whether we like those actions or not. As groups are interdependent in a society and nations are interdependent in the world, each individual is in some ways karmically linked with all others, and we all share in the outcome of world events.

Thus in a sense our actions do affect all mankind. We tend to see our lives as in a limited sphere, our influence extending only to those in our immediate vicinity. But, as we have seen, the universe is not created from isolated bits. It is a vast network of interconnections in all directions, at all levels. Our actions do not stop at the periphery of our vision but affect the whole of life in some measure, one way or another.

In *Light on the Path*, a mystical work by Mabel Collins, there is a small essay on karma attributed to a great sage and Master. He likens the individual life to a rope composed of innumerable fine threads. From time to time some of these threads get caught or attached to something, creating a tangle and disorder in the whole. Sometimes one or more of the threads becomes stained, and the stain spreads and discolors other strands. But in time the threads pass out of the shadow into the shine, where they become golden and lie together straight and even. At last harmony is established. This revealing image illustrates the holistic nature of karma. The essay goes on to say:

> What it is necessary first to understand is not that the future is arbitrarily formed by any separate acts of the present, but that the whole of the future is in unbroken continuity with the present, as is the present with the past.[22]

As each individual life is composed of intertwined threads, so the whole of humanity is composed of individual lives intertwined and continually influencing one another. To the degree that we deliberately try to improve the energies we contribute to the whole, so in this world of interconnections will we be able to "lift a little of the heavy karma of the world."

References

1. H. P. Blavatsky, *The Secret Doctrine*, (Adyar: Theosophical Publishing House, 1978). 2:361.
2. H. P. Blavatsky, *The Key to Theosophy*, Joy Mills, ed. (Wheaton, IL: Theosophical Publishing House, 1981).
3. *Secret Doctrine*, 2:359.

4. Ibid., 3:306.
5. Ibid., 2:360.
6. H. P. Blavatsky, *Key to Theosophy* (see chap. 2, n. 6), p. 121.
7. *Secret Doctrine*, 2:368.
8. *Key to Theosophy*, p. 124.
9. *Secret Doctrine*, 3:306.
10. *Key to Theosophy*, p. 124.
11. Prem and Ashish, *Man, the Measure of All Things*, (Wheaton, IL: Theosophical Publishing House, 1969), p. 210.
12. *Secret Doctrine*, 2:367.
13. Ibid., 3:60.
14. Ibid., 2:362.
15. Ibid., 2:366.
16. *Key to Theosophy*, p. 16.
17. *Secret Doctrine*, 2:364.
18. Ibid., 2:365.
19. *Key to Theosophy*, p. 121.
20. Prem and Ashish, *Man, the Measure*, p. 114-5.
21. *Secret Doctrine*, 2:369.
22. Mabel Collins, *Light on the Path* (Pasadena: Theosophical University Press, 1976), p. 88.

3

Compensation

RALPH WALDO EMERSON

The wings of Time are black and white,
Pied with morning and with night.
Mountain tall and ocean deep
Trembling balance duly keep.
In changing moon, in tidal wave,
Glows the feud of Want and Have.
Gauge or more and less through space
Electric star and pencil plays.
The lonely Earth amid the balls
That hurry through the eternal halls,
A makeweight flying to the void,
Supplemental asteroid,
Or compensatory spark,
Shoots across the neutral Dark.

Man's the elm, and Wealth the vine,
Stanch and strong the tendrils twine:
Though the frail ringlets thee deceive,
None from its stock that vine can reave.
Fear not, then, thou child infirm,
There's no god dare wrong a worm.
Laurel crowns cleave to deserts
And powers to him who power exerts;
Hast not thy share? On winged feet,
Lo! it rushes thee to meet;
And all that Nature made thy own,
Floating in air or pent in stone,
Will rive the hills and swim the sea
And, like thy shadow, follow thee.

Ever since I was a boy I have wished to write a discourse on Compensation; for it seemed to me when very young that on this subject life was ahead of theology and the people knew more than the preachers taught. The documents too from which the doctrine is to be drawn, charmed my fancy by their endless variety, and lay, always before me, even in sleep; for they are the tools in our hands, the bread in our basket, the transactions of the street, the farm and the dwelling-house; greetings, relations, debts and credits, the influence of character, the nature and endowment of all men. It seemed to me also that in it might be shown men a ray of divinity, the present action of the soul of this world, clean from all vestige of tradition; and so the heart of man might be bathed by an inundation of eternal love, conversing with that which he knows was always and always must be, because it really is now. It appeared moreover that if this doctrine could be stated in terms with any resemblance to those bright intuitions in which this truth is sometimes revealed to us, it would be a star in many dark hours and crooked passages in our journey, that would not suffer us to lose our way.

I was lately confirmed in these desires by hearing a sermon at church. The preacher, a man esteemed for his orthodoxy, unfolded in the ordinary manner the doctrine of the Last Judgment. He assumed that judgment is not executed in this world; that the wicked are successful; that the good are miserable; and then urged from reason and from Scripture a compensation to be made to both parties in the next life. No offense appeared to be taken by the congregation at this doctrine. As far as I could observe when the meeting broke up they separated without remark on the sermon.

Yet what was the import of this teaching? What did the preacher mean by saying that the good are miserable in the present life? Was it that houses and lands, offices, wine, horses, dress, luxury, are had by unprincipled men, whilst the saints are poor and despised; and that a compensation is to be made to these last hereafter, by giving them the like gratifications another day,—bank-stock and doubloons, venison and champagne? This must be the compensation intended; for what else? Is it that they are to have leave to pray and praise? to love and serve men? Why, that they can do now. The legitimate inference the disciple would draw was,—'We are to have *such* a good time as the sinners have now;'—or, to push it to its extreme import,—'You sin now, we shall sin by and by; we would sin now, if we could; not being successful we expect our revenge tomorrow.'

The fallacy lay in the immense concession that the bad are successful; that justice is not done now. The blindness of the preacher consisted in deferring to the base estimate of the market of what constitutes a manly success, instead of confronting and convicting the world from the truth; announcing the presence of the soul; the omnipotence of the will; and so establishing the standard of good and ill, of success and falsehood.

I find a similar base tone in the popular religious works of the day and the same doctrines assumed by the literary men when occasionally they treat the related topics. I think that our popular theology has gained in decorum, and not in principle, over the superstitions it has displaced. *But men are better than their theology.* Their daily life gives it the lie. Every ingenuous and aspiring soul leaves the doctrine behind him in his own experience, and all men feel sometimes the falsehood which they cannot demonstrate. For men are wiser than they know. That which they hear in schools and pulpits without afterthought, if said in conversation would probably be questioned in silence. If a man dogmatize in a mixed company on Providence and the divine laws, he is answered by a silence which conveys well enough to an observer the dissatisfaction of the hearer, but his incapacity to make his own statement.

I shall attempt in this and the following chapter to record some facts that indicate the path of the law of Compensation; happy beyond my expectation if I shall truly draw the smallest arc of this circle.

Polarity, or action and reaction, we meet in every part of nature; in darkness and light; in heat and cold; in the ebb and flow of water; in male and female; in the inspiration and expiration of plants and animals; in the equation of quantity and quality in the fluids of the animal body; in the systole and diastole of the heart; in the undulations of fluids and of sound; in the centrifugal and centripetal gravity; in electricity, galvanism, and chemical affinity. Superinduce magnetism at one end of a needle, the opposite magnetism takes place at the other end. If the south attracts, the north repels. To empty here, you must condense there. An inevitable dualism bisects nature, so that each thing is a half, and suggests another thing to make it whole; as, spirit, matter; man, woman; odd, even; subjective, objective; in, out; upper, under; motion, rest; yea, nay.

Whilst the world is thus dual, so is every one of its parts. The entire system of things gets represented in every particle. There is somewhat that resembles the ebb and flow of the sea, day and night, man and woman, in a single needle of the pine, in a kernel of corn, in each individual of every animal tribe. The reaction, so grand in the elements, is repeated within these small boundaries. For example, in the animal kingdom the physiologist has observed that no creatures are favorites, but a certain compensation balances every gift and every defect. A surplusage given to one part is paid out of a reduction from another part of the same creature. If the head and neck are enlarged, the trunk and extremities are cut short.

The theory of the mechanic forces is another example. What we gain in power is lost in time, and the converse. The periodic or compensating errors of the planets is another instance. The influences of climate and soil in political history are another. The cold climate invigorates. The barren soil does not breed fevers, crocodiles, tigers or scorpions.

The same dualism underlies the nature and condition of man. Every excess causes a defect; every defect an excess. Every sweet hath its sour; every evil its good. Every faculty which is a receiver of pleasure has an equal penalty put on its abuse. It is to answer for its moderation with its life. For every grain of wit there is a grain of folly. For every thing you have missed, you have gained something else; and for every thing you gain, you lose something. If riches increase, they are increased that use them. If the gatherer gathers too much, Nature takes out of the man what she puts into his chest; swells the estate, but kills the owner. Nature hates monopolies and exceptions. The waves of the sea do not more speedily seek a level from their loftiest tossing than the varieties of condition tend to equalize themselves. There is always some leveling circumstance that puts down the overbearing, the strong, the rich, the fortunate, substantially on the same ground with all others. Is a man too strong and fierce for society and by temper and position a bad citizen,—a morose ruffian, with a dash of the pirate in him?—Nature sends him a troop of pretty sons and daughters who are getting along in the dame's classes at the village school, and love and fear for them smooth his grim scowl to courtesy. Thus she contrives to intenerate the granite and felspar, takes the boar out and puts the lamb in and keeps her balance true.

The farmer imagines power and place are fine things. But the President has paid dear for his White House. It has commonly cost him all his peace, and the best of his manly attributes. To preserve for a short time so conspicuous an appearance before the world, he is content to eat dust before the real masters who stand erect behind the throne. Or do men desire the more substantial and permanent grandeur of genius? Neither has this an immunity. He who by force of will or of thought is great and overlooks thousands, has the charges of that eminence. With every influx of light comes new danger. Has he light? he must bear witness to the light, and always outrun that sympathy which gives him such keen satisfaction, by his fidelity to new revelations of the incessant soul. He must hate father and mother, wife and child. Has he all that the world loves and admires and covets?—he must cast behind him their admiration, and afflict them by faithfulness to his truth, and become a byword and a hissing.

The law writes the laws of cities and nations. It is in vain to build or plot or combine against it. Things refuse to be mismanaged long. *Res nolunt diu male administrari.* Though no checks to a new evil appear, the checks exist, and will appear. If the government is cruel, the governor's life is not safe. If you tax too high, the revenue will yield nothing. If you make the criminal code sanguinary, juries will not convict. If the law is too mild, private vengeance comes in. If the government is a terrific democracy, the pressure is resisted by an over-charge of energy in the citizen, and life glows with a fiercer flame. The true life and satisfactions of man seem to elude the utmost rigors or felicities of condition and to establish themselves with great indifferency under all varieties of circumstances. Under the governments the influence of character remains the same,—in Turkey and in New England about alike. Under the primeval despots of Egypt, history honestly confesses that man must have been as free as culture could make him.

These appearances indicate the fact that the universe is represented in every one of its particles. Every thing in nature contains all the powers of nature. Every thing is made of one hidden stuff; as the naturalist sees one type under every metamorphosis, and regards a horse as a running man, a fish as a swimming man, a bird as a flying man, a tree as a rooted man. Each new form repeats not only the main character of the type, but part for part all the details, all the aims, furtherances, hindrances, energies and whole system of every other. Every occupation, trade, art, transaction, is a compend of the world and correlative of every other. Each one is an entire emblem of human life; of its good and ill, its trials, its enemies, its course and its end. And each one must somehow accommodate the whole man and recite all his destiny.

The world globes itself in a drop of dew. The microscope cannot find the animalcule which is less perfect for being little. Eyes, ears, taste, smell, motion, resistance, appetite, and organs of reproduction that take hold on eternity,—all find room to consist in the small creature. So do we put our life into every act. The true doctrine of omnipresence is that God reappears with all his parts in every moss and cobweb. The value of the universe contrives to throw itself into every point. If the good is there, so is the evil; if the affinity, so the repulsion; if the force, so the limitation.

Thus is the universe alive. All things are moral. That soul which within us is a sentiment, outside of us is a law. We feel its inspiration; out there in history we can see its fatal strength. "It is in the world, and the world was made by it." Justice is not postponed. A perfect equity adjusts its balance in all parts of life. 'Aεἰ γὰρ εὖ πίπτουσιν οἱ Διὸς κύβοι, —The dice of God are always loaded. The world looks like a multiplication-table, or a mathematical equation, which, turn it how you will, balances itself. Take what figure you will, its exact value, nor more nor less, still returns to you. Every secret is told, every crime is punished, every virtue rewarded, every wrong redressed, in silence and certainty.

What we call retribution is the universal necessity by which the whole appears wherever a part appears. If you see smoke, there must be fire. If you see a hand or a limb, you know that the trunk to which it belongs is there behind.

Every act rewards itself, or in other words integrates itself, in a twofold manner; first in the thing, or in real nature; and secondly in the circumstance, or in apparent nature. Men call the circumstance the retribution. The causal retribution is in the thing and is seen by the soul. The retribution in the circumstance is seen by the understanding; it is inseparable from the thing, but is often spread over a long time and so does not become distinct until after many years. The specific stripes may follow late after the offense, but they follow because they accompany it. Crime and punishment grow out of one stem. Punishment is a fruit that unsuspected ripens within the flower of the pleasure which concealed it. Cause and effect, means and ends, seed and fruit, cannot be severed; for the effect already blooms in the cause, the end pre-exists in the means, the fruit in the seed.

Whilst thus the world will be whole and refuses to be disparted, we seek to act partially, to sunder, to appropriate; for example,—to gratify the senses we sever the pleasure of the sense from the needs of the character. The ingenuity of man has always been dedicated to the solution of one problem,—how to detach the sensual sweet, the sensual strong, the sensual bright, etc., from the moral sweet, the moral deep, the moral fair; that is, again, to contrive to cut clean off this upper surface so thin as to leave it bottomless; to get a *one end*, without an *other end*. The soul says, 'Eat'; the body would feast. The soul says, 'The man and woman shall be one flesh and one soul'; the body would join the flesh only. The soul says, 'Have dominion over all things to the ends of virtue'; the body would have the power over things to its own ends.

The soul strives amain to live and work through all things. It would be the only fact. All things shall be added unto it,—power, pleasure, knowledge, beauty. The particular man aims to be somebody; to set up for himself; to truck and higgle for a private good; and, in particulars, to ride that he may ride; to dress that he may be dressed; to eat that he may eat; and to govern, that he may be seen. Men seek to be great; they would have offices, wealth, power and fame. They think that to be great is to possess one side of nature,—the sweet, without the other side, the bitter.

This dividing and detaching is steadily counteracted. Up to this day it must be owned no projector has had the smallest success. The parted water reunites behind our hand. Pleasure is taken out of pleasant things, profit out of profitable things, power out of strong things, as soon as we seek to separate them from the whole. We can no more halve things and get the sensual good, by itself, than we can get an inside that shall have no outside, or a light without a shadow. "Drive out Nature with a fork, she comes running back."

Life invests itself with inevitable conditions, which the unwise seek to dodge, which one and another brags that he does not know, that they do not touch him;—but the brag is on his lips, the conditions are in his soul. If he escapes them in one part they attack him in another more vital part. If he has escaped them in form and in the appearance, it is because he has resisted his life and fled from himself, and the retribution is so much death. So signal is the failure of all attempts to make this separation of the good from the tax, that the experiment would not be tried,—since to try it is to be mad,—but for the circumstance that when the disease began in the will, of rebellion and separation, the intellect is at once infected, so that the man ceases to see God whole in each object, but is able to see the sensual allurement of an object and not see the sensual hurt; he sees the mermaid's head but not the dragon's tail, and thinks he can cut off that which he would have from that which he would not have. "How secret art thou who dwellest in the highest heavens in silence, O thou only great God, sprinkling with an unwearied providence certain penal blindless upon such as have unbridled desires!"

The human soul is true to these facts in the painting of fable, of history, of law, of proverbs, of conversation. It finds a tongue in literature unawares. Thus the Greeks called Jupiter, Supreme Mind; but having traditionally ascribed to him many base actions, they involuntarily made amends to reason by tying up the hands of so bad a god. He is made as helpless as a king of England. Prometheus knows one secret which Jove must bargain for; Minerva, another. He cannot get his own thunders; Minerva keeps the key of them:—

> *Of all the gods, I only know the keys*
> *That ope the solid doors within whose vaults*
> *His thunders sleep.*

A plain confession of the in-working of the All and of its moral aim. The Indian mythology ends in the same ethics; and it would seem impossible for any fable to be invented and get any currency which was not moral: Aurora forgot to ask youth for her lover, and though Tithonus is immortal, he is old. Achilles is not quite invulnerable; the sacred waters did not wash the heel by which Thetis held him. Siegfried, in the Nibelungen, is not quite immortal, for a leaf fell on his back whilst he was bathing in the dragon's blood, and that spot which it covered is mortal. And so it must be. There is a crack in every thing God has made. It would seem there is always this vindictive circumstance stealing in at unawares even into the wild poesy in which the human fancy attempted to make bold holiday and to shake itself free of the old laws,—this back-stroke, this kick of the gun, certifying that the law is fatal; that in nature nothing can be given, all things are sold.

This is that ancient doctrine of Nemesis, who keeps watch in the universe and lets no offense go unchastised. The Furies they said are attendants on justice, and if the sun in heaven should transgress his path they would punish him. The poets related that stone walls and iron swords and leathern thongs had an occult sympathy with the wrongs of their owners; that the belt which Ajax gave Hector dragged the Trojan hero over the field at the wheels of the car of Achilles, and the sword which Hector gave Ajax was that on whose point Ajax fell. They recorded that when the Thasians erected a statue to Theagenes, a victor in the games, one of his rivals went to it by night and endeavored to throw it down by repeated blows, until at last he moved it from its pedestal and was crushed to death beneath its fall.

This voice of fable has in it somewhat divine. It came from thought above the will of the writer. This is the best part of each writer which has nothing private in it; that which he does not know; that which flowed out of his constitution and not from his too active invention; that which in the study of a single artist you might not easily find, but in the study of many you would abstract as the spirit of them all. Phidias it is not, but the work of man in that early Hellenic world that I would know. The name and circumstance of Phidias, however convenient for history, embarrass when we come to the highest criticism. We are to see that which man was tending to do in a given period, and was hindered, or, if you will, modified in doing, by the interfering volitions of Phidias, of Dante, of Shakespeare, the organ whereby man at the moment wrought.

Still more striking is the expression of this fact in the proverbs of all nations, which are always the literature of reason, or the statements of an absolute truth without qualification. Proverbs, like the sacred books of each nation, are the sanctuary of the intuitions. That which the droning world, chained to appearances, will not allow the realist to say in his own words, it will suffer him to say in proverbs without contradiction. And this law of laws, which the pulpit, the senate and the college deny, is hourly preached in all markets and workshops by flights of proverbs, whose teaching is as true and as omnipresent as that of birds and flies.

All things are double, one against another.—Tit for tat; an eye for an eye; a tooth for a tooth; blood for blood; measure for measure; love for love.—Give, and it shall be given you. —He that watereth shall be watered himself.—What will you have? quoth God; pay for it and take it.—Nothing venture, nothing have.—Thou shalt be paid exactly for what thou hast done, no more, no less.—Who doth not work shall not eat.—Harm watch, harm catch.—Curses always recoil on the head of him who imprecates them.—If you put a chain around the neck of a slave, the other end fastens itself around your own. Bad counsel confounds the adviser.—The Devil is an ass.

It is thus written, because it is thus in life. Our action is overmastered and characterized above our will by the law of nature. We aim at a petty end quite aside from the public good, but our act arranges itself by irresistible magnetism in a line with the poles of the world.

A man cannot speak but he judges himself. With his will or against his will he draws his portrait to the eye of his companions by every word. Every opinion reacts on him who utters it. It is a thread-ball thrown at a mark, but the other end remains in the thrower's bag. Or rather it is a harpoon hurled at the whale, unwinding, as it flies, a coil of cord in the boat, and, if the harpoon is not good, or not well thrown, it will go nigh to cut the steersman in twain or to sink the boat. You cannot do wrong without suffering wrong. "No man had ever a point of pride that was not injurious to him," said Burke. The exclusive in fashionable life does not see that he excludes himself from enjoyment, in the attempt to appropriate it. The exclusionist in religion does not see that he shuts the door of heaven on himself, in striving to shut out others. Treat men as pawns and ninepins and you shall suffer as well as they. If you leave out their heart, you shall lose your own. The senses would make things of all persons; of women, of children, of the poor. The vulgar proverb, "I will get it from his purse or get it from his skin," is sound philosophy.

All infractions of love and equity in our social relations are speedily punished. They are punished by fear. Whilst I stand in simple relations to my fellow-man, I have no displeasure in meeting him. We meet as water meets water, or as two currents of air mix, with perfect diffusion and interpenetration of nature. But as soon as there is any departure from simplicity and attempt at halfness, or good for me that is not good for him, my neighbor feels the wrong; he shrinks from me as far as I have shrunk from him; his eyes no longer seek mine; there is war between us; there is hate in him and fear in me.

All the old abuses in society, universal and particular, all unjust accumulations of property and power, are avenged in the same manner. Fear is an instructor of great sagacity and the herald of all revolutions. One thing he teaches, that there is rottenness where he appears. He is a carrion crow, and though you see not well what he hovers for, there is death somewhere. Our property is timid, our laws are timid, our cultivated classes are timid. Fear for ages has boded and mowed and gibbered over government and property. That obscene bird is not there for nothing. He indicates great wrongs which must be revised.

Of the like nature is that expectation of change which instantly follows the suspension of our voluntary activity. The terror of cloudless noon, the emerald of Polycrates, the awe of prosperity, the instinct which leads every generous soul to impose on itself tasks of a noble asceticism and vicarious virtue, are the tremblings of the balance of justice through the heart and mind of man.

Experienced men of the world know very well that it is best to pay scot and lot as they go along, and that a man often pays dear for a small frugality. The borrower runs in his own debt. Has a man gained any thing who has received a hundred favors and rendered none? Has he gained by borrowing, through indolence or cunning, his neighbor's wares, or horses, or money? There arises on the deed the instant acknowledgement of benefit on the one part and of debt on the other; that is, of superiority and inferiority. The transaction remains in the memory of himself and his neighbor; and every new transaction alters according to its nature their relation to each other. He may soon come to see that he had better have broken his own bones than to have ridden in his neighbor's coach, and that "the highest price he can pay for a thing is to ask for it."

A wise man will extend this lesson to all parts of life, and know that it is the part of prudence to face every claimant and pay every just demand on your time, your talents, or your heart. Always pay; for first or last you must pay your entire debt. Persons and events may stand for a time between you and justice, but it is only a postponement. You must pay at last your own debt. If you are wise you will dread a prosperity which only loads you with more. Benefit is the end of nature. But for every benefit which you receive, a tax is levied. He is great who confers the most benefits. He is base,—and that is the one base thing in the universe,—to receive favors and render none. In the order of nature we cannot render benefits to those from whom we receive them, or only seldom. But the benefit we receive must be rendered again, line for line, deed for deed, cent for cent, to somebody. Beware of too much good staying in your hand. It will fast corrupt and worm worms. Pay it away quickly in some sort.

Labor is watched over by the same pitiless laws. Cheapest, say the prudent, is the dearest labor. What we buy in a broom, a mat, a wagon, a knife, is some application of good sense to a common want. It is best to pay in your land a skillful gardener, or to buy good sense applied to gardening; in your sailor, good sense applied to navigation; in the house, good sense applied to cooking, sewing, serving; in your agent, good sense applied to accounts and affairs. So do you multiply your presence, or spread yourself throughout your estate. But because of the dual constitution of things, in labor as in life there can be no cheating. The thief steals from himself. The swindler swindles himself. For the real price of labor is knowledge and virtue, whereof wealth and credit are signs. These signs, like paper money, may be counterfeited or stolen, but that which they represent, namely, knowledge and virtue, cannot be counterfeited or stolen. These ends of labor cannot be answered but by real exertions of the mind, and in obedience to pure motives. The cheat, the defaulter, the gambler, cannot extort the knowledge of material and moral nature which his honest care and pains yield to the operative. The law of nature is, Do the thing, and you shall have the power; but they who do not the thing have not the power.

Human labor, through all its forms, from the sharpening of a stake to the construction of a city or an epic, is one immense illustration of the perfect compensation of the universe. The absolute balance of Give and Take, the doctrine that every thing has its price,—and if that price is not paid, not that thing but something else is obtained, and that it is impossible to get any thing without its price,—is not less sublime in the columns of a ledger than in the budgets of states, in the laws of light and darkness, in all the action and reaction of nature. I cannot doubt that the high laws which each man sees implicated in those processes with which he is conversant, the stern ethics which sparkle on his chisel-edge, which are measured out by his plumb and foot-rule, which stand as manifest in the footing of the shop-bill as in the history of a state,—do recommend to him his trade, and though seldom named, exalt his business to his imagination.

The league between virtue and nature engages all things to assume a hostile front to vice. The beautiful laws and substances of the world persecute and whip the traitor. He finds that things are arranged for truth and benefit, but there is no den in the wide world to hide a rogue. Commit a crime, and the earth is made of glass. Commit a crime, and it seems as if a coat of snow fell on the ground, such as reveals in the woods the track of every partridge and fox and squirrel and mole. You cannot recall the spoken word, you cannot wipe out the foot-track, you cannot draw up the ladder, so as to leave no inlet or clew. Some damning circumstance always transpires. The laws and substances of nature,—water, snow, wind, gravitation,—becomes penalties to the thief.

On the other hand the law holds with equal sureness
for all right action. Love, and you shall be loved. All love
is mathematically just, as much as the two sides of an alge-
braic equation. The good man has absolute good, which like
fire turns everything to is own nature, so that you cannot
do him any harm; but as the royal armies sent against
Napoleon, when he approached cast down their colors and
from enemies became friends, so disasters of all kinds, as
sickness, offence, poverty, prove benefactors:—

> *Winds blow and water roll*
> *Strength to the brave and power and deity,*
> *Yet in themselves are nothing.*

The good are befriended even by weakness and defect.
As no man had ever a point of pride that was not injurious
to him, so no man had ever a defect that was not somewhere
made useful to him. The stag in the fable admired his horns
and blamed his feet, but when the hunter came, his feet
saved him, and afterwards, caught in the thicket, his horns
destroyed him. Every man in his lifetime needs to thank
his faults. As no man thoroughly understands a truth until
he has contended against it, so no man has a thorough
acquaintance with the hindrances or talents of men until
he has suffered from the one and seen the triumph of the
other over his own want of the same. Has he a defect of
temper that unfits him to live in society? Thereby he is
driven to entertain himself alone and acquire habits of
self-help; and thus, like the wounded oyster, he mends his
shell with peal.

Our strength grows out of our weakness. The indignation
which arms itself with secret forces does not awaken until
we are pricked and stung and sorely assailed. A great man
is always willing to be little. Whilst he sits on the cushion
of advantages, he goes to sleep. When he is pushed, tormented, defeated, he has a chance to learn something; he
has been put on his wits, on his manhood; he has gained
facts; learns his ignorance; is cured of the insanity of conceit;
has got moderation and real skill. The wise man throws
himself on the side of his assailants. It is more his interest

than it is theirs to find his weak point. The wound ciatrizes and falls off from him like a dead skin and when they would triumph, lo! he has passed on invulnerable. Blame is safer than praise. I hate to be defended in a newspaper. As long as all that is said is said against me, I feel a certain assurance of success. But as soon as honeyed words of praise are spoken for me I feel as one that lies unprotected before his enemies. In general, every evil to which we do not succumb is a benefactor. As the Sandwich Islander believes that the strength and valor of the enemy he kills passes into himself, so we gain the strength of the temptation we resist.

The same guards which protect us from disaster, defect and enmity, defend us, if we will, from selfishness and fraud. Bolts and bars are not the best of our institutions, nor is shrewdness in trade a mark of wisdom. Men suffer all their life long under the foolish superstition that they can be cheated. But it is as impossible for a man to be cheated by any one but himself, as for a thing to be and not to be at the same time. There is a third silent party to all our bargains. The nature and soul of things takes on itself the guaranty of the fulfillment of every contract, so that honest service cannot come to loss. If you serve an ungrateful master, serve him the more. Put God in your debt. Every stroke shall be repaid. The longer the payment is withholden, the better for you; for compound interest on compound interest is the rate and usage of this exchequer.

The history of persecution is a history of endeavors to cheat nature, to make water run uphill, to twist a rope of sand. It makes no difference whether the actors be many or one, a tyrant or a mob. A mob is a society of bodies voluntarily bereaving themselves of reason and traversing its work. The mob is man voluntarily descending to the nature of the beast. Its fit hour of activity is night. Its actions are insane, like its whole constitution. It persecutes a principle; it would whip a right; it would tar and feather justice, by inflicting fire and outrage upon the houses and persons of those who have these. It resembles the prank of boys, who run with fire-engines to put out the ruddy aurora streaming to the stars. The inviolate spirit turns their spite against the wrongdoers. The martyr cannot be dishonored. Every lash inflicted is a tongue of fame; every prison a more illustrious abode; every burned book or house enlightens the world; every suppressed or expunged word reverberates through the earth from side to side. Hours of sanity and consideration are always arriving to communities, as to individuals, when the truth is seen and the martyrs are justified.

Thus do all things preach the indifferency of circumstances. The man is all. Every thing has two sides, a good and an evil. Every advantage has its tax. I learn to be content. But the doctrine of compensation is not the doctrine of indifferency. The thoughtless say, on hearing these representations,—What boots it do well? There is one event to good and evil; if I gain any good I must pay for it; if I lose any good I gain some other; all actions are indifferent.

There is a deeper fact in the soul than compensation, to wit, its own nature. The soul is not a compensation, but a life. The soul *is*. Under all this running sea of circumstance, whose waters ebb and flow with perfect balance, lies the aboriginal abyss of real Being. Essence, or God, is not a relation or a part, but the whole. Being is the vast affirmative, excluding negation, self-balanced, and swallowing up all relations, parts and times within itself. Nature, truth, virtue, are the influx from thence. Vice is the absence or departure of the same. Nothing, Falsehood, may indeed stand as the great Night or shade on which as a background the living universe paints itself forth, but no fact is begotten by it; it cannot work, for it is not. It cannot work any good; it cannot work any harm. It is harm inasmuch as it is worse not to be than to be.

We feel defrauded of the retribution due to evil acts, because the criminal adheres to his vice and contumacy and does not come to a crisis or judgment anywhere in visible nature. There is no stunning confutation of his nonsense before men and angels. Has he therefore outwitted the law? Inasmuch as he carries the malignity and the lie with him he so far deceases from nature. In some manner there will be a demonstration of the wrong to the understanding also; but, should we not see it, this deadly deduction makes square the eternal account. Neither can it be said, on the other hand, that the gain of rectitude must be bought by any loss. There is no penalty to virtue; no penalty to wisdom; they are proper additions of being. In a virtuous action I properly *am*; in a virtuous act I add to the world; I plant into deserts conquered from Chaos and Nothing and see the darkness receding on the limits of the horizon. There can be no excess to love, none to knowledge, none to beauty, when these attributes are considered in the purest sense. The soul refuses limits, and always affirms an Optimism, never a Pessimism.

His life is a progress, and not a station, His instinct is trust. Our instinct uses "more" and "less" in application to man, of the *presence of the soul*, and not of its absence; the brave man is greater than the coward; the true, the benevolent, the wise, is more a man and not less, than the fool and knave. There is no tax on the good of virtue, for that is the incoming of God himself, or absolute existence, without any comparative. Material good has its tax, and if it came without desert or sweat, has no root in me, and the next wind will blow it away. But all the good of nature is the soul's, and may be had if paid for in nature's lawful coin, that is, by labor which the heart and the head allow. I no longer wish to meet a good I do not earn, for example to find a pot of buried gold, knowing that it brings with it new burdens. I do not wish more external goods,—neither possessions, nor honors, nor powers, nor persons. The gain is apparent; the tax is certain. But there is no tax on the knowledge that the compensation exists and that it is not desirable to dig up treasure. Herein I rejoice with a serene eternal peace. I contract the boundaries of possible mischief. I learn the wisdom of St. Bernard,—"Nothing can work me damage except myself; the harm that I sustain I carry about with me, and never am a real sufferer but by my own fault."

In the nature of the soul is the compensation for the inequalities of condition. The radical tragedy of nature seems to be the distinction of More and Less. How can Less not feel the pain; how not feel indignation or malevolence towards More? Look at those who have less faculty, and one feels sad and knows not well what to make of it. He almost shuns their eye; he fears they will upbraid God. What should they do? It seems a great injustice. But see the facts nearly and these mountainous inequalities vanish. Love reduces them as the sun melts the iceberg in the sea. The heart and soul of all men being one, this bitterness of *His* and *Mine* ceases. His is mine. I am my brother and my brother is me. If I feel overshadowed and outdone by great neighbors, I can yet love; I can still receive; and he that loveth maketh his own the grandeur he loves. Thereby I make the discovery that my brother is my guardian, acting for me with the friendliest designs, and the estate I so admired and envied is my own. It is the nature of the soul to appropriate all things. Jesus and Shakespeare are fragments of the soul, and by love I conquer and incorporate them in my own conscious domain. His virtue,—is not that mine? His wit,—if it cannot be made mine, it is not wit.

Such also is the natural history of calamity. The changes which break up at short intervals the prosperity of men are advertisements of a nature whose law is growth. Every soul is by this intrinsic necessity quitting its whole system of things, its friends and home and laws and faith, as the shellfish crawls out of its beautiful but stony case, because it no longer admits of its growth, and slowly forms a new house. In proportion to the vigor of the individual these revolutions are frequent, until in some happier mind they are incessant and all worldly relations hang very loosely about him, becoming as it were a transparent fluid membrane through which the living form is seen, and not, as in most men, an indurated heterogeneous fabric of many dates and of no settled character, in which the man is imprisoned. Then there can be enlargement, and the man of today scarcely recognizes the man of yesterday. And such should be the outward biography of man in time, a putting off of dead circumstances day by day, as he renews his raiment day by day. But to us, in our lapsed estate, resting, not advancing, resisting, not cooperating with the divine expansion, this growth comes by shocks.

We cannot part with our friends. We cannot let our angels go. We do not see that they only go out that archangels may come in. We are idolators of the old. We do not believe in the riches of the soul, in its proper eternity and omnipresence. We do not believe there is any force in today to rival or recreate that beautiful yesterday. We linger in the ruins of the old tent where once we had bread and shelter and organs, nor believe that the spirit can feed, cover, and nerve us again. We cannot again find aught so dear, so sweet, so graceful. But we sit and weep in vain. The voice of the Almighty saith, 'Up and onward for evermore!' We cannot stay amid the ruins. Neither will we rely on the new; and so we walk ever with reverted eyes, like those monsters who look backwards.

And yet the compensations of calamity are made apparent to the understanding also, after long intervals of time. A fever, a mutilation, a cruel disappointment, a loss of wealth, a loss of friends, seems at the moment unpaid loss, and unpayable. But the sure years reveal the deep remedial force that underlies all facts. The death of a dear friend, wife, brother, lover, which seemed nothing but privation, somewhat later assumes the aspect of a guide or genius; for it commonly operates revolutions in our way of life, terminates an epoch of infancy or of youth which was waiting to be closed, breaks up a wonted occupation, or a household, or style of living, and allows the formation of new ones more friendly to the growth of character. It permits or constrains the formation of new acquaintances and the reception of new influences that prove of the first importance to the next years; and the man or woman who would have remained a sunny garden-flower, with no room for its roots and too much sunshine for its head, by the falling of the walls and the neglect of the gardener is made the banyan of the forest, yielding shade and fruit to wide neighborhoods of men.

4

Karma and Reincarnation

L. H. LESLIE-SMITH

The themes of karma and reincarnation have been current and familiar in the East for many centuries. They have been progressively introduced into the West and have now permeated the thought of the world, at any rate as ideas. Whether accepted as hypotheses, beliefs, or possibilities, these subjects can be discussed in any assembly of intelligent persons. The thinking may be vague, for notions will commonly have been gathered from novels, poems, and plays rather than from any considered presentation. But such media have proved excellent for putting forward fresh or unorthodox concepts. Whereas a well prepared and reasoned statement is apt to be rejected out of hand as at variance with conventional thought and belief, the same ideas in the form of entertainment, or in a cultural setting, raise no automatic barriers. The ordinary reactive defenses are bypassed because the challenge is not made in real life but in a kind of fantasy world of the arts.

Obviously, belief has nothing to do with fact. The disbelief of the majority of men cannot make a truth false; and an untrue statement is rendered nonetheless so because the whole world believes it to be correct. Nor can our earnest desire that something may be true affect its validity in the least. Further, it is no use trying to fit facts into some theory. We must seek a postulate that is not only warranted by the facts but is also a reasonable theory that explains things previously obscure. Thus, though half the peoples of the earth believe in reincarnation, that in itself is no reason for accepting the doctrine, but only for carefully examining it, the evidence for it, and its rationale, in order to form our own opinion. This investigation must be done objectively, with a mind free from bias and preconception and an attitude of openness and receptivity, yet with the critical faculty fully alert. Both karma and reincarnation are vast subjects in their complex application, but their general principles are easy to understand. Let us look at them briefly.

That the universe runs according to law. Every discovery of science seems to confirm it so far as the physical world is concerned. Only on such a basis could technologists have achieved the superb feat of putting men on the moon. H. P. Blavatsky* said, "Deity is Law and vice-versa." So-called miraculous occurrences are due to the operation or use of some law, within the all-embracing law of nature, of which we are mostly yet ignorant. Enough "miracles" have been performed by physical means in this century to make this clear. Few people, however, have applied this principle to the more subtle psychic realms. Yet when a law is found working at one level of existence, one can be sure that it works correspondingly at all other levels, though seemingly different, perhaps, because operating in other circumstances and conditions. The whole of nature is one, a unity. "As above, so below" is an occult maxim, which is equally true the other way around. Law is fundamental to all existence.

The most important aspect of universal law, according to H. P. Blavatsky, is the law of adjustment, of balance, of causation, called karma. She calls it "the *Ultimate Law* of the Universe, the source, origin and fount of all the laws which exist throughout Nature. Karma is the unerring law which adjusts effect to cause on the physical, mental and spiritual planes of being." Whenever and wherever imbalance is produced, the self-adjusting intelligent "mechanism" comes into play to restore equilibrium. The root meaning of "karma" is action; hence it applies to the whole of nature,

---

*Author of *The Secret Doctrine*, a seminal source of esoteric wisdom.

including humanity, for action is involved in all manifestation.

It is somewhat confusing that the same word is used for the relation of cause to effect in the lower kingdoms of nature as for humanity, where alone "whatsoever a man soweth, that shall he also reap." Karma not only keeps the stars on their courses and every atom in being, but it also adjusts moral relationships resulting from the power of choice, which is one of the distinguishing characteristics of man. Blavatsky gives the difference when she says that karma is the "law of adjustment which ever tends to restore disturbed equilibrium in the physical and broken harmony in the moral world." To A. P. Sinnett,* karma was "the law of ethical causation," which would restrict it to the human race; in that context it seems a fair definition. Repeatedly, Blavatsky speaks of the law of retribution. To modern ears this suggests vengeance, but formerly the word included the meaning of compensation or recompense. Having moral significance, this also can apply to human beings.

The doctrine of karma is nowhere more clearly and yet more profoundly expounded than in *The Key to Theosophy* by H. P. Blavatsky, from which the quotations given above and those to follow are taken unless otherwise stated. Universally, "Karma is that unseen and unknown law *which adjusts wisely, intelligently and equitably* each effect to its cause." Humanly, "Karma gives back to every man the actual consequences of his own action." It follows that it is "an unfailing redresser of human injustice; a stern adjuster of wrongs; a retributive law which punishes and rewards with equal impartiality. It is no respecter of persons" and it "can neither be propitiated nor turned aside by prayer." Inexorably thus it achieves not only the Mikado's sublime object of letting "the punishment fit the crime"; it also complements it justly by making the reward fit the merit. We have to take responsibility for our own actions; the law will surely return results to us. The small boy's plea, "He

---

*An early member of the Theosophical Society and recipient of most of the Mahatma letters.

told me to do it," is no excuse; nor is an order from one in authority; or that other common plaint, "I didn't mean to do it." Motive is indeed important and must mitigate the moral force of any action, though it cannot affect the physical result.

The general principle is simple. "It does not require metaphysics or education to make a man understand the broad truths of Karma and Reincarnation." It is one of the splendid features of the theosophical philosophy that the general outline can be easily grasped; yet the greatest minds cannot fully comprehend the implications and ramifications. One is apt to think that one knows about karma. But it is not much that one knows.

Since no person can live to himself or herself and is inevitably caught up in human relationships, the application of karma is bound to be complex. For "the aggregate of individual Karma becomes that of the nation to which those individuals belong, and the sum of national Karma is that of the world." And again, "The interdependence of humanity is the cause of what is called Distributive Karma, and it is the law which affords the solution to the great question of collective suffering and its relief." The individual karma of every man and woman is inextricably linked with that of the group, and through the group with the entire human race.

"Karma is the force that impels to Reincarnation, and that Karma is the destiny man weaves for himself." In any one life we sow the seeds of the personality of the next incarnation. That is the hypothesis. Reincarnation is the method by which human karma, at any rate, works. The two are inseparably interwoven.

This concept offers greater understanding of our lives and of those of the people around us. The circumstances that make things easy for some, hard for others, and well-nigh impossible for still others, are karmic—the precise outcome of their own behavior in the past. That, however, is no reason for not giving anyone all the help we can. Indeed, not to do so would be to build an appropriate failure into our future, in this incarnation or another. That is why today is of the utmost importance; not only today, but this hour, this minute, for by what we do this very moment, every present moment, we mold our tomorrow.

The interdependence of humankind involves group and national karma. We are all intimately linked both with the cultural group into which we are born and with the race or nation of which that group is part. Karma of our own making placed us in the setting of a mystique that is the cumulative result of the nation's history—an aura or mental-emotional atmosphere created by untold generations of our forefathers. This brings in distributive karma, by which the doings of a group involve all members of that group, whether or not they approve of them. This could possibly explain the statement that after death the Ego (the reincarnating individuality, not the personality, which modern psychology calls the "ego") receives only "the reward for the unmerited suffering endured during its past incarnation." At any rate, just as we cannot avoid the results of our own actions, so no one can stay or turn aside the karma of our group. We cannot run away and opt out of it. If its problems are not faced now, we will remain tied to them karmically in future lives, in future nations perhaps, until proper balance is restored. This raises interesting and cogent points. Is the minority that deserts its native land to settle elsewhere a band of heroes or a bunch of escapists? This question becomes more fascinating in the case of those emigrants who in their new world persecuted those who disagreed with them as fiercely as they themselves had been persecuted before they left their homeland.

Karmic forces return to their individual originators; but with the intricate network in any group they would seem likely to meet and be affected by other forces. The result would thus be a modification of the original. Karmic debts have to be paid. Yet, like ordinary ones, may they not sometimes be met by an altruistic benefactor? Can this not also be within the province of distributive karma? Blavatsky says that "no man can rise superior to his individual failings without lifting, be it ever so little, the whole body of which he is an integral part." Thus one eases a little of the "heavy karma of the world," as it has been put, for one's fellows and thereby may be said to a small extent to redeem them. Is not this, raised to a superlative degree, what those great ones have done who have been called the saviors of humankind? All students of Theosophy are familiar with a further aspect of universal law: the law of cycles or of periodicity. This is self-evident in nature—ebb and flow, night and day, waking and sleeping, and so on. A period of activity and growth is followed by one of assimilation and rest. Reincarnation is another example of the same process. After death, Devachan. But death is not just the dissolution of the physical body. That is said to be followed by a widely varied period during which base desires are worked out and purged. The successive breaking up of the lower aspects of the personality culminates in the "second death," which marks the end of that mortal personality. All its spiritual aspirations and higher qualities—"eternal qualities such as love and mercy"—are transferred to the spiritual Ego. The complex of body, emotions, brain, of each of us, answering to a certain name, will vanish and its various constituents be resolved again into the matter of their respective planes— "dust to dust" at the physical level, and so forth. "Personal consciousness can hardly last longer than the personality itself." Hence a personality can win relative immortality only by rejecting its lower life of personal desire for one of devotion to unselfish service, whose spiritual qualities can be absorbed by the Ego.

Successive personalities are likened to parts in a series of dramas—or comedies—played by the same actor, the reincarnating individuality. This Ego "retains during the Devachanic period merely the essence of the experience of its past earth life or personality"; but "all that constituted during life the *spiritual* bundle of experiences, the noblest aspirations and *unselfish* nature, clings for the time of the Devachanic period of the Ego. The *actor* is so imbued with the role just played that he dreams of it during the whole Devachanic night." So, "collecting from every terrestrial personality, into which Karma forces it to incarnate, the nectar alone of the spiritual qualities and self-consciousness, it unites all these into one whole and emerges from its chrysalis as the glorified *Dhyan Chohan.* So much the worse for the personalities from which it could collect nothing. Such personalities cannot assuredly outlive consciously their terrestrial existence."

The karmic connection between lives is made by *skandhas,* bundles of attributes. These are psychomental link mechanisms by which characteristics are passed from one personality to its successors. They correspond to the DNA, gene, chromosome arrangement of inherited qualities in the physical bodies. They are, as it were, the seeds of character, representing innate faculty and capability—or lack of it. At death they "remain as karmic effects, as germs, in the atmosphere of the terrestrial plane to attach themselves to the new personality of the Ego when it reincarnates."

What of Devachan? "Devachan is a state of mental bliss . . . analogous to but far more vivid and real than the most vivid dream." It is an idealistic and subjective continuation of earth life, a dream world of our own fashioning. The world of this present life is also the creation of our own minds through sense impressions made on the brain—also an illusion, we are told. After the death of Keats, Shelley wrote, "He hath awakened from the dream of life." Are both this life and the post-mortem one simply dreams, seemingly very real, one more highly colored than the other? Again, Blavatsky said "Death is sleep." What relation have sleep and dreams to Reality? These are questions worth pondering. Maybe our concepts need looking at again. We can accept without reservation the validity of the cyclic law, but we may well be cautious with interpretations of its application on the various planes of being and guard against the tendency to fixed ideas.

"The period between births is said to extend to ten to fifteen centuries." *The Mahatma Letters to A. P. Sinnett,* however, gives a hundred times longer "in the transitory sphere of *effects* than on the globes." Was 1,500 reckoned to be a hundred times the average length of life in those days—

fifteen years, owing to the high mortality rate in infancy?*
There is this also: "In eternity the longest periods of time
are as the wink of an eye." Then surely a seeming period
of fifteen centuries might actually pass in a few minutes,
hours, days, weeks. There is no common time scale, and
comparisons could easily lead us astray in our thinking.
Maybe in meditation sometime a flash of illumination
and understanding will come.

The theories, hypotheses, doctrines—as suits us best—of
karma and reincarnation present a scheme of law that can
throw light on evolution and can make some sense of life
and death, rendering the former intelligible and the latter
negligible. They show a pattern that explains the world
as it is with its many human problems. They offer a unique
philosophy for living and an unrivaled basis for moral values.

Human potentialities unfold slowly yet surely under
the law of adjustment, which is wholly educative, teaching
people by experience until they come to realize their
responsibility, not only to their fellows but also to the
other kingdoms of nature. Only what is worthy of the immortal center within each one of us can survive. All the
separative qualities—pride, possessiveness, selfishness—
have to go. By stripping away these, by discarding the illusory
toys on which the world sets great store, we may return
to our native purity of soul, through which divine light
and wisdom may be manifested in a human being.

The modern course is for us to take charge of our destiny.
Unconsciously we have always been responsible, for present
actions mold our future, just as our own past actions have
predestined the present. But if we are consciously to shape
the future—a task that evolution is steadily forcing on us—
then only a knowledge of the great laws of karma and reincarnation can enable us to do so wisely.

---

*Other sources, such as the Cayce readings, indicate a much shorter period
between lives.

5

God Is Not Mocked

ALDOUS HUXLEY

Why hast thou said, "I have sinned so much,
And God in His mercy has not punished my sins"?
How many times do I smite thee, and thou knowest not!
Thou art bound in my chains from head to foot.
On thy heart is rust on rust collected
So that thou art blind to divine mysteries.
When a man is stubborn and follows evil practices,
He casts dust in the eyes of his discernment.
Old shame for sin and calling on God quit him;
Dust five layers deep settles on his mirror,
Rust spots begin to gnaw his iron,
The colour of his jewel grows less and less.

Jalal-uddin Rumi

If there is freedom (and even Determinists consistently act as if they were certain of it) and if (as everyone who has qualified himself to talk about the subject has always been convinced) there is a spiritual Reality, which it is the final end and purpose of consciousness to know; then all life is in the nature of an intelligence test, and the higher the level of awareness and the greater the potentialities of the creature, the more searchingly difficult will be the questions asked. For, in Bagehot's words, "we could not be what we ought to be, if we lived in the sort of universe we should expect. . . . A latent Providence, a confused life, an odd material world, an existence broken short in the midst and on a sudden, are not real difficulties, but real helps;

46

for they, or something like them, are essential conditions of a moral life in a subordinate being." Because we are free, it is possible for us to answer life's questions either well or badly. If we answer them badly, we shall bring down upon ourselves self-stultification. Most often this self-stultification will take subtle and not immediately detectable forms, as when our failure to answer properly makes it impossible for us to realize the higher potentialities of our being. Sometimes, on the contrary, the self-stultification is manifest on the physical level, and may involve not only individuals as individuals, but entire societies, which go down in catastrophe or sink more slowly into decay. The giving of correct answers is rewarded primarily by spiritual growth and progressive realization of latent potentialities, and secondarily (when circumstances make it possible) by the adding of all the rest to the realized kingdom of God. *Karma* exists; but its equivalence of act and award is not always obvious and material, as the earlier Buddhist and Hebrew writers ingenuously imagined that it should be. The bad man in prosperity may, all unknown to himself, be darkened and corroded with inward rust, while the good man under afflictions may be in the rewarding process of spiritual growth. No, God is not mocked; but also, let us always remember, He is not understood.

> *Però nella giustizia sempiterna*
> *la vista che riceve vostro mondo,*
> *com'occhio per lo mar, dentro s'interna,*
> *chè, benchè dalla proda veggia il fondo,*
> *in pelago nol vede, e non di meno*
> *è lì, ma cela lui l'esser profondo.*

("Wherefore, in the eternal justice, such sight as your earth receives is engulfed, like the eye in the sea; for though by the shore it can see the bottom, in the ocean it cannot see it; yet none the less the bottom is there, but the depth hides it.") Love is the plummet as well as the astrolabe of God's mysteries, and the pure in heart can see far down into the depths of the divine justice, to catch a glimpse, not indeed of the details of the cosmic process, but at least of its principle

and nature. These insights permit them to say, with Juliana
of Norwich, that all shall be well, that, in spite of time, all
is well, and that the problem of evil has its solution in the
eternity, which men can, if they so desire, experience, but
can never describe.

But, you urge, if men sin from the necessity of their nature,
they are excusable; you do not explain, however, what
you would infer from this fact. Is it perhaps that God will
be prevented from growing angry with them? Or is it rather
that they have deserved that blessedness which consists
in the knowledge and love of God? If you mean the former,
I altogether agree that God does not grow angry and that
all things happen by his decree. But I deny that, for this
reason, all men ought to be happy. Surely men may be
excusable and nevertheless miss happiness, and be tormented
in many ways. A horse is excusable for being a horse and
not a man; but nevertheless he must needs be a horse and
not a man. One who goes mad from the bite of a dog is
excusable; yet it is right that he should die of suffocation.
So, too, he who cannot rule his passions, nor hold them
in check out of respect for the law, while he may be excusable
on the ground of weakness, is incapable of enjoying con-
formity of spirit and knowledge and love of God; and he is
lost inevitably.

                                                    Spinoza

Horizontally and vertically, in physical and temperamental
kind as well as in degree of inborn ability and native goodness, human beings differ profoundly one from another.
Why? To what end and for what past causes? "Master, who
did sin, this man or his parents, that he was born blind?"
Jesus answered, "Neither hath this man sinned nor his
parents, but that the works of God should be made manifest
in him." The man of science, on the contrary, would say
that the responsibility rested with the parents who had
caused the blindness of their child either by having the
wrong kind of genes, or by contracting some avoidable
disease. Hindu or Buddhist believers in reincarnation
according to the laws of *karma* (the destiny which, by their
actions, individuals and groups of individuals impose upon
themselves, one another and their descendants) would
give another answer and say that, owing to what he had

done in previous existences, the blind man had predestined himself to choose the sort of parents from whom he would have to inherit blindness.

These three answers are not mutually incompatible. The parents are responsible for making the child what, by heredity and upbringing, he turns out to be. The soul or character incarnated in the child is of such a nature, owing to past behaviour, that it is forced to select those particular parents. And collaborating with the material and efficient causes is the final cause, the teleological pull from in front. This teleological pull is a pull from the divine Ground of things acting upon that part of the timeless now, which a finite mind must regard as the future. Men sin and their parents sin; but the works of God have to be manifested in every sentient being (either by exceptional ways, as in this case of supernormal healing, or in the ordinary course of events)—have to be manifested again and again, with the infinite patience of eternity, until at last the creature makes itself fit for the perfect and consummate manifestation of unitive knowledge, of the state of "not I, but God in me."

> "*Karma*," according to the Hindus, "never dispels ignorance, being under the same category with it. Knowledge alone dispels ignorance, just as light alone dispels darkness."

In other words, the causal process takes place within time and cannot possibly result in deliverance from time. Such a deliverance can only be achieved as a consequence of the intervention of eternity in the temporal domain; and eternity cannot intervene unless the individual will makes a creative act of self-denial, thus producing, as it were, a vacuum into which eternity can flow. To suppose that the causal process in time can of itself result in deliverance from time is like supposing that water will rise into a space from which the air has not been previously exhausted.

> The right relation between prayer and conduct is not that conduct is supremely important and prayer may help it, but that prayer is supremely important and conduct tests it.
> Archbishop Temple

The aim and purpose of human life is the unitive knowledge of God. Among the indispensable means to that end is right conduct, and by the degree and kind of virtue achieved, the degree of liberating knowledge may be assessed and its quality evaluated. In a word, the tree is known by its fruits; God is not mocked.

6
The Source of Becauses

CLARENCE R. PEDERSEN

"All things have 'becauses,' " wrote Arthur Koestler in his book, *Act of Creation*,[1] in what may be the most succinct explanation of the *modus operandi* of nature ever offered by a philosopher. For of the many questions which puzzle the mind, the concept of karma as cause and effect, or action and reaction, has long been one of the most challenging and disturbing. Throughout history this concept has been debated, described, defied, and denied. It has been the basis of much philosophical theory, religious dogma, and scientific deduction. The ontologist finds this aspect of nature intrinsic to life, for ontology becomes meaningless unless karma is incorporated as one of the fundamental aspects of being. Sociologically, karma, even when unrecognized as such, has been the rationale behind our concept of justice.

To those who have studied reincarnation as a doctrine essential to the theory of evolution, karma is a most meaningful concept. Regarding karma as action plus the results of action, the student recognizes that the proper consideration of events cannot be complete unless the preceding related activity, plus the sequel to an event, then the sequel to the sequel, *ad infinitum*, are all considered as integral parts of the entire chain of action.

Defining karma in *The Secret Doctrine*,[2] H. P. Blavatsky wrote: "Karma . . . is eternity itself; and as such, since no act can be co-equal with ETERNITY, it cannot be said to act, for it is **ACTION** itself." It would seem from this definition that karma must have come into operation with the first instant of manifestation, the first instant of creation. For manifestation is action; in addition, it automatically establishes a dichotomy between the source of the creation and the created, a bifurcation which is, so to speak, the very "nature of nature." Thus there is this act of separation which might be termed "First Cause."

According to the theosophical philosophy, it was from this original act of creation that vast numbers of microcosmic units of consciousness, all deriving from the Absolute Principle, began their evolution. Each of these units, being essentially a spark of the Divine, became a microcosmic world in itself, each able to create in its own right by projecting portions of itself into the world outside. It is suggested that as the act of creation by Deity is the beginning of macrocosmic karma, so the first reaching out of the individual soul is the beginning of karma at the microcosmic level. Here too, although on an infinitely smaller scale, there is the creator and the created, with action as the relationship between them. It is implied, of course, that at the earliest stage of evolution, the mental capacities of the units of consciousness are still latent, and thus no personal responsibility is attached to action. In this highly undifferentiated state, karma is simply physical cause and effect, involving groups of dimly conscious units.

Nevertheless, because the superficial diversity of these sparks of consciousness leads to a vast assortment of conflicting creativity, and because the unpolarized noumenon always resists the establishment of polarized phenomena, we find that the projection of consciousness creates an "unnatural" tension, an imbalance within the universe. We note an incessant tug of war throughout creation, first a pulling away from the center of being (centrifugal force), then a compensatory reaction, a pulling back to the center (centripetal force). This rubber-band-like quality of nature eliminates imbalance and restores the universal ethic of harmony.

We find further that within the localization of each unit

of consciousness, as the personality moves from a state of latency, there is the development of a subjective dichotomy due to the relatedness between various components of the psyche. Here also nature strives to overcome the resulting disharmony.

Thus we find that the act of creation is basically divisive, but that nature, the moment it creates this diversity, immediately demands the reunion of the separate parts.

We may say that there appears to be within nature an exquisite tendency toward maintaining the status quo of pure spirit—spirit unsullied and unencumbered by the matter of manifestation. God, we may say, observing what he has wrought, immediately repents his rashness. Unable to recall that portion of his consciousness which he has willed forth, he now does the next best thing and proceeds to negate the effects of First Cause. It is, then, this need to eliminate polarity which seems to be the "cause" of cause and effect. This is an underlying quality of nature, and its manifested result is the law of compensation.

There have of course been many different interpretations of karma and how it affects life. As with all laws which operate in realms not susceptible to empirical evidence, the various conclusions reached concerning karma have been conditioned by the limited nature of human knowledge and by the desire to adjust philosophy to meet one's needs and inclinations. Under these limitations, complete objectivity of interpretation is impossible, and so we find that karma frequently means different things to different people.

For instance, many people believe that karmic law is based upon an ethical interpretation of action—that the nature of reaction is dependent upon an evaluation of action in relation to certain ethical standards. As these standards vary with the psychological uniqueness of the individual, they cannot be designated as universal moral imperatives, and it would therefore be inaccurate to interpret karma on this basis.

The belief in karma as an evaluator of the ethics of human behavior has at times led to the conclusion that karmic

reaction is instigated by a force or forces extraneous to the
perpetrator of the action. Such a conclusion is not surprising
if we consider the background of many major religions.
Here we find that commandments for ethical behavior have
traditionally been "given" to man by Deity. Therefore,
karma, accepted in this sense, has also assumed the status
of divinity. We find, in the Hindu religion, that the *Lipika*
(Lords of Karma) have become the personal karmic administrators in the same way that Jehovah, the God of the
Jews, Gentiles, and Moslems, has been personalized as a
stern but just God. As an evaluator of ethics, karma has
become a guarantee of justice, *as justice is understood from
the point of view of the personality*; consequently it has become
a concept restricted by the limits of the human psyche.

However, as all action is related either directly or indirectly
to First Cause, and as it appears that the nature of the
primordial Source reflects an inherent need to expand
creativity through the unfoldment of its basic integrative
nature, it would appear that action which deviates from
this original impulse would be subject to corrective influences. Thus, any action which tends to hurt or dwarf
life might be considered unethical, and the reaction might
tend to redirect the drive of the actor.

But, if karma is truly the need of the Creator to dispel
the polarity of manifestation, this need must perforce
apply to *all* activity, and thus it would seem that morality
would not be a necessary factor. In this sense, karma would
simply be the agent which in effect nullified all action by
means of reaction.

One effect of (or reaction to) this ethical interpretation
of karma has sometimes been a fear of acting because of
the consequences which might follow. Thus we find the
development within some people of an inclination toward
noninvolvement in the human scene, toward abstinence
from action. This manifests in many cases as a strong
tendency to live what might be called a "karmaless" existence.
This situation might possibly be compared to the germination of a physical antibody, an attempt to instill within
the psyche an antikarma serum composed of anti-emotional

matter, which manifests as a strong desire to repress activity.

Now if we accept the fact that part of the reason for physical incarnation is objective experiencing through relationship, it appears that such a nihilistic approach to life would be contrary to our basic will to act. It seems that life, to fulfill its *dharma* (purpose), must include both subjective and objective activity, the degree of each depending upon the stage of development of the individual Ego.* Thus, inordinate deliberate withdrawal from life would seem to be in opposition to the natural unfoldment of human consciousness. In other words, the greatest "sin" might be an attempt to avoid one's karma; the attempt by the personality to achieve morality by becoming amoral. Such an attempt to circumvent natural law cannot succeed, of course, for an "attempt" implies action to which there would be a reaction. The karma which would follow this negative approach to life would seem to be in the nature of emotional distortion of the psyche; the result might be that, in the future, before engaging in the normal activity of living, the personality would have to overcome the tendency to repress action. This "need to overcome" would be the karma of the Ego and would presumably manifest in the psyche as a specific attribute based on fear.

"Karma," wrote Arthur Robson in his book, *Look at Your Karma*,[3] "means 'actions,' 'doing,' but is used of those things only that we do by natural impulse, innate tendency. In other words one's karma is the sum of one's habits, tendencies, mannerisms and peculiarities of nature, as manifested in what one does."

According to this definition, it would seem that karma proceeds invariably from the psychic force field of the "doer" and never from the occasion itself; that for the occasion to be reactive, to be an effect of a cause previously traced to the "doer," there must be an active acceptance of the occasion by the "doer," whether this acceptance be positive or negative.

---

*Understood here as the true identity, the reincarnating entity, rather than the ego as identified in modern psychology.

Karma in this sense is simply doing and redoing by the unit of consciousness and makes consciousness synonymous with action. In no way does it imply a reaction by the "not-I." Thus, events emanating from the "not-I" cannot be considered as retributive, edifying, or rewarding in themselves. Rather, their effects upon the psyche depend upon the manner of acceptance by the psyche, and this acceptance is subject to the amplifications or modifications of the will of the center of consciousness.

Examining our concept from this point of view, it might be helpful to divide the consideration of karma into three categories: the karma of anticipation; the karma of realization; the karma of remembrance. This last is, of course, a correlative of the first but is used here in the sense of regretting or enjoying a past activity. There is little room for debating the complete subjectivity of the first and third categories. Anticipation and remembrance of relationships with the "not-I" are qualities unique to each localization of consciousness. This leaves the karma of realization as the only type of karma which might be instigated by outside influences.

However, if we accept the fact that the Ego is autonomous within the limits of its psychic force field, that each unit of consciousness is a self-sustaining microcosm within the limits of macrocosmic law, then it seems logical to conclude that the unfoldment of consciousness is dependent upon the will of the Ego. The Ego is stimulated by outside energies only after it determines the need for a specific relationship and guides the consciousness correspondingly. Frequently such subjective motivation is generated from the deep layers of the unconscious, and thus may not be recognized by the waking consciousness.

Of course, Egoic action implies self-awareness but, as has been suggested, this condition is not manifest at the outset of creation.

Prior to what might be termed the "humanization" of the unit of consciousness, before the mental principle with its quality of reflection and judgment becomes manifest, there appear to be certain general guidelines arranged to direct the consciousness to an environment suitable for its evolutionary needs. Although karma, as action and reaction, is a factor in this "gestation period" of the Ego, there is as yet no self-awareness, and thus no basis for judging action in relation to development needs. Yet there is relative importance in this early activity, for the manner of acceptance by the consciousness of the original outside stimulus is the first transmutation of an attribute, a transmutation from a state of latency to one of manifested activity. The energies used in absorbing this experience will be converted into habit, so that subsequent experience will be correspondingly conditioned. Thus it seems that our first manner of accepting experience might be the most important, much as the training of an infant is more vital than that of later years.

It is suggested however that once consciousness has reached human status, the threads of the web of life are created solely by the Ego. Thereafter, at no time does any outside force penetrate within the "ring pass not" of the evolving consciousness. Indeed such an intrusion would seem to be contrary to the pattern of creation as understood by Theosophy, for inasmuch as the Ego bears complete responsibility for its actions, the will of the Ego, within the limits of natural law, must decide what relationships it should have.

Thus we find that karma is the web of life, the total pattern of cause and effect: causes originated by the Ego; effects depending upon the manner of acceptance by the Ego.

Granting the individual psyche this degree of autonomy helps to change our perspective of the influences of outside forces of human life. No longer will the "Lords of Karma"—a vaguely anthropomorphic group of superhumans—be our personal administrators; rather are we subject only to impersonal principle, to natural law. No longer will parochial morality be confused with the universal ethic. Rather, karma will tend to be accepted as a philosophy of complete self-responsibility, so complete that we ourselves must undertake any necessary corrective measures. We may see more clearly that each of us is a god unto himself or herself; that we must not—nay, cannot—rely on outside circumstance to guide our evolution. For all necessary forces are available to each of us; being essentially divine, we can summon to our assistance the powers of divinity at any time we will. These powers of divinity are essential aspects of our own nature, not a part of life outside ourselves. As C. G. Jung remarks in his introduction to *The Tibetan Book of the Dead*, "The Soul [or, as here, the individual consciousness] is assuredly not small, but the radiant Godhead itself . . . even the gods are the radiance and reflections of our own souls. . . . The world of gods and spirits is truly 'nothing but' the collective unconscious inside me."[4]

From this it would seem that you as a person are the "doer," the creator of the occasion, or the responder to the occasion, or both. This of course means that there is never an event in the course of evolution which is in any way fortuitous or fatalistic. There is no arbitrariness in action. Purpose predominates. For karma, beginning with creation, will control creation until the time arrives for the Sound of Silence to return once more.

References

1. Arthur Koestler, *Act of Creation*, New York: The Macmillan Co., 1964, p. 616.
2. H. P. Blavatsky, *The Secret Doctrine*, Adyar: The Theosophical Publishing House, 1938, vol. 3, p. 306.
3. Arthur Robson, *Look at Your Karma*, Adyar: Vasanta Press, 1964, p. 2.
4. W. Y. Evans-Wentz, *The Tibetan Book of the Dead*, New York: Oxford University Press, 1960. Introduction by C. G. Jung, pp. xxxix, li, lii.

II
Karmic Principles in World Religions

The concept behind the term "karma" comes from India, where it has played a vital role in Hindu philosophy for thousands of years. Yet similar concepts can be found within cultures and religious systems throughout the world, expressed in a variety of ways. This section briefly explores versions of the karmic principle within some of these contexts, both Eastern and Western.

Joseph Goldstein looks at karma in Buddhism and considers the importance of compassion and mindfulness in approaching this doctrine. Ananda Coomaraswamy addresses the problem of how karma connects with the specifically Buddhist doctrine of no-self: if there is no independent self, how can karma be transmitted from lifetime to lifetime? Haridas Chaudhuri discusses the philosophy of Integral Yoga as developed by Aurobindo, emphasizing that we humans can learn to cooperate with the law of karma in its role of forwarding cosmic evolution. Geddes MacGregor looks at karma in the light of Christian teaching and addresses several questions and objections commonly raised by Christians regarding karma. He shows how karmic ideas can be found in Christian scripture and also discusses the relation of karma to the Christian concept of grace. Edward Hoffman, in the context of Kabbalistic mysticism, discusses such Jewish notions as tikun *(to make whole) and* gilgulim *(incarnation) and their relation to karma and dharma (one's mission).*

7

A Buddhist View of Karma

JOSEPH GOLDSTEIN

The law of karma is one of the most important laws governing our lives. When we understand it, and live our understanding, when we act on what we know, then we experience a sense of wholeness and peace. If we live in a way that is out of harmony, ignoring the nature of things, we then experience dissonance, pain, and confusion. The law of karma is one of the fundamental natural laws through which we create these vastly different realities. It is as though we are all artists, but instead of canvas and paint, or marble or music, as our medium, our very bodies, minds, and life experience are the materials of our creative expression. A great sense of fulfillment in dharma practice comes from knowing this and from actively creating and fashioning our lives.

Karma is a Sanskrit word (*kamma* in Pali) that means "action." The law of karma refers to the law of cause and effect: that every volitional act brings about a certain result. If we act motivated by greed, hatred, or delusion, we are planting the seed of suffering; when our acts are motivated by generosity, love, or wisdom, then we are creating the karmic conditions for abundance and happiness. An analogy from the physical world illustrates this: if we plant an apple seed, the tree that grows will bear apples, not mangoes. And once the apple seed is planted, no amount of manipulation or beseeching or complaining will induce the tree to yield a mango. The only meaningful action that will produce a mango is to plant a mango seed. Karma is just such a law of nature, the law of cause and effect on the psycho-physical plane.

The Buddha used the term *karma* specifically referring to volition, the intention or motive behind an action. He said that karma is volition, because it is the motivation behind the action that determines the karmic fruit. Inherent in each intention in the mind is an energy powerful enough to bring about subsequent results. When we understand that karma is based on volition, we can see the enormous responsibility we have to become conscious of the intentions that precede our actions. If we are unaware of the motives in our minds, when unskillful volitions arise we may un-mindfully act on them and thus create the conditions for future suffering.

The law of karma can be understood on two levels, which indicate the vast scope of its implications in our lives. On one level, karma refers to the experience of cause and effect over a period of time. We perform an action, and sometime later we begin to experience its results. We plant a mango seed, and many years later we taste the fruit. The other level of understanding karma has to do with the quality of mind in the very moment of action. When we experience a mind state of love, there comes naturally along with it a feeling of openness and joy that is its immediate fruit; similarly, when there are moments of greed or hatred, in addition to whatever future results will come, we also experience the painful energies that arise with those states. Our direct awareness of how the karmic law is working in each moment can be a strong motivation to develop skillful states of mind that create happiness for us in the moment, as well as produce the fruit of well-being in the future.

Another dimension of the law of karma helps in understanding how individual personalities develop. While it is true that there is no enduring entity, no unchanging self that can be called "I," it is also quite obvious that each of us is a uniquely changing and recognizable pattern of elements. This comes about because each of us has in our own way, both consciously and unconsciously, cultivated different mind states. If we cultivate loving-kindness, we experience its taste in the moment and at the same time are strengthening it as a force in the mind, making it easier for it to arise again. When we are angry, we experience the suffering of that anger as present karma and are also strengthening that particular pattern of mind. Just as we condition our bodies in different ways through exercise or lack of it, so we also condition our minds. Every mind state, thought, or emotion that we experience repeatedly becomes stronger and more habituated. Who we are as personalities is a collection of all the tendencies of mind that have been developed, the particular energy configurations we have cultivated.

We tend not to pay attention to this conditioning factor of our experience, thinking instead that once an experience has passed it is gone without residue or result. That would be like dropping a stone in water without creating any ripples. Each mind state that we experience further conditions and strengthens it. . . .

[This is true of both "positive" and "negative" mental states; yet it poses a particular challenge in the latter case, because of the momentum generated by such experiences.] One unwholesome mind state conditions another in a downward cycle of greed, hatred, and delusion. Reflecting on the law of karma brings an appreciation of the preciousness of one's life and a sense of the urgent importance not to squander the rare opportunity we have to hear and practice the dharma. Countless times a day intentions arise in the mind creating the karmic force that brings results. With a careful attention and awareness of volitional activity, we can take active responsibility for the unfolding of our lives.

Once a man asked the Buddha what it is that makes for the different qualities, characteristics, and circumstances among people. Why is it that some people die young and others die old? Why are some rich and some poor? Why are some beautiful and others ugly? Some wise and some foolish? In response, the Buddha explained the actions that produce each of these various results.

Nonkilling results in long life. The result of taking the

lives of other beings is that in the future one's own life will be shortened. Why is it that some people are healthy and others sickly? Nonharming is the karmic force for health, while hurtful actions create the condition for disease. Anger and hatred are the conditions for ugliness, and loving care, gentleness, and kind speech are the conditions for beauty. When someone is very angry, we can see what anger does to his or her expression. The energy that we see clearly manifesting in that moment has a continuing force and power. Previous actions motivated by generosity are the karmic conditions for wealth, and those motivated by greed create the conditions for poverty. Why are some people wise and others dull? The mind that inquires, investigates, and explores conditions wisdom. The minds of those not interested in understanding and insight become dull.

It is said that on the eve of his enlightenment, the Buddha, with the power of his mind, reviewed the births and deaths of countless beings wandering throughout the cycle of existence in accordance with their karma. His great compassion was awakened when he saw all those beings wanting happiness, striving for happiness, yet performing the very actions that would lead to suffering. When we do not understand the unfolding of karmic law, when we are deluded about the nature of things, then we continually create the conditions for greater suffering for ourselves and others, even when we are wishing and hoping for peace. There are those even today who have developed the power of mind to see karmic unfolding through past and future lifetimes. But it is not necessary to be able to see our past lives in order to understand the principles of karmic law. If we pay attention and carefully observe our own lives, it can become very clear how our actions condition certain results.

The Buddha spoke often about right and wrong view with regard to the effects of one's actions. Right view is the understanding that our actions do bring results, both in the present and in the future, while wrong view denies this cause-and-effect relationship. Our culture is generally geared to the pursuit of immediate gratification of desires, and this reinforces the view that what we do will not have effects, that there is no karmic result from our actions that will come back to us. But when we step back and take a broader perspective, we begin to understand that we are the heirs of our own motives and deeds and that our lives do not unfold randomly or haphazardly. It is important to see what our motives and volitions are and to understand the results they condition.

Mindfulness plays a critical role in understanding the unfolding of karma. Two aspects of mindfulness that are particularly relevant to this are clear comprehension and suitability of purpose. Clear comprehension means paying attention to what we are doing, being fully aware of what is actually happening. When we stand up, we know we're standing; when we walk, we know we're walking. Clear comprehension of what we are doing in the moment then allows us to consider the suitability of purpose. This means knowing whether the actions are skillful or unskillful, whether or not they will bring the results that we want.

When mindfulness is weak, we have little sense of clear comprehension or suitability of purpose. Not only may we be unaware of our intentions, we often are not even paying attention to the action itself, hence we may be propelled by habitual patterns into actions that bring painful results. The deep understanding that actions condition results creates a compelling interest in what we do. We begin to pay quite meticulous attention; we begin to awaken. Not only does each action, no matter how insignificant it may seem, condition a future result, it also reconditions the mind. If a moment of anger arises in the mind and we get lost in it, we are then actually cultivating anger. If we get lost in greed, we are cultivating greed. It is like a bucket being filled with water, drop by drop. We think each drop is so tiny, so insignificant, that it doesn't matter at all. Yet drop by drop the bucket gets filled. In just this way, the mind is conditioned by each experience in every moment, and moment after moment the mind gets filled. We should have a tremendous respect for the conditioning power of the mind, not only in terms of our present experience, but also in terms of our future direction.

For a moment now, imagine being on your deathbed and in your last moments looking back upon your life. How would you like to have lived? What would you have wanted to do? What qualities would you wish to have developed? Our lives are a dynamic process of energy transformation, constantly flowing and changing, and we each have the power to determine the direction of our lives and to live in accord with our deepest values. If we become more conscious and awake, developing the ability to observe clearly, we can begin to use our energy creatively and not be bound so blindly to past conditioning. We need not wait until we're dying to reflect on the course of our lives. Reflection on the law of karma, right now, can bring a very strong motivation and inspiration to practice and to live one's life in the best possible way. . . .

During a visit to the United States, His Holiness the Dalai Lama gave a talk about emptiness of self and the karmic law of cause and effect. In the course of the talk, he said that given a choice between understanding karma and understanding emptiness, one should try to understand karma. To many that was surprising, because the very heart of the wisdom of Buddhism is understanding the empty, selfless, insubstantial nature of phenomena. His point of emphasis, though, is extremely important for us to grasp, because without an understanding of karma, of the effect of our actions, the aspect of the emptiness of phenomena can be used as a rationale for not taking responsibility in our lives. To think that nothing matters, that we can do anything because it's all empty anyway, is a serious misunderstanding of the teaching and a poor justification for unskillful behavior. If we are sensitive to the law of karma and become responsible for our actions and their results, then it will help us come to a genuine understanding of emptiness.

Compassion, as well as insight, arises from understanding karma. When we understand that unfair, harmful, or hateful actions rebound in suffering to the person committing them as well as to the recipient, we can respond to both with compassion rather than with anger or resentment.

This in no way means that our response is weak or indecisive. In fact, seeing people act out of ignorance in ways that cause themselves or others great pain can inspire a very strong and direct response to that ignorance, but it is a response of compassion.

The Buddha at one point remarked that only a buddhamind could fully grasp the fullness and complexity of karmic law, the way in which it unfolds, not only within one lifetime, but over countless lives. There are, however, many stories illustrating how karmic destiny unfolded for various people according to their actions. Most are straightforward accounts of the very widespread understanding that we reap as we sow. There are some stories, though, that have particular twists in the plot. These stories are very simple, but they point out some of the complexities and subtleties of the law of karma. One story tells of a man in the Buddha's time who, seeing a monk passing by, thought to offer him food. The man offered the food to the monk but afterward regretted having done so, thinking that it was a waste. The monk was an arhant, a fully enlightened being, and it is said that offering food to an arhant has a very powerful wholesome karmic effect. The result of having offered food to the monk was that the man was reborn as a millionaire for seven consecutive lifetimes. But the karmic fruit of his having regretted his own generosity was that he had a miserly disposition throughout those seven lifetimes and was unable to enjoy his great wealth: the ironies of karmic justice. Each mind moment brings its own appropriate result, and an action can bring mixed results if the mind moments surrounding it are mixed. If a wholesome action is surrounded by a feeling of appreciation, the power of its wholesome karmic force is increased. . . .

In explaining the workings of karma, the Buddha spoke of the potency of different actions. He spoke often of the great power of generosity, explaining that an act of generosity is purified and empowered in three ways. It is purified by the giver, by the receiver, and by that which is given. The purity of mind of the one giving and of the one receiving, and the purity of the gift itself (that is, the means by which the gift came into one's possession), strengthen the karmic force of each act of generosity.

And many times more powerful than giving a gift even to the Buddha and the whole order of enlightened disciples is one moment in which the mind is fully concentrated on extending thoughts of loving-kindness toward all beings. When we genuinely open our hearts, the deep feeling of our connectedness to all beings is a tremendously effective force, which can then motivate a wide variety of skillful actions.

The Buddha went on to say that even more powerful than that moment of loving-kindness is one moment of deeply seeing the impermanent nature of phenomena. This moment of insight is so profound because it deconditions attachment in the mind and opens up the possibility of true non-attachment. When we deeply see the impermanent, ephemeral nature of the mind and body, how they are in constant flux, we develop detachment and equanimity toward the dreamlike elements of our experience. Sometimes in meditation practice when we are dealing with the pain, restlessness, boredom, and other difficulties that come up, we may lose sight of the larger context of what the practice is about. It is helpful to remember that the karmic energy generated by the repeated observation and awareness of the changing nature of things is a tremendously powerful karmic force that leads to many kinds of happiness and to freedom.

Understanding the law of karma is known as the light of the world because through this understanding we can take responsibility for our destinies and be more truly guided to greater fulfillment in our lives.

8

Karma, the Link Between Lives

ANANDA COOMARASWAMY

[When approaching the teachings of the Buddha, it is important that we understand the specific and unique sense in which he adopted the existing terminologies of Hinduism.] The term *Samsara* is a case in point; for this "Wandering" is not for Guatama the wandering of any *thing*. Buddhism nowhere teaches the transmigration of souls, but only the transmigration of character, of personality without a person. Many are the similes employed by Gautama to show that no *thing* transmigrates from one life to another. The ending of one life and the beginning of another, indeed, hardly differ in kind from the change that takes place when a child becomes an adult—that also is a transmigration, a wandering, a new becoming.

Among the similes most often used we find that of flame especially convenient. Life is a flame, and transmigration, new becoming, rebirth, is the transmitting of the flame from one combustible aggregate to another; just that, and nothing more. If we light one candle from another, the communicated flame is one and the same, in the sense of an observed continuity, but the candle is not the same. Or, again, we could not offer a better illustration, if a modern instance be permitted, than that of a series of billiard balls in close contact: if another ball is rolled against the last stationary ball, the moving ball will stop dead, and the foremost stationary ball will move on. Here precisely is Buddhist transmigration: the first moving ball does not pass over, it remains behind, it dies; but it is undeniably the *movement of that ball*, its momentum, its *karma*, and not any newly created movement, which is reborn in the foremost ball. Buddhist reincarnation is the endless transmission of such an impulse through an endless series of forms; Buddhist salvation is the coming to understand that the forms, the billiard balls, are compound structures subject to decay, and that nothing is transmitted but an impulse, a *vis a tergo*, dependent on the heaping up of the past. It is a person's character, and not the self, that goes on.

It is not difficult to see why Gautama adopted the current doctrine of karma (action, by thought, word, or deed). In its simplest form, this doctrine merely asserts that actions are inevitably followed by their consequences, "as a cart a horse." So far as the experience of one life goes, it is simply the law of cause and effect, with this addition, that these causes are heaped up in *character*, whereby the future behaviour of the individual is very largely determined.

Karma must not be confused with mechanical predestination. It does not eliminate responsibility nor invalidate effort: it merely asserts that the order of nature is not interrupted by miracles. It is evident that I must lie on the bed I have made. I cannot effect a miracle, and abolish the bed at one blow; I must reap as "I" have sown, and the recognition of *this* fact I call karma. It is equally certain that my own present efforts repeated and well directed will in course of time bring into existence another kind of bed, and the recognition of *this* fact I also call karma. So far, then, from inhibiting effort, the doctrine of karma teaches that no result can be attained without "striving hard." There is indeed nothing more essential to the Buddhist discipline than "Right Effort."

If we combine the doctrine of karma with that of samsara, "deeds" with "wandering," karma represents a familiar truth—the truth that the history of the individual does not begin at birth. "Humanity is born like a garden ready planted and sown."

> *Before I was born out of my mother generations*
> *guided me. . . .*
> *Now on this spot I stand.*

This heredity is thinkable in two ways. The first way, the truth of which is undeniable, represents the action of past lives on present ones;[1] the second, which may or may not be true, represents the action of a single continuous series of past lives on a single present life. The Buddhist theory of karma plus samsara does not differ from its Brahmanical prototype in adopting the second view. This may have been because of its pragmatic advantage in the explanation of apparent natural injustice; for it affords a reasonable answer to the question, "Who did sin, this person or the parents, that he or she was born blind?" The Indian theory replies without hesitation, *this person*.

Buddhism, however, does not explain in what way a continuity of cause and effect is maintained as between one life A and a subsequent life B, which are separated by the fact of physical death; the thing is taken for granted.[2] Brahmanical schools avoid this difficulty by postulating an astral or subtle body (the *linga-sarira*), a material complex, not the Atman, serving as the vehicle of mind and character, and not disintegrated with the death of the physical body. In other words, we have a group, of body, soul, and spirit; where the two first are material, complex and phenomenal, while the third is "not so, not so." That which transmigrates, and carries over karma from one life A to another life B, is the soul or subtle body (which the Vedanta entirely agrees with Gautama in defining as non-Atman). It is this subtle body which forms the basis of a new physical body, which it moulds upon itself, effecting as it were a spiritualistic "materialization" which is maintained throughout life.

---

1. That the human individual is *polypsychic*, that an indefinite number of streams of consciousness coexist in each of us which can be variously and in varying degrees associated or dissociated is now a doctrine widely accepted even by "orthodox psychology." (G. W. Balfour, *Hibbert Journal*, No. 43) The same thought is expressed more Buddhistically by Lafcadio Hearn: "For what is our individuality? Most certainly it is not individuality at all; it is multiplicity incalculable. What is the human body? A form built up out of billions of living entities, an impermanent agglomeration of individuals called cells. And the human soul? A composite of quintillions of souls. We are, each and all, infinite compounds of fragments of anterior lives." In the Psalm of Ananda: "a congeries diseased, teeming with many purposes and places, and yet in whom there is no power to persist."
2. T. W. Rhys Davids, *Early Buddhism*, p. 78.

The principle is the same wherever the individual is reborn, in heaven or purgatory or on earth.

In this view, though it is not mentioned by Buddhists,[3] there is nothing contrary to Buddhist theory. The validity of the dogma of non-eternal-soul remains unchallenged by the death survival of personality; for that survival could not prove that the personality constitutes an eternal unity, nor can it prove that anything at all survived the attainment of *nirvana*. We may indeed say that Buddhism, notably in the Jatakas, takes the survival of personality (up to the time of attaining nirvana) for granted; and were it otherwise, there would be little reason for the strong Buddhist objection to suicide, which is based on the very proper ground that it needs something more powerful than a dose of poison to destroy the illusion of I and Mine. To accomplish that requires the untiring effort of a strong will.

---

3. Ibid., p. 78. That the theory of the subtle body is not mentioned accords with Gautama's general objection to the discussion of eschatology. It is, however, a tribute to the value of Buddhist thought, that even the proof of the survival of the person would not affect the central doctrine of the soul's complexity and phenomenal character.

9
The Meaning of Karma in Integral Philosophy

HARIDAS CHAUDHURI

Volumes have been written on the Law of Karma and its manifold ethico-religious implications as well as practical bearings upon human life and self-development. The purpose of this paper is to provide a brief account of the ultimate philosophical significance of the Law of Karma, especially in the light of Integralism;[1] the latest development in the Hindu-Buddhist tradition of India.

The fundamental concepts and principles of Integralism have been developed by the author from the teachings of Sri Aurobindo with necessary modifications suggested by the discoveries of modern science and psychology. In respect of its ontological root, it will be shown how the Law of Karma is a logical sequel to the integral world-view or comprehensive awareness of Being.

The major premise of integral philosophy may be spelled out in the form of the following ontological equation:

$$\text{Being} = \text{Cosmic Energy} = \text{Entropy-Negentrophy-Balance}$$
$$\text{Brahman} = \text{Mahashakti} = \text{Tamas-Rajas-Sattva}$$

The meaning of the above question is that Being (ultimate reality or Brahman) is perfectly identical with, or rather non-different from (advaita), cosmic energy (Mahashakti), which is the fundamental energy of the cosmic whole.[2] The sign of equation is in this instance the mathematical symbol of the philosophical concept of nonduality. Nonduality means that we are dealing here not with two separate realities, but with one and the same reality endowed with two inseparable aspects and functions.

Cosmic energy is the basic energy of the cosmic whole from which endless diversities of empirical existence spring into being, in which they all abide, and into which they are dissolved again. The categories of our ordinary thought such as substance, antecedent linear cause, unity, plurality, etc., are inapplicable to the cosmic whole or fundamental energy. Such categories are developed in the human mind as practically useful tools of self-adjustment to the everchanging environment. In consequence, their scope of application is strictly limited to finite empirical existents or observable phenomena, such as oceans and mountains, rivers and trees, animals and humans, stars and galaxies. In so far then as cosmic energy itself is beyond the conceptual tools of intellect, it is incapable of further verbalization (nirguna, anirvachaniya). In respect of its essential being, it is the same as indefinable Being (nirguna Brahman).

Being is the externally self-existent and self-sufficient ground of the entire universe and its bewildering varieties of existence (namarupa). In so far as it is beyond the scope of application of such ordinary categories of human consciousness as space, time, unchanging substance, antecedent cause, etc., it is logically indeterminable (nirguna, nirakara). But so far as it is the creative source of the cosmic manifold, it is entirely nondifferent from cosmic energy. It is presumptuous on the part of the human mind to fathom the mystery of Being-Energy (Brahman-Shakti) by thoughtless application of such perceptual categories as space, time, substance, cause, etc.; or such metaphysical categories as matter and mind, nature and spirit; or such theological categories as body and soul, world and God, God and Satan; or such ethical categories as right and wrong, good and evil.

The Triune Structure of Cosmic Energy

The variegated universe in its primordial essence is then cosmic energy. Energy is the harmonious and dynamic unity of three inseparably interrelated forces. The dynamic interactions of these three interrelated modalities of energy give rise to all the fundamental laws of the universe governing our life and destiny. These forces are:

Material force:	inertia	entropy	tamas	body
Vital force:	activity	negentropy	rajas	life
Mental force:	balance	syntropy	sattva	mind

The material force or physical energy is outward self-expression, space-time expansion, extroversion or gradual dissipation of energy. Traceable to this material aspect of energy is the recently discovered scientific truth that the universe in which we live is an expanding universe. Galaxies are tearing away from one another with tremendous speed, as it were, seized with some kind of cosmic hate or repulsion. In the process they are all losing energy little by little, slowly dissipating their life substance in an irretrievable manner. This is known in modern science as the Law of Entropy, the second law of thermodynamics.[3] The law applies not only to intergalactic relations, but to our human relations, too. The more we live an extroverted pattern of living, the more we dissipate our vital energies. The more we engage in the life style of fierce competition and hateful exclusion of one another, the more we squander our spiritual potential and tread the path of perdition. Herein we find the first important implication—the implication on the material level—of the Law of Karma. It is the ethical correlate, in the sphere of human relations, of the scientific Law of Entropy. As we live and act, so we enjoy or suffer, endure or die. The path of hate and exclusion is the path of gradual self-dissipation. The path of competition is the sure way to the abyss of annihilation.

The essence of the vital force (rajas, prana, elan) consists in inward self-gathering, self-centering, increasing self-organization and structural complexification. This gives rise to Nature's evolutionary process and man's historical order. The creative flow of evolution running through cosmic Nature is conditioned by increasing complexification of structure accompanied by corresponding simplification of function and behavior. The truth of this observation is exemplified even in such primordial energy structures as electrons, protons, atoms, molecules, cells, cellular societies, etc.

The one remarkable offshoot of this self-centering and self-structuring of energy is the creative emergence at critical moments of higher and higher qualities, functions, values and levels of being. For instance, when such divergent molecules as carbon, hydrogen, oxygen, nitrogen, etc., combine in definite proportions, a qualitative novelty, a unique and unprecedented modality of being, namely the living cell, is born. It shows the emergent ability for such new functions as spontaneous mobility, immanent growth from within, self-reparation, self-regulation, self-reproduction, etc. This is known in modern philosophy as the law of emergent or creative evolution. This law represents a higher synthesis in which the religious theory of creation out of nothing and the Darwinian theory of mechanistic evolution through natural selection are harmonized. In the course of evolution, new forms, new qualities, new values continually emerge into being.[4] Life evolved out of the abysmal depths of matter; animal sentience evolved out of the impetus of life; human rational self-consciousness evolved out of the spiraling matrix of animal sentience. In the course of the creative advance of human evolution we know that god-like, illuminated persons endowed with cosmic truth-vision, evolve through prodigious centralization of consciousness. In yoga philosophy this is known as the Law of Tapas-Sristi. This means that when persons by virtue of long practice of intelligent and purposive self-organization (Brahmacharya) generate the internal psychic heat of creative spiritual energy (Tapas),[5] then new visions of truth, beauty, and perfection illuminate their mental horizon and transform their total being into a channel of creativity. Herein lies the secret of original creativity of all such masterminds as the Buddha, Krishna, Christ, Moses, Muhammad, Zoroaster, Lao-tze, and the like.

According to a Hindu legend, at the beginning of a new cycle of creation, the creator Brahma was wondering what kind of fresh novelty he could produce this time. Suddenly he heard a voice from the void, declaring loud and clear: "Tapas, Tapas, Tapas," which means: "Go into the depth of your being, marshal all energy toward the center, and generate the internal heat of new creativity." It is this heat and flame of creativity which is variously known as the mystic fire, the splendor of inner lightening, the pure flame of divine love; the kundalini.

In our human life if we take to heart this principle of novel creation and develop a life style of self-centering and sincere dedication to some such supreme value as truth, beauty, goodness, perfection, peace, freedom and the like, then we are launched upon the path of increasing spiritual unfoldment. Self-development brings in an increasing measure the divine blessings of expanding knowledge, broadening compassion, intrinsic joy, and illumined action. We see here the law of Karma operative on the evolutionary level. Viewed from the evolutionary perspective, the law of karma may then be stated somewhat as follows:

> The more you intensify your consciousness in search of the true Self or the ultimate meaning of life, the more you gain access to unexpected treasures of the spirit.

The Law of Karma on the Cosmic Level

The inner evolutionary process eventually leads one to the cosmic vision of truth suffused with the sweetness of love and compassion. Revealed to the eye of cosmic vision is the essential structure of the cosmic whole as an all-encompassing, self-coherent system, which is self-adjusting, self-regulating and self-manifesting. Cosmic balance and harmony is the name of its essential form.

Viewed from different standpoints the cosmic balance acquires different names. When we look at it from the standpoint of intellect or reason, the cosmic balance appears as the rational structure of the universe or as the system of all systems. Herein lies the fundamental faith of the scientist and the philosopher. This faith consists, as Albert Einstein puts it, in "profound reverence for the rationality made manifest in existence." The more the scientist contemplates the operation of laws in nature, the more he or she is inspired with a religious attitude of awe and humility "towards the grandeur of reason incarnate in existence."[6]

It is by the way of developing the same attitude that the systems view[7] of the universe has evolved in contemporary scientific thought. From the philosophical viewpoint then the highest law of the universe, the supreme and eternal law (Dharma), appears as perfect self-consistency (Satyam). The world's various philosophical schools (darsanas) try to articulate this cosmic self-coherence in various conceptual frameworks.

The fundamental laws of science, such as the law of conservation of energy, and that of cause and effect, are expressions of the eternal Dharma on the scientific level. They may be said to constitute the intellectual aspect of the Law of Karma. In other words, from the intellectual standpoint, the Law of Karma means that nothing happens in this world without a definite cause. It follows that we can control any special kind of happening by suitably changing its cause. If for instance we know the cause of a particular kind of suffering, we can eliminate that suffering by rooting out its cause.

Viewed from the esthetic standpoint, the cosmic balance appears as the harmony of multitudinous sense-impressions. The human mind experiences this harmony of sensations as the beautiful (Sundaram). Since both the true and the beautiful are modes of expression of the spirit of harmony, they are certainly very akin to each other.

Viewed from the standpoint of volition and action, the universe as a self-coherent and self-adjusting system appears as an inviolable ethical order (Sivam). Our practical reason or moral sense perceives in the cosmic harmony an active principle of cosmic justice (Ritam, Bhadram, Subham) controlling the operations of Nature and the human destinies.[8] Herein lies the specific meaning of the Law of Karma, as ordinarily understood—our faith in the moral structure of the universe. Moral faith can be formulated thus: as you sow, so you reap; like action, like consequence (jeman karma teman phal). Mahatma Gandhi laid special stress upon this implication of the Law of Karma: violence begets violence, hatred begets hatred, so love alone can lift humanity from the self-destructive vicious circle of mutual negativity.

Another way the Law of Karma can be expressed is, "He who lives by the sword, perishes by the sword"; conversely, he who lives in the love of truth shines on the lotus of love. Whereas he who thrives on greed perishes in the mud, he who delights in self-giving for the good of others, receives the blessings of God in abundant measure.

In the biological sphere, the Law of Karma assumes the form of ecological balance. The quality of life degenerates if the proper balance is not maintained in the interrelationship of various life forms and in the interaction between life and the physical environment. Violation of this law in the shape of indiscriminate commercial exploitation of the precious resources of Nature has brought us today to the verge of serious ecological crisis. Mother Nature is warning us to the effect: control your greed, or perish.

In the sphere of international relations the Law of Karma is revealed in terms of the balance of power and justice. This means that military power should be employed in international politics only as a handmaid to international justice. Otherwise it is bound to prove self-destructive and internecine.

Unfortunately, at our present stage of evolution, there is a tragic divorce, a yawning chasm, between political power and ethical justice. Until and unless this gulf is bridged by bringing sanity into the sphere of political action the chances of abiding world peace are very slim indeed.

Thus it is the spirit of balance and harmony which sustains the universe in its proper course. Without the force of balance (sattva) holding sway over the opposite forces of tamas and rajas, matter and life, outward self-expansion and inward self-organization, the universe would cease to be the cosmic order that it is. It is the spirit of harmony that creatively holds together the disintegrating entropy of matter and the evolutionary negentropy of life. In consequence, the evolutionary process in humanity continuously advances toward higher and higher levels of consciousness— toward the heavenly boons of immortality (amiritam), truth, love and beauty (satyam, sivam, sundaram).

It is thus the law of harmony which constitutes the ultimate foundation of both science and religion. On the one hand it guarantees the conservation of all energy which is the cornerstone of science; on the other it guarantees the conservation of all values which is the cornerstone of ethics and religion. By harmonizing seemingly conflicting forces such as matter and life, nature and spirit, body and mind, existence and essence, fact and value, it provides the right kind of environment within which the process of creative evolution may go on and the precious fruits thereof be duly preserved.

On the cosmic scale, the spirit of balance (sattva) makes our universe a self-maintaining, self-adjusting, self-regulating system. Instead of an amorphous mass of chaos and confusion it is a self-coherent whole. This basic structural feature of the universe is personified in Hindu philosophy in the image of Lord Vishnu, the supreme God of harmony and love. He is associated with two seemingly conflicting symbols: the infinite serpent (Ananta) and the Sun-bird (Garuda).[9] This bears a striking resemblance to the image of Zarathustra whose two animal companions were, as Nietzsche points out, the serpent and the eagle. The serpent symbolizes the vital energy, the unconscious instinctual drive (libido), which has a tendency to dissipate itself in extroversion. But the same energy is also capable of being rechanneled in an entirely different direction—upward.

The sun-bird garuda is the symbol of the power of spirit. It is the spirit of freedom in upward evolution which transforms instinctual energy and carries it upward on the sunlit path toward the thousand-petalled blossoming of man's divine potential (Kundalini). This upward evolutionary movement is triggered by the ingathering and inwardly focussing concentration of consciousness (pratyahara, dharana and dhyana) oriented to the ultimate goal of life.

The Convergence of Science and Mysticism

It is an exciting development of our present time that modern science, as a result of its recent revolutionary discoveries, has come very close to the eternal truths of mysticism. Contemporary science, following the lead of Einstein and Planck, has rejected the atomistic, mechanistic, and reductionistic outlook of older scientists. It is developing a systemic world view of enormous significance. Implicit in this development is a perfect reversal of outlook revealing the cosmic manifold as the diversification of one unified field of energy.

Bringing together the laws of science and the truths of mysticism, Integral Philosophy contemplates the cosmic whole as a superorganic unity and self-harmonizing system of divergent forces imperceptibly jostling and blending with one another within the limits of an all-controlling order (eternal dharma). Integral Yoga, which is the practical application of the integral worldview, lays its major emphasis upon the need for total integration of personality with a view to perfecting the art of harmonious living in tune with the creative urge of Being (Brahman).[10]

Let us now turn to a brief consideration of the implication of the Law of Karma in regard to the trend of human self-development. We as humans hold in the depth of our being a profound spiritual potential, a divine spark for endless perfectibility. This is our *swadharma*, distinctive human essence. The law of cosmic balance (viswa dharma), mentioned before, maintains the dynamic and evolutionary balance of life by harmonizing opposite forces such as matter and life, devolution and evolution, regress and progress. In our human life the two most fundamental dynamic forces are *karma* and *swadharma*, the conative thrust of the past and the developmental attraction of the future, the drive of desire embodied in samskara and the dream of self-perfection embodied in spiritual aspiration (aspriha, sankalpa).

In other words, all our dynamic thinking oriented to the future is the result of constant interaction between the forces of the past and the future, between *karma* and *swadharma*, between samskara and sankalpa, between the will to live and enjoy, and the will to love and be one with Being. To put it in still other words, the dynamics of our

self-enfoldment are the result of active interplay between
the unseen force of past actions (adrista) and the free initiative
for higher development (purusakara), between the force of
past history and the light of potential liberation (moksa).

The more our knowledge expands, the more we learn to
make a judicious adjustment between the karmic dynamism
of the past and the creative urge of our inner potential
oriented to the future. The motivations flowing from such
interaction ultimately determine our course of evolution.

Be it noted here in passing that Karma does not mean
any external coercive agency. It does not mean the kind
of supernatural fate which was illustrated in the tragic
dramas of the ancient Greeks. Nor does it mean any arbitrary
fiat or predetermined command of the divine will (kismet).
That would be a violation of the ethical order of life (Ritam)
which the Law of Karma presupposes.

Be it also noted that true freedom does not mean absolutely
arbitrary action or irrational choice which some modern
existentialist philosophers eulogize. Rightly understood,
freedom means our ability to act and live in the light of
our own human essence (swadharma), the inner light revealing the purpose of our being as a unique mode of
manifestation of Being, a distinctive creative center of the
cosmic whole (Brahman, Purnam).

In an attempt to actualize the spiritual potential, some
mystics aspire for immortality after death on the supernatural plane. If they follow the right path, they surely can
attain such supernatural self-fulfillment. The Bhakti Yoga
tradition of India,[11] as well as the currents of devotional
mysticism flowing through Judaism, Christianity and
Sufism, emphasize this Karmic connection between
authentic divine love and rapturous communion with
God, the supernatural Lord of the universe.

Some spiritual seekers focus the deep longing of their
hearts upon blissful union with transcendent Being, the
eternal Spirit or indeterminable Godhead beyond God.
This is especially emphasized in the contemplative approach
of the Yoga of Knowledge in India,[12] and in the mystical
traditions of Plato and Plotinus, Jacob Boehme and Meister

Eckhart, Jalal Uddin Rumi and pseudo-Dionysius and others.

It should be noted here that the Theosophical Movement has rendered a signal service to sincere spiritual seekers all over the world by laying stress upon the validity of all major religious and spiritual paths as means of ultimate spiritual fulfillment.

Integral Yoga shares with Theosophy this universality of spiritual outlook. Its special emphasis is geared to the evolutionary potentials of the emerging New Age—the Supramental Age. A suitable integration of the future-oriented spiritual values in the world's major mystical traditions is the dominant keynote of this new yoga dedicated to the outflowering of the Divine in global humanity.

The Karmic significance of Integral Yoga is that if we learn how to cooperate consciously with the creative force of planetary evolution as it is shaping up with the passage of time, humankind's age-old dream of the kingdom of heaven on earth, i.e., an internationally unified world order controlled by the power of truth, justice and love, can inevitably come true.

So the focus of integral self-discipline does not lie on mystic self-realization, whether on the supernatural level or on the transcendental level. Its focus is rather on the paramount desirability of harmonizing the mystic realization with the evolutionary perspective as well as the in-dividuated self-discovery. United with the eternal, the integrated individual would joyfully cooperate with the process of evolution toward the emergence of a new global society.[13]

References

1. Haridas Chaudhuri, *Being, Evolution & Imortality*. Wheaton, Illinois: Quest Books, 1974.
2. Ibid., Ch. VII.
3. Isaac Asimov, *The New Intelligent Man's Guide to Science*. New York: Basic Books, 1965, p. 328.
4. Samuel Alexander, *Space, Time, and Deity*. Vol. 1. London: George Allen & Unwin.

5. S. Radhakrishnan, *The Principal Upanishads*. New York: Harper, 1953. p. 253-54.
6. Albert Einstein, *Out of My Later Years*. New York: Wisdom Library, a division of Philosophical Library, 1950. p. 33.
7. Ervin Laszlo, *The Systems View of the World*. New York: George Braziller, 1972.
8. S. Chatterjee & Datta, *An Introduction to Indian Philosophy*. Calcutta: University of Calcutta, 1950. p. 14-15.
9. Heinrich Zimmer, *Myths and Symbols in Indian Art & Civilization*. New York: Pantheon Books, 1947. p. 76.
10. Haridas Chaudhuri, *Integral Yoga: The Concept of Harmonious and Creative Living*. Wheaton, Illinois: Quest Books, 1974. Ch. 1.
11. Ibid., pp. 67-71.
12. Ibid., pp. 62-66.
13. Ibid., pp. 51-52, 81-82.

10

The Christening of Karma

GEDDES MacGREGOR

The concept of karma, even when properly understood as specifying a universal moral principle that entails profound individual responsibility for one's actions, generally alarms Christians. That is partly because for various complex reasons reincarnationism has had a bad press in the history of Christian thought and practice. Despite the enormous body of literature in which it has appeared in the West, it still seems to many an alien and essentially Indian notion, as ill-fitted to a Christian outlook as would be a stupa or pagoda atop a Gothic church. Apart, however, from such widespread and perhaps not unnatural prejudices against the doctrine of karma and the reincarnationism with which it is associated (prejudices that are hardly worth considering here), some serious objections are raised by informed Christians to the proposal that the doctrine of karma may be with propriety christened as eminently reconcilable with Christian faith, even as that faith is interpreted by the most orthodox and traditionalist of Christians.

One of the most obvious of such objections is that Christian faith, being grounded in the recognition of the power of Jesus Christ to save me and, through his death and resurrection, to raise me (my sins notwithstanding) to everlasting life, can have no place for an inexorable moral law such as is implied in the concept of karma. This type of objection is likely to be raised more vehemently among those Christians who account themselves "Protestant" than among those who regard themselves as "Catholics." That this should be so looks at first somewhat paradoxical to those of us who recall that Kant, who has been traditionally revered in Protestant thought and feared by traditionalist Catholic thinkers, argues in the *Critique of Practical Reason* for a view that is almost an exact occidental counterpart of the oriental doctrine of karma. His "categorical imperative" expresses in encapsulated form the basic moral principle at the heart of the universe: duty. Not only is the universe subject to "physical laws" (the law of "the starry heavens above"); it is governed no less inexorably by another law, "the moral law within." This law, according to Kant, operates just as surely as the law of gravity or any other of the so-called "laws of physics." It is I alone, moreover, who am responsible for my actions, as are you for yours. If Kant's ethical teachings could be, as they have been, so palatable to Protestant Christian thought and so acceptable even to Catholic thought (for Catholic objection to his thought was not directed to his ethics but, rather, to his metaphysical skepticism), why should the notion of karma strike such terror in so many Christian hearts?

But let us probe deeper and into canonical Christian Scripture itself. In the Sermon on the Mount, that most venerated collection of the utterances of Jesus, these words are attributed to the Lord himself: "Do not imagine that I have come to abolish the Law or the Prophets. I have come not to abolish but to complete them. I tell you solemnly, till heaven and earth disappear, not one dot, not one little stroke, shall disappear from the Law until its purpose is achieved." (Matthew 5.17f Jerusalem Bible) Jesus is speaking, of course, of the Torah—to Jews still the most sacred part of the Bible. He is saying that the *formulations* of the moral law that is at the heart of all things may be inadequate and so may be improved or enriched; but the Law itself is unchangeable. It is, as the psalmist had said long before, "perfect, new life for the soul." (Psalm 19.7 Jerusalem Bible) So Jesus goes on: "Therefore, the man who infringes even one of the least of these commandments and teaches others to do the same will be considered the least in the kingdom of heaven; but the man who keeps them and teaches them will be considered great in the kingdom of heaven. For I tell you, if your virtue goes no deeper than that of the scribes and Pharisees, you will never get into the kingdom of heaven." (Matthew 19f Jerusalem Bible) These words, from him whom Christians acknowledge as Lord and acclaim as Savior and Redeemer, leave one in no doubt that no Christian dare pretend to a means of by-passing the moral law which Jesus describes in almost exactly the terms in which one would describe the law of karma.

The karmic law does not exclude grace and redemption any more than does the Torah to which Jesus was referring. Paul rejoices, as must all Christians, that grace has come through Jesus Christ; but he deplores those (and no doubt there were many then as there are today) who proposed to ignore the Law and let grace take over and replace it, making the Law redundant. "Does it follow that we should remain in sin so as to let grace have greater scope?" he asks rhetorically and immediately answers his own question: "Of course not." (Romans 6.1 Jerusalem Bible) Grace gives me a unique opportunity; it puts me in a privileged position by providing conditions of unheard-of advantage; but it no more erases the Law than my good fortune in having a good teacher absolves me from the need to learn. A good teacher helps me to learn. He or she may even make my education possible where otherwise it would have been, for all practical purposes, a hopeless enterprise. So Christianity can take the karmic law with all its entailments under its wing as, following its Master's precept, it must take the Torah.

Why, then, is there so much resistance to the concept of karma and its entailments on the part of those who look to Jesus as Savior and Lord? It is not easy to avoid the conclusion that antinomianism (the view that Christians are by grace freed from the need to obey the Law or even to recognize it) is, under various guises and sometimes ingenious disguises, more widespread in the Christian Church than is commonly supposed either within it or outside it. A genuinely deep concern for morality and righteousness cannot be said to be strikingly characteristic either of the leaders of the Church or of the average churchgoer. A passion for justice is certainly no more characteristic of the assemblies of the Church than is a passionate concern for the truth, the absence of which was cited by Lord Russell as his fundamental reason for not being a Christian. Yet every educated Christian must surely know that to talk of grace without the Law is like talking of literature without language. Indeed, it is much worse: it is like talking of love without sacrifice.

What, according to Christian teaching, does Christ do for the Christian? What is the nature of his redemptive work? The answer, however formulated, is essentially this: he puts the Christian in the right way, providing the conditions that make possible his or her salvation. Through faith in Christ the Christian is "justified," that is, "put right," so that it is now possible for him or for her, as before it was not, to be "sanctified," that is, to get out of the bind and make progress in spiritual development. It is the discovery of the aid that Christ provides in this undertaking that causes the Christian to be, in C. S. Lewis's felicitous phrase, "surprised by joy."

More serious is the theological objection that, while a program of spiritual evolution attained through reincarnation, may be thinkable for Christian believers, it cannot apply to Christ himself who, according to Christian orthodoxy, is "fully God" and "fully man." Since he is God, how can he (as God is conceived in the biblical, Judaeo-Christian tradition) need to progress anywhere at all? Yet if he is also, as Church doctrine insists, "fully man," how can he *not* need to progress, since this is the nature of humanity, and the humanity of Christ, according to orthodox Christian doctrine, must be preserved: to do injury to the one is as bad as to do injury to the other. Such reflections lead us to a more profound one still. When the early Christians acknowledged Jesus Christ as Lord and Savior of the world, what precisely did they mean? Not only were they far from thinking in terms of possibly inhabited planets on solar systems in distant galaxies, as surely we must think today; their knowledge of planet Earth itself was very limited.

Their world extended little beyond the Mediterranean basin.
May not it be that other planets in the trillions of galaxies
in the universe have their own counterparts to Jesus Christ,
their own unique incarnations of God? A Savior who is
"True God and True Man" is fitting indeed for "us men
and for our salvation," as the Christian creed has it; but
suppose there are Martians on Mars. He would not be fitting
for them. They would presumably need a Savior who is
True God and True Martian. So then, since we are being
for the moment so speculative, suppose that we have just
had a radio signal from a planet in some distant galaxy.
We should all be very excited, of course. Christians would
be eager to know whether the inhabitants had heard of
Jesus Christ. Suppose that they had not but that they had
had on their own planet a Being who was the focus of one
of their major religions and seemed to function in it precisely the way in which Jesus Christ functions in orthodox
Christianity. Would a Christian then be justified in saying,
in effect: "No, no, that will not do at all. We must collect
money and see that messages are transmitted at once to
the other planet to bring them the Good News that the
True Savior, the unique Son of God, chose this planet
Earth, and that they must therefore acquaint themselves
without delay with him and his teaching and accept him
as their Savior?" Would a Christian then also feel bound
in conscience, the first time that a spaceship went to the
other planet, to see that included in the passenger list was
a team of missionaries armed with a large supply of Bibles
duly translated into whatever language was appropriate
to the planetary needs of the new missionary field? Would
that spaceship cross one coming in the other direction
with emissaries from the other planet addressed to the
Patriarch of Constantinople, the Archbishop of Canterbury,
the Pope, and the President of the World Council of
Churches, in hope of converting their faithful to an allegiance
to *their* Savior and Lord?

If that seems absurd, as surely many will perceive it to
be, a way is open for the orthodox Christian to say, in effect:
"I cannot tell what has been the pilgrimage of Jesus Christ

before his incarnation on this planet of ours, nor can I dare to prognosticate what his future role on other planets may be. I cannot see, however, why he should not be part of an evolutionary process too, although his stage in the process is infinitely beyond the one in which, by his grace, I am mercifully making some little progress here and now." So not even this objection need have the weight it seems to many Christians to carry.

The next objection to the reincarnational implicates of the karmic law that I should like to consider here is partly philosophical, partly theological. According to reincarnational teaching, the Self transcends in some way the personalities into which it is periodically incarnated. We know, however, that the brain functions as a computer and that this computer not only deteriorates with age but can be irreparably injured by an automobile accident or other traumatic experience in such a way as to destroy memory. The claims of reincarnationists notwithstanding, it is plain that most people remember nothing of a previous life and if what has just been noticed about the functioning of the brain be true, that is unsurprising. For many Christians the notion of a "subtle body" or "etheric double" or "store of energy" to carry over from one incarnation to another the memory-function seems fanciful, no less than does Plato's symbol of the waters of Lethe through which souls pass on their way to the next incarnation, so that all but a few indomitable and advanced souls who manage to keep their heads just a little above these waters of forgetfulness are completely deprived of the power to remember anything of an alleged past life.

This is, of course, a standard and serious philosophical objection (however answerable it may seem) to reincarnationism in general. We should notice, however, that what applies to the reincarnational goose applies no less to the Christian gander. Central to all Christian orthodoxy and the supreme focus of the *kerygma* or proclamation of the first apostles of Christianity is the doctrine of Resurrection. Because Jesus Christ has been "raised from the dead," those who acknowledge and receive him will rise too; that is, they will die but eventually receive a new body. Paul calls it a "glorious" body, one that is presumably finer and better, more ductile and of greater luminosity than our present one. But now, suppose that I have died and have been invested with this new and glorious body of which Paul so eloquently writes. Surely I must be filled with gratitude for what Christ did for me to make all this possible; yet how can I be able to have such thankfulness if I cannot remember my life in the physical body, the life in which my salvation was begun? And how can I remember anything about this life by means of my "glorified" brain or whatever instrument is its counterpart in the luminous body I have now been accorded? In short, whatever difficulties attend reincarnationist doctrine apply in exactly the same way to the indubitably orthodox Christian doctrine of the resurrection of the body.

Christians, especially those with a Catholic background, also often feel that the karmic principle and its reincarnational implicates encourage an individualist approach to such an extent as not only to remove the need for the Church, its ministry, and its sacraments which the Church deems necessary for salvation, but also to eliminate all need of guidance and help. True, reincarnationism, grounded in the karmic principle, does make a "lone walk" possible. It does abolish the need to depend absolutely on the Church's ministry and sacraments. That is not to say, however, that any sane man or woman, Christian or otherwise, would fail to use any help he or she can find in so momentous an enterprise as one's salvation. The fact that I can, if I am reasonably intelligent, educate myself entirely from books does not imply that I shall on that account decline the services of good teachers. On the contrary, the more intelligent I am the more readily shall I see their value to me. Nevertheless, *in extremis* I can do without a teacher and fend for myself. If it should happen that I can find only very bad teachers I may well prefer to manage on my own, for a bad teacher may be even worse than none. He may impede an intelligent person's progress. So a stupid priest or ignorant rabbi or lazy guru could be an impediment that I might well be better without.

A thorough knowledge of the history of the Christian Church leaves us in little doubt that much of the prejudice against karmic and reincarnationist teaching has been generated by the fears of those bad bishops and pedestrian priests who, having no spirituality of their own to offer, perceive the danger that such spiritual independence poses to their power over the lives of men and women. Good priests, however, have nothing to fear and indeed everything to welcome from the development of spiritual independence among the faithful. In fact, many of the greatest Christians, those who plainly have been conspicuously able to fend for themselves in their spiritual development have been no less conspicuously ready to learn from any teacher or confessor or friend and also to participate in the life of the Church with the simplest of "babes" in the faith. One thinks, for instance, of Teresa of Avila, of George Tyrrell, of Kierkegaard, of Simone Weil, to mention only a random few. They have deeply loved the Church without finding it absolutely indispensable. I very much love my home without deeming it absolutely essential to life and happiness.

The suspicion, voiced long ago by A. E. Taylor in *The Faith of a Moralist*, that reincarnationism encourages procrastination also warrants notice. Of course one can put off reform to another life, but one knows all the while that one is only making things more difficult for oneself. Most people manage to procrastinate copiously even with no expectation of the "second chance" that reincarnationism provides. Augustine's youthful prayer, "Give me chastity but not yet," is as possible without a karmic view as with one. The deathbed-repentance syndrome is familiar to all pastors and confessors. The moral urgency implied in either a reincarnationist or a non-reincarnationist view is always there. The sooner I reform, the easier my reformation will be; the longer I delay, the more trouble I make for myself. Every drunk learns that.

Some Christians object that reincarnationism is inconsistent with the Christian teaching that our destiny is settled once for all at death. There is, however, no such clear

Christian teaching. Indeed, the Christian teaching on the afterlife is, for various reasons, by far the most confused part of traditional theology. It is so for some very good reasons, one of which is that in the first century of the Christian Way people did not give it much thought because they expected the end of the world imminently, perhaps literally on the morrow. In such circumstances one does not readily engage in eschatological speculations. When eventually that expectation died down, churchmen were confronted with a vast panorama of possibilities from both their Hebrew heritage and their Hellenistic surroundings. The most promising line of early Christian thought was that which pointed to a state of purgation and growth, a notion which, found in Clement of Alexandria and others among the early Fathers, was later developed in singularly unfortunate ways in the Latin West as the medieval doctrine of purgatory. Along with this doctrine of an "intermediate state," however, were developed the notions of heaven and hell, states generally presented as unchanging conditions, the one of eternal bliss, the other of eternal torment. Such notions are in fact unthinkable not only because the doctrine of hell is incompatible with the doctrine of God's love and mercy, but because both heaven and hell exclude growth, which is of the very nature of all finite being. Most educated Christians have quietly set aside the notions of heaven and hell in the form in which they were presented in the Middle Ages and by the Reformation Fathers.

The objection that it is immoral to be held accountable for sins one has committed in a previous life and has therefore forgotten deserves some attention, since at first sight it seems plausible. How can I have the disposition of penitence for my misdeeds if I cannot even remember them? We may well argue that if a child is to be punished the punishment should be swift, since otherwise the child will soon have forgotten the wrong it did and therefore rightly resent the punishment. But while that may be sound parental practice for the training of the very young, life operates on different lines. Modern psychoanalysis recognizes that what gives us most trouble is what lies buried in our un-conscious. It is our forgotten misdeeds and evil thoughts that take the worst toll. Christian theology abundantly recognizes the fact that we do not know how distorted we are. Like it or not, we do have to pay the price for past wrong-doing we have long forgotten about. It is so easy to injure my brother and then forget about it. The greater the injury the more ready I am to forget, that is, to push the memory of it down into my unconscious. There, however, it continues to fester. The reincarnationists, grounded as they are in the karmic principle, are only extending the scene, knowing as they do that humans have a much longer history than the date on their birth certificates. They have also a longer future than the date that is to be on their death certificates: a future they can make or mar.

Many Christians believe in a literalistic way in the Second Coming of Christ as a "day," the *dies irae*, the Day of Judgment. Is not that alien to a reincarnationist view? It may be incompatible with some forms of reincarnationism, but not all. We can still interpret the Day of Judgment as the end of the present age and the beginning of a new one, which is indeed in accord with the biblical witness. The new age, if this planet Earth be destroyed, might begin on another planet in another galaxy, if not on one in our own. The holocaust that many Christians envision on that "terrible day" would presumably in any case wipe out all life, including the vast animal kingdom to which we are biologically re-lated through evolution: a relationship to which, by the way, Christian theologians have never given adequate attention, despite the poetry of Francis of Assisi and the Gospel assurance that God notes the fall of the smallest sparrow to the ground.

The Cambridge moralist, A. C. Ewing, in a sympathetic but critical reference to reincarnationism and the karmic principle, suggested that it has too much of a "mercantile flavor," too much of "an exact proportion between such incommensurables as goodness and happiness." In such a scenario, he suggests, there could be no genuine self-sacrifice. True, Christian love knows nothing of moral accountancy. Christ, far from calculating the cost of our redemption, pours forth his blood for us on the Cross with infinite abandon. The cost of our redemption, however, may be even greater than Ewing perceived. Thomas Aquinas, preeminent among the medieval schoolmen, taught that grace presupposes nature and perfects it. If then, God, in his self-humbling, must reckon with both law and nature, the cost of sacrificial love must surely be incalculably higher than we can imagine. The karmic principle abides.

What the karmic principle and its reincarnational implicates do provide is a mitigation of, if not a complete solution to, the most intractable problem in Christian theology: the problem of evil. They spread the story of the individual on to a much larger canvas, so that in looking at our present life we are looking at only a slice (indeed a very slim slice) of the moving picture that stretches far into the future as well as deeply into the past.

Long before anyone knew of outer galaxies or could have thought seriously about the possibility of interplanetary travel, Alice Meynell (1847-1922), a profoundly mystical English Catholic poet, hinted in a poem at the problem that the magnitude of the universe posed for Christology even in her time. Entitled *Christ in the Universe*, it contains allusions such as these:

> *No planet knows that this*
> *Our wayside planet, carrying land and wave,*
> *Love and life multiplied, and pain and bliss,*
> *Bears as chief treasure one forsaken grave.*

> *Nor, in our little day,*
> *May his devices with the heavens be guessed;*
> *His pilgrimage to thread the Milky Way,*
> *Or His bestowals there be manifest.*

> *But in the eternities*
> *Doubtless we shall compare together, hear*
> *A million alien gospels, in what guise*
> *He trod the Pleiades, the Lyre, the Bear.*[1]

---

1. *The Golden Book of Modern English Poetry*, 1870-1920 (London and Toronto: Dent and Sons, 1927), p. 51.

O, be prepared, my soul!
To read the inconceivable, to scan
The myriad forms of God those stars unroll
When, in our turn we show to them a Man.

Perhaps, however, nothing so much impedes the
christening of karma as does an objection and misunderstanding that we considered near the outset: the notion
that emphasizing individual responsibility for salvation
undercuts the operation of Christ's redemptive act. Since
this is probably the most popular misconception on the
subject, especially among Protestant Christians, I wish to
make abundantly clear to readers of this essay, Christian
or otherwise, that this objection arises more from a misunderstanding of Christian doctrine than from a misunderstanding of the karmic principle itself.

The notion that, when one is captured by the power of
Christ's love and responds in fervent gratitude for the
salvation he assures the recipient of his grace, that is the
end of the matter, is not a Christian notion at all. It is a
pernicious travesty of Christian doctrine as taught in the
New Testament, the early Fathers, and not least the Reformation Fathers. A tradition that runs all the way from Paul
through Augustine to Luther and Calvin demands that
Christians be especially on their guard against the notion
that when one has become aware of the saving act of Christ
in the soul there is nothing more to be done.

I have elsewhere told the story of a stuttering Christian
missionary who, on being taunted that Christ did not seem
to have healed him, replied: "But b-b-before he h-h-healed
me I was a d-d-deaf-m-m-mute." Until his conversion his
condition had been hopeless; now it was remediable. There
is also an old Victorian poem about a little girl who, having
covered her school "slate" with figures in trying to solve an
arithmetic problem, comes weeping to the teacher who,
being a good and kind teacher, sits down beside the child,
cleans the slate and says, "Now let us do it together." The
teacher's action becomes, in the poem, a parable of the work
of salvation that Christ begins in the soul. Would such
an action diminish the gratitude of such a child? Should

such a recognition of the nature of Christ's saving love diminish a Christian's appreciation and gratitude? Of course not. If you had a mental block against mathematics that made math a fruitless pain to you, its removal would make doing math a pleasure; the last thing it would do for you would be to cause you to stop doing mathematics. If you were an alcoholic down and out in the gutter and then through Christ found your way to redemption from your vice and the path to a productive and creative life, the last thing you would do would be to insist that you had no longer any need to consider the tendency that had brought you so low in the first place. On the contrary, you would be all the more aware of it and at the same time aware of your power to overcome it, which you did not have before.

"So then, my dear friends," writes Paul to the Church at Philippi, "continue to do as I tell you, as you always have; not only as you did when I was there with you, but even more now that I am no longer there; and work for your salvation 'in fear and trembling.' It is God, for his own loving purposes, who puts both the will and the action into you." (Philippians 2.12f. Jerusalem Bible)

Is there, then, any sound theological reason from any Christian point of view, orthodox or heterodox, traditionalist or experimental, against the christening of karma and its reincarnational implicates? Personally I cannot see any at all. The influence on Christianity of Hellenistic ideas, including of course the Platonic tradition, was not merely something that developed after the apostles of the Christian Way had spread their message to the Gentile world; it was present, to say the least, in the Judaism in which the Christian Way was cradled. During what Christian scholars have customarily called the "intertestamental period" (that is, approximately 165 B.C. through A.D. 48, the interval between the last book of the Hebrew canon, Daniel, and the earliest of the New Testament writings), the Jews were exposed to vast extraneous influences. Jewish thought, even in Palestine, was profoundly affected by these. The kind of movement of which Jesus was the center, however we may choose to interpret it, would have been unthinkable in Palestine a few centuries earlier. By his time, however, the situation had so altered that Hellenistic ideas could be commingled with traditional Jewish faith and practice in a rabbi's teaching. In Alexandria, the chief intellectual center of the Diaspora, the Hellenistic influence was overwhelming, having a most able spokesman in Philo, a contemporary of Jesus; but even in the Jewish Homeland its effects, if less enduring, were considerable. Greek architectural ideas affected even the way in which synagogues were built and Greek administrative practices were adopted by Jewish communities in their government and organization. Hellenism was fostered, at least for a time, by the priestly aristocracy. While Jesus himself encouraged the veneration of the Torah and in principle honored the traditional Jewish ritual and other customs, his leadership of the kind of celibate religious community into which he organized his disciples was alien to classical Hebrew practice. The *extent* to which Hellenistic ideas affected his teaching is controversial; what is indisputable is that Hellenistic ideas permeated the thought of his times. To suggest otherwise would be like suggesting that an educated American today could be ignorant of Darwin or of Freud or that he or she might not have heard of nuclear fission.

We all know that Plato, following the Pythagorean tradition, accepted the ancient doctrine of reincarnation, very explicitly putting it into the mouth of the Socrates of the Dialogues. Long before Christianity was in the way of being directly influenced by Platonistic and Neoplatonistic ideas in the pagan world, however, it had emerged in an atmosphere in which reincarnationist ideas such as Plato took as part of the ideological scenery were at least an ingredient. Christians of the first century would not but have imbibed such ideas and there is some evidence to show that they did not by any means necessarily repudiate them. Some seem to have found them congenial. In the Alexandrian tradition that developed, in which Clement and Origen played leading roles, the thought of Plato loomed very large indeed.

Why, then, did reincarnationist teaching get such a bad

press in the Christian Church and come to be so much distrusted, not to say feared? Only a combination of circumstances that included the inchoate state of Christian eschatology and the second-century Church leaders' suspicion of Gnostic teaching, could have led to the ousting of a reincarnationist interpretation of the life of the world to come that was and is the Christian hope. I think this result has gravely impoverished the Church's official presentation of the nature of the afterlife. As we have seen, there is really not the slightest reason for the fear or the distrust.

Of course that is not to say that reincarnationism in every form in which it happens to appear is necessarily reconcilable with Christian faith or that the Church ought to welcome Gnosticism no matter in what guise it comes. In some forms it can lead to and indeed express a selfish unconcern for others that would be radically antithetical to the *agape* that Paul exalts above all else in one of his most eloquent passages (I Corinthians 13) and that is universally acclaimed by Christians as of the very life of the Church. Any *such* reincarnationism would be, on that account alone, entirely out of court. Moreover, reincarnationist teaching is sometimes so closely tied to certain metaphysical presuppositions not easily if at all reconcilable to Christian faith that a Christian with any pretensions to loyalty to the central creeds of the Church would be rightly cautious in regard to such forms of it. Nevertheless, when all that is said, there is nothing in the notion itself and certainly nothing in the karmic principle that lies behind it (whatever name be given to that principle) that need give a Christian of even the strictest orthodox stance the slightest pause. On the contrary, the karmic principle and its reincarnationist implicates can be warmly embraced by any such Christian as a means of greatly illuminating his or her understanding of the nature of the life of the world to come, belief in which is solemnly affirmed in the final article of the Nicene Creed with no specifying or limiting details of any kind. Cardinal Mercier is among the distinguished Roman Catholics who have declared that reincarnationism has never really been officially or explicitly condemned by the Church. The bad press it received was partly through a sort of guilt by association with other ideas and partly because of the fears we have considered earlier.

To such Christians as are interested in the karmic principle and the concept of reincarnation, I would say: by all means diligently study it through theosophical or any other well-informed channels and, bearing in mind the considerations I have laid before you here, discover through critical thought and earnest prayer whether it might not greatly clarify your understanding of the Christian hope and. illumine your vision of your own destiny in the life of the world to come.

11

A Kabbalistic View of Karma

EDWARD HOFFMAN, Ph.D.

In the modern era, Jewish concepts about the human soul and its journey through earthly existence became almost totally eclipsed by the scientific ethos. Outside of the various Hasidic groups, founded in eighteenth-century Eastern Europe, few Jewish theologians or philosophers in modern society paid even scant attention to metaphysics or mysticism. Today, however, with the burgeoning interest in Eastern spiritual traditions, there has been a marked fascination in the West, among people of all backgrounds, in the Kabbalah, the esoteric branch of Judaism. It has become increasingly clear to many around the globe that Kabbalistic ideas are both fascinating and relevant to our contemporary lives. What the Kabbalah has to say is not only interesting in its own right, but also provides some startling parallels to ideas set forth in other paths, such as Hinduism and Tibetan Buddhism.

The Hebrew term *tikun* derives from the root-word meaning "to rectify," "to redeem," or "to make whole." In essence, the Kabbalah has long taught that every human soul is created by God (the *Ein Sof* or "Infinite") in order to fulfill a unique role in the divine plan, a notion that recalls the Hindu concept of one's *dharma*. Every soul is wholly unique and precious, and each has a vital part to play. Kabbalists have always insisted, too, that one single lifetime is seldom sufficient for the soul to complete its mission on earth, so that several incarnations—called *gilgulim* in Hebrew—are almost always necessary.

Overt references to reincarnation can be found as early as the *Sefer Bahir* (*Book of Brilliance*), which first appeared around the year 1175 in southern France. About a century later, the *Zohar* (*Book of Splendor*) dealt more extensively with this theme. But with the tremendous Kabbalistic germination in the land of Israel during the sixteenth century, this provocative doctrine became a key element in the Jewish esoteric tradition. In fact, during this period, as Professor R. J. Zwi Werblowsky of Hebrew University notes, "Trying to identify the souls inhabiting their colleagues became a passionate and serious [activity]. . . . Rabbi Isaac Luria was considered by his followers as the supreme authority." The Hasidic masters likewise ascribed to this notion and incorporated it as a significant feature in their message for the discouraged and impoverished masses of East European Jewry.

Though Kabbalists emphasize the existence of a spiritual realm beyond the physical world, they also stress that each soul must return to earth until all its tasks are completed. In heaven only the Self gains a deeper understanding of its corporal life. It is essential, the Kabbalah affirms, that the soul reincarnate, in order to fulfill all of its unmet commandments. These might vary radically from person to person—hence, the basic Kabbalistic view that we each have a unique mission to accomplish. Indeed, works such as the *Zohar* assert that the very fact of our physical existence indicates our incomplete inner development. Except for one rather notable exception—to be discussed shortly—we would not even be here in material form unless it were necessary.

> The Holy One . . . permits [the human being] . . . to start anew, and labor for himself in order to make good his deficiency. In addition, it must be remembered that the man has to undergo transmigration because he is not, in any case, of great merit; since if he were so he would not have had to pass into another form and live again upon the earth, but would at once have "a place better than sons and daughters."

The *Book of Splendor* specifically mentions several causes that necessitate additional lifetimes in the physical realm.

One of these is the failure to raise a child, another is not having married. Thus, we are told, if an individual marries but dies without children, husband and wife undergo reincarnation and unite again as they were before. For the Kabbalists, the union between man and woman—encompassing physical, emotional, and spiritual dimensions—is a key pathway to the divine. Not surprisingly, therefore, initiates have viewed marriage—as well as other close relationships—as almost inevitably involving reincarnational dramas.

In fact, in the Jewish mystical tradition, spouses are regarded as having typically known each other in past lives. For example, Rabbi Joseph Karo was a great sage who lived in the town of Safed, in the Land of Israel, during the sixteenth century. He experienced deep trance states for many decades, in which he felt a spirit-guide (known in Hebrew as a *maggid*) communicated to him secrets about the universe. Karo's *maggid* thus declared that one of Karo's wives had actually been a well-known male scholar in an earlier existence. The *maggid* intriguingly stated:

> Since she is a male soul she is not really your mate; you received her as "ownerless property" [i.e., not as your true partner]. . . . Because her soul is essentially a male soul, she could not produce offspring for you.

In another discourse on reincarnation, the *maggid* related:

> You already know that she has lived twice before and that in her second existence she was a miser . . . transmigrated this time in order . . . to be perfected through you. . . . She too will acquire merits, for through the money that she has brought you and through her serving you, you will be privileged to teach *Torah*.

Throughout its exotic messages, Karo's *maggid* expounded upon a favored theme among the Safed Kabbalists: that the arena of sexuality and marriage is an important testing ground for our spiritual development. Spouses are here together to work out unresolved conflicts impeding inner growth. In this context, the *Zohar* tersely observes that each spouse gets the one he or she deserves. Similarly, the

child-rearing experience is seen as an important aspect
of earthly existence, and no one is considered able to pass
beyond this realm without having raised—in at least one
lifetime—a child to adulthood.

Isaac Luria and his followers devoted a great deal of
attention to the subject of the transmigration of souls.
They elevated this earlier concept to a key element in their
entire teaching about the nature of human destiny and the
divine order. In his book, *Sefer Ha Gilgulim* (*The Book of
Transformations*), Chaim Vital discussed this issue in detail.
To summarize his rather elaborate system, one could say
that he argued that each person must normally carry out
all of the various commandments. If a single commandment
is not fully observed, then transmigration has to occur.
But Vital drew a distinction between those commandments
which the person is capable of fulfilling and those which
he or she is not. For instance, a woman is obviously unable
to complete tasks that Judaism specifies for men only. In
such cases, Luria's protege explained, if we do not have
the opportunity to fulfill them, we need not transmigrate
because of their incompletion. Moreover, every commandment must ultimately be carried out not just physically,
but with the proper intentionality and concentration. "If
some spark of a soul has not fulfilled even one aspect of
those three—deed, speech, and thought—it must transmigrate
until it fulfills all of them," he wrote.

Chaim Vital also helped to promulgate the evocative
Lurianic doctrine that various people on earth are secretly
or inwardly related to one another because of their joint
origin in the same "family of souls," or, in Eastern terminology,
they have mutual karma. Many historical developments
among apparently disparate groups or nations, therefore,
are seen to stem from longstanding reincarnational ties.
The early Hasidic leaders, more than two hundred years
later, stressed this same concept to their minions; in fact,
some Hasidic founders explicitly identified their colleagues
—and even themselves—as prominent biblical figures in
prior lifetimes. Inevitably, the Kabbalah tells us, our purpose
on earth relates to our own previous lifetimes and those

of others around us, especially intimates, a thought which might be expressed as having karmic ties. "As a result of this," Rabbi Moses Chaim Luzzatto, an Italian Kabbalist of the eighteenth century commented, "all men [are] bound to each other."

In the Jewish esoteric discipline, the goal of the *gilgulim* is for each soul to end its repetitive cycles of death and rebirth in the physical world. This viewpoint is strikingly similar to Buddhist and Hindu teachings, which likewise preach that when we attain sufficient spiritual awareness, we break free of karma and the cycle is finally over. Thus, in *The Tantric Mysticism of Tibet*, John Blofeld observes:

> Clinging to the false notion of its permanency, the wretched ego suffers successive rounds of death and rebirth, aeon upon aeon. . . . None of the infinite number of states . . . is altogether satisfactory. . . . The remedy lies in freeing oneself from [the cycle] forever by destroying the last shreds of egohood.

In an identical belief, Jewish mystics have seen the necessity to return to earthly existence as a distinct burden. Thus, Chaim Vital relates that Moses died in bitterness because he knew that he had not yet fulfilled all of the commandments and would therefore need to reincarnate. Indeed, the *Zohar* stresses that in the World to Come souls must oftentimes be forced to transmigrate as they are not eager and even unwilling to return voluntarily to the obvious travails of this domain.

The Kabbalah emphasizes that in all matters of earthly life—encompassing our health, livelihood, and social relationships—the crucial perspective to adopt is that everything is part of the divine plan. Our *tikun* is never suffering for its own sake, but ultimately knowing God better through joy. It is normal and natural to feel helpless or victimized by the vagaries of a seemingly blind and uncaring universe. But in Kabbalistic terms, virtually all that we experience as major life events are part of a destiny in which various souls are linked through countless unseen ways. The more we grow in wisdom and discernment, Kabbalists have always stressed, the better able we are to perceive the hidden patterns and workings of the Holy One in our lives.

Coincidence and Tikun

How do we come to recognize and stay committed to our *tikun* in life? One key way, Jewish mystics have insisted, is through recognizing *Divine Providence* as a guide for helping us to maintain direction in our day-to-day endeavors. The Jewish visionary tradition explains this phenomenon as encompassing events in our daily lives that are in some way uncanny, startling, or unbelievably coincidental so as to serve as clear signposts for us along the way. Such incidents can exert a tremendous force over the everyday world that lifts our routine frame of mind out of its doldrums. By remaining open and receptive to happenings around us, we become alert to such occurrences, the Kabbalists have stressed. Thus, for instance, Rabbi Luzzatto observed that there are many different reasons for everything that occurs to an individual in this world, for good or otherwise. "The Highest Wisdom," he noted, "perceives and knows what is best to rectify all creation." Because everything that exists is in constant interplay, each element of the cosmos moves in correspondence to all others.

As we gain in our own understanding of the cosmos, we can more easily read the pattern that lies behind outward events. We begin to see the common threads that bind seemingly unrelated occurrences. Whereas before we saw merely apparent chaos or misfortune—what Shakespeare's Hamlet bemoaned as the "slings and arrows of outrageous fortune"—now we perceive a unity. Rabbi Luzzatto gives such examples as that of a man whose cow broke its foot and fell, thereupon causing the irate owner to find a buried treasure. Also, he recounts the anecdote—familiar to many of us through our own lives—of a person who wants to embark on a trip and is suddenly detained, only to learn later that the journey would have ended in disaster. "Means such as these can be destined to affect the individual himself or to influence others," Rabbi Luzzatto writes. "Something can thus happen to a person in order to bring good or evil to someone else."

Of course, we cannot always subject the most minute features of our days to great scrutiny. But the Kabbalists have always insisted that beneath the surface of what appear to be random events is actually a tightly woven pattern of meaning. With wisdom comes the gift of discernment, we are told, a power more prized than the simple flexing of extrasensory abilities.

This idea was similarly emphasized by the early Hasidim several generations later. They viewed odd or strange turns of events as very meaningful, to be interpreted on several levels. In one well-known Hasidic tale which illustrates this point, a disciple of the Koretzer *Rebbe* was accidentally marooned on a deserted isle while en route to perform a *mitzvah* (good deed) for his mentor. He kept himself alive by eating wild fruit and berries. Eventually, he was picked up by a passing ship. Upon returning with remorse to the House of Study, he met the Rabbi, who told him, "There were sparks of holiness on the island which it was necessary . . . to restore to their source. Regret not the opportunity granted you, for you served the Lord well."

In another anecdote, the Baal Shem Tov (Hasidic founder) and a disciple were walking along the road. There was no water available for miles on the hot and dusty path; the disciple complained bitterly of his thirst. When asked whether he believed in Divine Providence, the disciple replied, "Yes." Suddenly a person appeared bearing a pail of water and offered a drink to the astonished Hasidic initiate. The Baal Shem Tov asked the man how he had come to be in such an out-of-the-way spot, ferrying water from a long distance. The man answered, "My master has just fainted not far from here, and I was compelled to bring water from a spring several miles distant." Thereupon, the Hasidic founder turned to his disciple and said, "You see, there are no coincidences in the universe."

This Kabbalistic notion is quite similar to Carl Jung's interesting concept of *synchronicity.* In his last two decades of life, the Swiss psychoanalyst developed a theory to explain the phenomenon of "meaningful coincidences." He believed that a divine harmony pervades the cosmos and that such events point to the fact that everything is ultimately inter-related. In his therapeutic work with patients, Jung stressed that these occurrences may provide deep significance and direction to those who feel trapped and lost.

Interestingly, evidence from his personal correspondence indicates that Jung was familiar with the Kabbalah and the Hasidic tradition, though he could not read Hebrew. It is fascinating to speculate whether his concept of syn-chronicity was influenced by such sources, which he apparently studied at the same time he began to articulate this theory, which is now attracting increasing attention among physicists as well as psychologists.

However successful we are in heeding such striking events as secret clues to our lives, the Kabbalah affirms, physical existence must come to an end. Its major thinkers have suggested that when the person's chief life-task is completed, his or her mission on earth is likewise over. It becomes time to move on. This notion was well accepted by the early Hasidim. In various anecdotes, they expounded upon the Lurianic doctrine.

In one incident, Rabbi Yekuthiel Teitelbaum became dangerously ill in old age. He declined to call in a doctor. When questioned by his amazed disciples, he explained that his work had ended, and therefore no physician could help him. As he predicted, he never recovered. In another tale, a Hasidic leader criticized a colleague for assuming massive responsibilities for his congregation at too early an age. When pressed for an explanation, the older *Rebbe* said, "Every [person] is allotted by Heaven a term of service lasting for a certain number of years. Had [he] waited to commence his term at a more mature age, he would have enjoyed a longer life." And, as the *Rebbe* had surmised, his cohort passed away while still young.

Aspects of Tikun

For many centuries, Kabbalists have regarded health and illness as important facets of our tikun. In their view, no major physical disorder, disability, or disease can be fully understood—or treated without seeing it from a larger, spiritual perspective. Congenital or lifelong disabilities have always been viewed by Jewish mystics as meaningful components of one's particular incarnation on earth. Yet the traditional outlook is *never* that the soul is being "punished" by being placed in a stricken or diseased body, but that it has been put in this difficult situation for reasons ultimately known only to the Creator. Our response—whether as a family member, friend, or simply fellow human—is expected to be compassion and aid, not sanctimonious judgment.

In this respect, Kabbalists take strong exception to the tendency among some espousing "New Age" ideas to blame the suffering individual for his or her condition. Sometimes, such blaming is tacit rather than overt, but it still represents a "holier than thou" attitude antithetical to the entire Kabbalistic perspective. In particular, Jewish mystics have long preached that a person's chronic illness or disability may actually be a divine lesson for others—usually, family members or friends—and that the sufferer may be gaining little for his or her *own* growth.

In our era, there are many benefits to be gained from adopting this viewpoint. Certainly it offers a much needed counterbalance to the pervasive cynicism and gloom in our wider culture today. For instance, in a recent discussion on Jewish mysticism and its contemporary relevance, a lively middle-aged woman related to our group that she had been burning with resentment several years earlier for having to care for her elderly, senile mother. The situation had begun to deteriorate for her into an intolerable burden, so she had sought the advice of her personal *rebbe*, who was both a practicing psychotherapist and a teacher of the Kabbalah.

"Would you be pleased if you were suddenly presented with a wonderful spiritual teacher meant just for you?" her *rebbe* asked.

"Of course," the woman instantly replied, "I'd be more than pleased. I'd be overjoyed!"

"Well," her *rebbe* continued, "you have your wonderful

spiritual teacher in your mother now. Go and learn from her."

The woman concluded this story by emotionally commenting that she immediately saw her whole, difficult relationship in a new light—and found that she possessed the strength to make her mother's last years rewarding for both of them.

From the Kabbalistic perspective, certainly there was tikun involved in this final, intense relationship between adult daughter and mother. The senility was not something that "accidentally" or "coincidentally" happened. But the tikun was *mutual*, generated by both souls, and multi-faceted in its effects. The daughter's proper response was humility, compassion, and gratitude for this opportunity to help another.

Turning to a more pleasant aspect of life, it is intriguing to learn that Kabbalists have traditionally seen travel as relevant to our tikun. The early Hasidic masters emphasized that by visiting new or distant places, we are often in a position better to fulfill our mission on earth.

In this context, Rabbi Nachman of Bratslav was once asked by a man whether he should make a certain journey.

"If you have occasion to travel," Rabbi Nachman replied, "you should not remain at home and stubbornly refuse to go. Wherever you travel, there are things you must rectify. Each person is destined from on high to be in a particular place at a given time. At that time and place, there is something that you must correct."

If we thus feel a longing to visit a far-off country or region, we should take this desire seriously. Especially if we repeatedly experience the yearning in dreams or meditation, the situation should be seen as a message from our higher self: your tikun now leads you there. The place may well represent "unfinished business" awaiting completion from a previous lifetime, or simply that we have a new, divinely mandated task to accomplish there.

The purpose may seem obvious once we arrive—for instance, "coincidentally" meeting a long-lost friend, or encountering an exciting opportunity. Or, we may never rationally understand our inner need to visit the particular locale. But, as Rabbi Nachman poetically urged his followers, "When you have occasion to travel, it is for your own good. If you would not make the journey voluntarily, you would be forced to go in chains." In a beautiful way, such advice is a metaphor, of course, for our entire physical existence.

Finally, Kabbalists have insisted, the notion of tikun ultimately involves faith in the Creator's goodness for all. Of course, we are encouraged to grow in wisdom and discernment; in this way, we are better able to sense the splendor of our existence, the radiant harmony of which the world's mystics have always spoken. But perhaps even more important—and this is why faith is cherished so highly—is that we experience our tikun with as much joy as possible. Indeed, the presence of joy in any endeavor is a key that we are following our tikun appropriately. Similarly, the absence of joy suggests that we have strayed from the path meant for us.

On a concrete level, this time-honored Hasidic principle can be very helpful for us. Look for guidance to those aspects of your own life that give you joyful feelings; they need not involve esoteric practices or exotic travels, for everything on earth can become a pathway to the divine. Such moments can be as simple as listening to beautiful music or gazing at a sunrise over the mountains or into the eyes of someone you love.

As much as possible, become aware of what gives you joy on a daily basis, and you will intuit your personal tikun far more easily. This does not mean that struggle or pain vanishes, but that it becomes subordinated to a much larger context. Every human life is infinitely precious, beyond our most imaginative comprehension. Regardless of its specifics, our sojourn here on earth is meant to bring us closer to our Creator with joy.

III

Karma, Psychology, and Astrology

Historically, the concept of karma reached its greatest development within the cosmological and psychological worldview of Hinduism. Yet the emergence of spiritual and transpersonal ideas in contemporary Western psychology offers the opportunity of gaining new insights into the ancient doctrine. The following set of essays explores karma in a psychological setting and also looks at ways it has influenced modern astrological thought.

*Harold Coward discusses the theory of karma in the light of transpersonal and Jungian psychology and the important role it played in Jung's formulation of the theory of archetypes. Roger Woolger focuses on karma as it helps explain psychological "scars" (*samskaras*) and the formation of major complexes over successive lifetimes. Psychologist and astrologer Stephen Arroyo looks at the important connection of both karma and modern psychology to the astrological chart, which, he argues, can be seen as a diagram of one's past karmas and the psychological tendencies they suggest for this lifetime. Liz Greene discusses the larger question of karma and its relation to the ideas of fate and destiny as they have unfolded in Western thought, focusing particularly on astrology's place in this still-developing debate.*

12

Karma, Jung and Transpersonal Psychology

HAROLD COWARD

Early in this century Western writers often pictured karma
and rebirth as resulting in a callous fatalism. J. N. Farquhar,
in his widely read, *The Crown of Hinduism*, portrayed the
Indian experience of karma as follows:

> Since the sufferings of these people were justly measured
> requital of their past sins, no power on earth could save them
> from any part of their misery. Their *karma* was working itself
> out and would inevitably do so. Thus, Hindus not only
> shared the common conviction of the ancient world, that
> degraded tribes were like animals and could not be civilized.
> Their highest moral doctrine taught them that it was useless
> to attempt to help them in the slightest; for nothing could
> prevent their *karma* from bringing upon them their full
> tale of misery.[1]

It is not surprising then that karma and rebirth have often
been understood in very negative and inhumane terms in
Western thought. While it is possible to find karma equated
with fate in Indian sources (e.g., in some Puranic materials),
in other instances (e.g., the *Mahābhārata*) the forces of
time and fate appear as non-karmic elements.[2] In Patañjali's
Yoga Sūtras 2:12-14 and 4:7-9, karma, rather than being
fatalistic or mechanistic, is understood as a memory trace
or disposition from previous thought or action—an impulse
which can either be acted upon and reinforced or negated
by the exercise of free choice.[3] Wendy Doniger O'Flaherty
has outlined the great variety of competing and contrasting

115

understandings of karma within the Indian sources themselves.[4] Thus, it is clear that Farquhar's early presentation
of karma and rebirth to the West is unfairly one-sided.
More recently the view of karma as a mental disposition
which may carry over from one birth to the next has been
picked up and given further development by some schools
of thought in modern Western psychology. The aim of this
essay is to examine the way in which karma and rebirth
have been understood in modern Western psychology, and
to identify the contribution these Indian concepts have
made to recent psychological theory. The approach taken
will be to examine the impact of karma and rebirth on
Carl Jung and the currently influential school of Transpersonal Psychology.

Karma and Rebirth in Carl Jung

There is no question that India had a major influence
upon Jung's thought. Although many Hindu and Buddhist
concepts fascinated him, it was the idea of karma and
rebirth that continued to play a central role in the development of Jung's thinking to the end of his life.[5]

Jung's encounter with Eastern thought is complex, and
in some respects can be described as a love/hate relationship.[6] After his break with Freud in 1910, and his 1912-1918
confrontation with the unconscious, one of the major sources
Jung turned to for support and new insight was Eastern
religion.[7] During the period 1920-1940, for example, the
Upanisadic notion of *ātman* played a major role in the
development of Jung's "Self" concept.[8] After 1940, and
especially after his trip to India, Jung tended to turn his
back on the East and adopt Western alchemy as his major
source of inspiration. But the Eastern concept of karma
and rebirth continued to reappear in Jung's thinking. In
fact, careful analysis demonstrates that his attitude to karma
and rebirth changed dramatically over the years. Throughout the last years his thinking came very close to the Indian
perspective. For Jung the study of the Eastern ideas of
karma and rebirth suggested that consciousness was wider

than the typical modern Western fixation on the scientific intellect.[9] As we shall see these Indian ideas played a major role in the formation of Jung's archetype concept, and they continued to provoke Jung's thinking even after he had left other Eastern notions such as yogic meditation far behind.

The main basis of Jung's understanding of karma probably came from his in-depth study of Patañjali's *Yoga Sūtras*. Evidence of this comes from notes taken by Barbara Hannah at Jung's lectures given at the Eidenössische Technische Hochschule, Zürich, October 1938-June 1939. During this period Jung gave a detailed commentary on the *Yoga Sūtras* including a thorough discussion of karma in terms of *kleśas*, previous lives, and unconscious potentiality for this life.[10] Although Jung was acquainted with the more fatalistic interpretations of karma, it was the Yoga analysis of Patañjali and Vyāsa that strongly influenced his thinking.

Karma as Archetype

Although the archetype came to be Jung's most significant psychological postulate, it was an idea that evolved slowly in his mind interacting constantly with the Indian notion of karma. In the list of definitions attached to his 1921 publication *Psychological Types*, archetype is not listed, indicating that the concept was not yet formed.[11] Direct influence from Indian thought is evidenced in Jung's 1932 lectures on Kundalini Yoga. In Lecture One Jung states, "There is a rich world of archetypal images in the unconscious mind, and the archetypes are conditions, laws or categories of creative fantasy, and therefore might be called the psychological equivalent of the samskāra."[12] And at the end of the Fourth Lecture, in answer to the question "Are the samskāras archetypes?" Jung replies, "Yes, the first form of our existence is a life in archetypes."[13] Three years later in his *Psychological Commentary on "The Tibetan Book of the Dead,"* Jung is more explicit in his formulation of archetype in terms of karma theory:

> According to the Eastern view, *karma* implies a sort of psychic theory of heredity based on the hypothesis of reincarnation . . . we may cautiously accept the idea of *karma* only if we

understand it as *psychic heredity* in the very widest sense of the word. Psychic heredity does exist—that is to say, there is inheritance of psychic characteristics, such as predisposition to disease, traits of character, special gifts and so forth.[14]

By 1942, in writing his definitive work *The Psychology of the Unconscious*, Jung admits to a deliberate extension of the archetype notion by means of karmic theory. Karma, he says, is essential to a deeper understanding of the nature of the archetype.[15] The influence of karma theory of the *Yoga Sūtra* type is especially evident in the way Jung here described archetypes as at first latent (*bīja* or seed states) which later filled out or actualized (*samskāras* which have "sprouted and flowered").

> ... the unconscious contains, as it were, two layers: the personal and the collective. The personal layer ends at the earliest memories of infancy, but the collective layer comprises the pre-infantile period, that is, the residues of ancestral life. Whereas the memory-images of the personal unconscious are, as it were, filled out, because they are images personally experienced by the individual, the archetypes of the collective unconscious are not filled out because they are forms not personally experienced. On the other hand, when psychic energy regresses, going even beyond the period of early infancy, and breaks into the legacy of ancestral life, then mythological images are awakened: these are the archetypes. An interior spiritual world whose existence we never suspected opens out and displays contents which seem to stand in sharpest contrast to all our former ideas.[16]

Although Jung himself clearly credits karma theory with the filling in of his notion of archetypes, it is interesting to note that little recognition is given to this major Eastern influence by either Jacobi, Jung's systematizer, or Jungian scholars. Instead, Jacobi credits Plato's "idea and Bergson's *éternels incréés*" as sources of Jung's thought. Jacobi also cites analogies with Gestalt psychology and acknowledges Augustine as the source of the term archetype, but nowhere is mention made of karma.[17] This apparent attempt to hide or ignore the Eastern content in Jung's archetype may be an example of Western bias, or of a fear among the Jungians that such an admission would make their already suspect psychology even less acceptable to the mainstream of Western psychology. Whatever the reason, the obscuring of Jung's considerable debt to karma theory—a debt which he himself openly acknowledged—has veiled a significant impact that Eastern thought has had upon the modern West. For it is precisely the archetypal notions in Jung's psychology that have proven productive in the applications of Analytical Psychology to Western art, literature, and religion.[18]

Personal Karma, Collective Karma and Rebirth

Just as there are a variety of views in Indian thought as to the personal or collective nature of karma,[19] so also there is uncertainty over the matter in Jung's thinking. Jung seems to have been acquainted with only the Indian doctrine of personal karma, which, in his earlier writings he tended to distinguish from his own position of collective karma in the Collective Unconscious. For example, in a 1937 letter to Swami Devatmananda, Jung describes and rejects the Indian doctrine of karma as teaching retribution for each individual action and thus determining an individual's fate in his next life.[20] In a 1946 letter to Eleanor Bertine, Jung notes that our life is not made entirely by ourselves.

> The main bulk of it is brought into existence out of sources that are hidden to us. Even complexes can start a century or more before a man is born. There is something like *karma*.[21]

A 1940 lecture entitled "Concerning Rebirth" cites the Buddha's experience of a long sequence of rebirths but then goes on to say, "it is by no means certain whether continuity of personality is guaranteed or not: there may only be a continuity of *karma*."[22]

The main statement of Jung's earlier position favoring collective rather than personal karma comes in his 1935 "Psychological Commentary on 'Tibetan Book of the Dead.' " After characterizing the *Sidpa Bardo* as the fierce wind of karma which whirls the dead man along until he comes to the "womb-door," and the *Chonyid Bardo* as a state of karmic illusions resulting from the psychic residue of previous existences, Jung observes that neither scientific knowledge nor reason can accept the hypothesis of reincarnation assumed in the Tibetan Buddhist understanding of *Bardo* karma. But he allows that we may accept the idea of karma if we understand it as the psychic heredity of broad psychic characteristics such as traits of character, special gifts, and so forth. Just as we have inherited characteristics like eye and hair color on the physical level, so on the psychic level there are the universal dispositions of the mind, the archetypes. These archetypes are "externally inherited forms and ideas which have at first no specific content. Their specific content only appears in the course of an individual's life, when personal existence is taken up in precisely these forms."[23] The source of the content of these inherited archetypes comes not from one's personal karma but from the collective karma of one's ancestors.[24] In a letter to E. L. Grant Watson, Jung clearly distinguishes his understanding of the personal experience of inherited karma from what he takes to be the Indian view.

> Inasmuch as *karma* means either a personal or at least individual inherited determinant of character and fate, it represents the individually differentiated manifestation of the instinctual behaviour pattern, i.e., the general archetypal disposition. *Karma* would express the individually modified archetypal inheritance represented by the collective unconscious in each individual. I avoid the term of *karma* because it includes metaphysical assumptions for which I have no evidence, i.e., that *karma* is a fate I have acquired in previous existence. . . .[25]

In Jung's early thinking, therefore, there is no personal inherited karma as such, there is only the collective inherited karma of one's ancestors, the archetypes, which one creatively individuates in one's own personality development. A contemporary Jungian, Edward Edinger, proposes the Catholic image of a "treasury of merits" as helpful in understanding Jung's thinking: ". . . the psychological accomplishments of the individual leave some permanent spiritual residue that augments the cumulative collective treasury, a sort of positive collective *karma.*"[26]

In a letter dated shortly before his death in 1961, Jung says that his continued wrestlings with the question of karma and rebirth has renewed his interest in the East, especially in Buddha.[27] During the last years prior to his death Jung seemed to soften his earlier rejection of the notion of personal karma and its psychological function in rebirth. The best insight into Jung's thought during this later period is found in the Chapter titled "On Life After Death" in his autobiography, *Memories, Dreams, Reflections.* Jung notes that the problem of karma and personal rebirth has remained obscure to him due to the lack of empirical evidence. But he then goes on to say:

> Recently, however, I observed in myself a series of dreams which would seem to describe the process of reincarnation . . . after this experience I view the problem of reincarnation with somewhat different eyes, though without being in a position to assert a definite opinion.[28]

Jung does not give any detailed analysis of the psychological processes which would be involved in personal reincarnation. However, he does offer a general speculation which brings him very close to traditional Indian thought.

> I could well imagine that I might have lived in former centuries and there encountered questions I was not yet able to answer; that I had to be born again because I had not fulfilled the task given to me. When I die, my deed will follow along with me—that is how I imagine it. I will bring with me what I have done.[29]

Karma as Motivation In This Life and The Next

In his later thought, Jung sees karma and rebirth in terms of a "motivation toward knowledge" which may be personal or impersonal in nature. Jung asks, "Is the *karma* I live the outcome of my past lives, or is it the achievement of my ancestors whose heritage comes together in me?"[30] He answers the question in terms of a psychological motivation toward knowledge—an approach to which Samkara would surely have given his blessing. Jung perceives the meaning of his existence in terms of a question which life has addressed him, a question which perhaps preoccupied him and/or his ancestors in a previous life, and which they could not answer. He admits that this question from the past could be the result of the collective karma of his ancestors or the result of his own karma acquired in a previous life. Either way it could be experienced today, suggests Jung, as "an impersonal archetype which presses hard on everyone and has taken particular hold on me—an archetype such as, for example, the development over the centuries of the divine triad and its confrontation with the feminine principle, or the still pending answer to the Gnostic question as to the origin of evil, or, to put it another way, the incompleteness of the Christian God-image."[31] Should Jung's way of posing the question or his answer prove unsatisfactory, then "someone who has my karma—or myself—would have to be reborn in order to give a more complete answer."[32] Thus the karmic motivation toward knowledge is the explanation for this life and the cause of the next.

Jung even goes so far as to entertain the Indian concept of release from *karma-samsāra* via the path of knowledge. He says:

> It might happen that I would not be reborn again so long as the world needed no [more complete] answer, and that I would be entitled to several hundred years of peace until someone was once more needed who took an interest in these matters and could profitably tackle the task anew.[33]

Thus, for Jung, motivation for knowledge is the karma which leads from past lives into this life and on into future lives.

The notion of "an earned otherworldly peaceful pause" and the idea of "a determinant or motivation for rebirth" are both consistent with Indian theories of karma and rebirth. Jung even goes so far as to suggest that once a completeness of understanding was achieved, there would then no longer be a need for rebirth. The karmic goal of motivation for knowledge would have been realized.

Then the soul would vanish from the three-dimensional world and attain what the Buddhists call *nirvana*. But if a *karma* still remains to be disposed of, then the soul relapses again into desires and returns to life once more, perhaps even doing so out of a realization that something remains to be completed.[34]

As to the exact motivation involved, Jung says that in his own case it must have been "a passionate urge toward understanding which brought about my birth."[35] He suggests that the psychological processes resulting in psychic dissociation illness (e.g., Schizophrenia) may provide an analogy for the understanding of life after death. Just as in a disturbed person a split-off complex can manifest itself as a projected personification, so rebirth might be conceived as a psychic projection. As evidence Jung offers one of his own dreams:

I was walking along a little road through a hilly landscape; the sun was shining and I had a wide view in all directions. Then I came to a small wayside chapel. The door was ajar, and I went in. To my surprise, there was no image of the Virgin on the altar, and no crucifix either, but only a wonderful flower arrangement. But then I saw that on the floor sat a yogi—in lotus posture, in deep meditation. When I looked at him more closely, I realized that he had my face. I started in profound fright and awoke with the thought: "Aha, so he is the one who is meditating me. He has a dream, and I am it." I knew that when he awakened I would no longer be.[36]

In terms of analytical psychology, Jung's meditating yogi is the symbol or psychic projection of his unified Self from the other worldly reality of the archetypes. Thus, the empirical world is merely the projected karmic illusion and is characterized by an ego-conscious focus. The decisive question for man, says Jung, is: "Is he related to something infinite or not?"[37] The problem with the modern Western world is that its karma is too ego-centered. What is needed is a shift of the karmic center of gravity from the ego to the Self. For Jung this is the essence of transcendence in religious experience. In psychological terms it requires the successful individuation of the Self or God archetype. It is worth noting in passing that Jung's karmic understanding of the religious experience has had a significant impact on at least one contemporary Christian theologian, namely Paul Tillich.[38]

Empirical Evidence For Karma and Rebirth

Throughout his life Jung admitted his strong attraction to Indian karma and reincarnation theory, but its lack of empirical verification was the obstacle to its full acceptance. Most often he would classify the doctrine of reincarnation as a belief which, like the belief in God, did not admit of scientific proof.[39] Although he searched Western experience broadly, he could find only testimonies to personal experiences which could not be scientifically tested. One wonders how Jung would respond to the current studies of reincarnation by Ian Stevenson.[40] Later in life, however, Jung's dreams, which for him were empirical reality, gave him evidence pointing to his own reincarnation. It was the evidence of his own dreams, plus those of a close acquaintance, which led to a very positive assessment of Indian karma and rebirth theory in the last years before his death. To Jung, the Indian understanding seemed a great advance on the common Western view that a person's character is the particular admixture of blessings or curses which fate or the gods bestowed on the child at birth—the Western version of prenatal karma.[41]

Karma and Rebirth In Transpersonal Psychology

The most recent development in modern Western Psychology, Transpersonal Psychology, adopts a methodology which explicitly opens the way for influence from Hindu and Buddhist notions of karma and rebirth. Transpersonal Psychology radically widens the scope and methodologies of psychology. Modern scientific psychology is seen simply as one form of psychology amongst many others. Other psychologies can be found as part of religious traditions which are thousands of years old. Such traditions did not just act as receivers of religious experience, they also developed systematic psychological interpretations of their experiences. Transpersonal Psychology suggests that each of these traditional interpretations is as much a psychology as is the modern Western scientific interpretation. Consequently, the plural form of the term in the title of Charles Tart's book, *Transpersonal Psychologies*.[42] As Bregman puts it:

> Scriptures, and the meditative and devotional practices which are taught in these traditions, represent a distillation of generations of psychological expertise. This expertise has been based on a kind of experimentation, and represents a massive effort of reflection and systematizing. What is being claimed is that Buddhists, for example, are not only religious experiencers, but possessors of a coherent system of concepts and practices which is at least potentially comparable to a Western, modern psychological theory.[43]

Thus, through Transpersonal Psychology, the door is opened wide for the direct exposure of modern psychology to the major roles occupied by karma and rebirth in the traditional Eastern psychologies.

Karma and Rebirth as a Basic Paradigm

According to T. S. Kuhn in his *The Structure of Scientific Revolutions*, a paradigm is a theoretical formulation which interprets a wide variety of data into an internally consistent and coherent body of knowledge.[44] It quickly becomes a philosophical predisposition that directs and interprets the activity of the adherents to that paradigm. Rather than a tentatively held theory, a paradigm rapidly becomes "a dogma and defines the parameters within which researchers conduct their inquiries."[45] In this way a paradigm serves as a prism through which certain phenomena are included for inquiry while others are excluded. Until now, modern psychology has largely held to the Western Scientific paradigm. But with the recognition of the religious traditions as valid paradigms by the Transpersonal Psychologists, karma and rebirth, as a fundamental paradigm of the Eastern religions, is being given serious consideration.

The karma and rebirth paradigm is extending boundaries for the understanding of human behavior in significant ways. The impact of this Eastern paradigm on theories of perception, cognition, motivation, self-regulation, and psychotherapy, may be considered as illustrative examples.

Karma Theory, Perception, Cognition and Motivation

The Eastern paradigm which sees karma functioning as a filtering device[46] has helped to focus attention on theories of constructive and/or reductive nature of cognition. Whereas modern scientific psychology has tended to adopt stimulus-response models which assume that we cognize what exists,[47] karma theories of the Jaina, Buddhist, and Hindu traditions presuppose that our ordinary awareness is a construction and not a mere registration of the external world. It is our past personal and cultural patterns of behavior that construct the karmic filters through which our present experience is passed. In modern psychology this Eastern paradigm provided support for some philosophers and psychologists who saw the mind functioning as a reducing valve. Bergson's general proposal in this regard has been elaborated by C. D. Broad and popularized by Aldous Huxley. In *The Doors of Perception and Heaven and Hell*, Huxley quotes C. D. Broad as follows:

> [Bergson's] suggestion is that the function of the brain and nervous system and sense organs is in the main *eliminative* and not productive. Each person is at each moment capable of remembering all that has ever happened to him and of perceiving everything that is happening everywhere in the universe. The function of the brain and nervous system is to protect us from being overwhelmed and confused by this mass of largely useless and irrelevant knowledge, by shutting out most of what we should otherwise perceive or remember at any moment, and leaving only that very small and special selection which is likely to be practically useful.[48]

Huxley comments that accordingly each one of us is Mind-at-Large. But to make biological survival possible, the brain and sense organs act as a reducing valve for Mind-at-Large.

"What comes out is a measly trickle of the kind of consciousness which will help us to stay alive on the surface of this particular planet."[49] Experimental studies, particularly on vision, support this view of perceptual and cognitive systems as reducers of information.[50] The eye, for example, responds to a limited range of stimuli, and once the sensory impulses reach the brain, different cells respond to different types of stimulation—certain cells detect edges and corners, others respond to movement on the retina, etc. Although sense organs have built-in ranges and limits of perception, our awareness and analysis of sense impulses is open to much construction or interpretation. Just as various computer programs can be created to sift input data, so the mind can create and change the cognitive programs by which the reported sensory stimuli are selected and acted upon. Within certain limitations we are able to reprogram and reconstruct our awareness in line with our motivations. Thus the reducing valve of the mind can be altered. Experimental work has begun to examine such mental programming activity. Karl Pribram, the neurophysiological psychologist, has demonstrated the mental filtering activity called habituation by which constancies in our environment are tuned out of awareness. For example, when we enter a room and a clock is ticking, we are aware of it for the first few minutes and then the sound is gradually tuned out. Any change in the loudness or speed of the ticking will immediately result in us hearing it again. Pribram pointed out an interesting example of this phenomenon. In New York a noisy train ran along Third Avenue at a certain time each night. When the train line was torn down people in the neighborhood began calling the police to report strange things occurring late at night, noises, thieves, etc. These calls came at about the time of the former train. What they were hearing was the absence of the familiar noise of the train.[51] Such habituation programming forms an additional reducing valve behind the reducing valves of the senses. Jerome Bruner has conducted experiments verifying the constructive nature of our awareness. Rather than seeing reality as it is, we categorize it in the perception process. Stereotyped systems are learned through past experience for sorting out the input that reaches us. For example, when subjects were confronted with a red ace of spades in a deck of cards they would mentally correct the image and perceive it as an ace of hearts.[52] Similarly, unless we are functioning as teachers in our correcting mode, we often miss typographical errors in what we read because as readers we do the mental correcting within ourselves under the category "correct English."

Karma theory not only provides supporting evidence and interpretation for such experiments, it suggests extrapolations which have not yet occurred to modern psychology. For example, if mental categorizing activity is learned from past behavior, then, under the theory of rebirth, the behavior of previous births, along with the behavior of this birth, helps produce the filtering categories of the mind. Karma suggests that the roots of habitual responses may be more deeply rooted in the psyche than modern psychology suspects. Much apparently pre-natal learning can be explained in terms of repeated karmic patterns. Thus our instincts, predispositions, and innate tendencies toward particular kinds of categorizations can be explained.

While the current work in American psychology parallels karma theory in understanding ordinary consciousness as a constructive process, the Eastern paradigm has clearly taken the lead in analyzing the ways in which the various filtering categories of the mind can be rendered inactive or perhaps even completely rooted out through the practise of meditation.

Karma, Meditation and the Opening-Up of Awareness

Without doubt, the strongest influence from karma theory via the Transpersonal psychologists to modern psychology has been focused on Eastern methods of meditation. The aim of the psychological techniques involving meditation is the opening-up or removal of the reducing-valve of the mind resulting in a corresponding expansion of awareness. The shutting down of the filtering activity of the mind is frequently accomplished through the repetition of the same karmic pattern over and over in the nervous system. The chanting of *mantras*, focusing upon a single visual image, regulating breathing and repeating the same body movement are all meditative tactics designed to disrupt the ordinary filtering activity of the mind and to open the way for new or fresh perception. In terms of Patañjali's Yoga, karmic patterns established in this and previous lives are being deconditioned and their filtering activity negated. *Yoga Sūtra* 2:52 states that the regulation of breathing removes the karma that covers discriminative awareness[53] and *Yoga Sūtra* 2:54 refers to "the withdrawal of senses" from their usual patterns of addiction to and perception of worldly objects.[54] In the karma and rebirth paradigm of the Eastern religions, such techniques are said to lead to a turning off of karmic filtering (i.e., habitual ways of perceiving and thinking of the external world) and a consequent opening up of a new state of awareness. The response of modern psychology to the meditation techniques of the karma paradigm have been of three general types: (1) empirical studies within the modern scientific paradigm aimed at verifying or discrediting the Eastern claims; (2) attempts at translating the esoteric meditation techniques into applications more in tune with modern technology, for example, biofeedback; and (3) applications in psychotherapy. We will briefly examine each of these responses. . . .

It is clear that by introducing the karma and rebirth paradigm into modern psychology, Transpersonal Psychology has prompted many important new developments. The major result would seem to be an extended concept of human consciousness,[55] and an approach to psychotherapy which emphasizes voluntary control and self-knowledge rather than manipulation by drugs or doctors. Thus karma theory is having a considerable impact on the way many modern psychologists are revising their basic concepts and assumptions relating to human nature. A notable factor in this regard is that since the karma paradigm has been introduced through the esoteric psychologies of the Eastern religions, the examination of spiritual experience is receiving more attention than is usual from modern psychology. For example, Ornstein's popular textbook, *The Psychology of Consciousness*, is structured around quotes from a Sufi source, "The Exploits of the Incomparable Mulla Nasrudin." It also includes a chapter, albeit brief, on the esoteric religious psychologies, while the companion book of readings includes some one hundred pages of traditional religious source materials.[56] Also featured are humanistic topics such as intuition and creativity, and psychologists such as William James, Carl Jung, Michael Polanyi and Lama Govinda. If nothing else the impact of the karma paradigm is certainly expanding the consciousness of at least some modern psychologists and their students. The assumed conceptual filters of the scientific psychology paradigm are being broken down or at least partially suspended to allow room for many traditional karma and rebirth categories, often appearing in new guises. Whether the outcome will be a synthesis of the two paradigms in a new psychology, as the Transpersonalists predict, remains to be seen.[57]

Conclusion

Our analysis of the impact of karma and rebirth upon modern psychology has come full circle. The Transpersonal psychologists, in opening the way for an expanded understanding of human nature, have returned with enthusiasm to the insights of Carl Jung and his openness to karma theory. Today, however, rather than through one isolated individual, karma theory is reaching out through the ever widening circles of Transpersonal Psychology to such diverse areas as neurophysiology, learning theory, perception, motivation, cognition, altered states of consciousness, psychotherapy, parapsychology, and psychology of religion. In effect some basic assumptions of modern scientific psychology are being challenged by those of karma and rebirth.

References

1. J. N. Farquhar, *The Crown of Hinduism.* New Delhi: Oriental Publishers Reprint Corporation, 1971, p. 142. (Originally published in 1913).
2. *Karma and Rebirth in Classical Indian Traditions.* ed. by Wendy Doniger O'Flaherty. Berkeley: University of California Press, 1980, p. xxiii.
3. See *The Yoga System of Patañjali* translated by J. H. Woods. Harvard Oriental Series, vol. 17. Delhi: Motilal Banarsidass, 1966.
4. *Karma and Rebirth in Classical Indian Traditions,* op. cit., pp. ix-xxv.
5. C. G. Jung, *Memories, Dreams, Reflections,* ed. by A. Jaffe. New York: Vintage Books, 1965, pp. 317-326.
6. Harold Coward, "Jung's Encounter with Yoga" in *The Journal of Analytical Psychology, 23,* 1978, pp. 339-357.
7. *Memories, Dreams, Reflections,* op. cit. Cps. V, VI, VII.
8. See C. G. Jung, *Psychological Types,* Collected Works (*CW*) 6, paras 188 & 189. Also Joseph L. Henderson, "The Self and Individuation" unpublished paper, 1975. All Jung's Collected Works (*CW*) are published by Princeton University Press.
9. "Jung's Encounter with Yoga," op. cit., p. 344.
10. Barbara Hannah, "The Process of Individuation: Notes on Lectures given at the Eidgenössische Technische Hochschule, Zurich, by C. G. Jung,",October, 1938-June, 1939, unpublished.
11. C. G. Jung, *Psychological Types, C.W.,* 6, 1975.
12. C. G. Jung, "Psychological Commentary on Kundalini Yoga," *Spring,* 1975, p. 8.
13. C. G. Jung, "Psychological Commentary on Kundalini Yoga," *Spring,* 1976, p. 30.
14. C. G. Jung, *Psychological Commentary on "The Tibetan Book of the Dead," C.W.* 11, p. 517.
15. C. G. Jung, *The Psychology of the Unconscious, C.W.* 7, 1942, p. 76.
16. Ibid.
17. Jolande Jacobi, *The Psychology of C. G. Jung.* New Haven: Yale University Press, 1973. See also her *Complex, Archetype and Symbol in the Psychology of C. G. Jung.* New York: Bollingen, 1959.
18. See for example the writings of Robertson Davies, Northrop Frye, Paul Tillich.
19. See Wendy O'Flaherty's summary of the various Indian views in her "Introduction" to *Karma and Rebirth in Classical Indian Traditions,* op. cit., pp. ix-xxv.
20. *C. G. Jung: Letters,* op. cit., vol. I., p. 226-227.
21. Ibid., p. 436.

22. C. G. Jung, *Concerning Rebirth, C.W.* 9, Pt. 1, p. 113.
23. C. G. Jung, *Psychological Commentary on "The Tibetan Book of of the Dead," C.W.* 11, p. 518.
24. C. G. Jung, *Memories, Dreams, Reflections,* op. cit., p. 317.
25. C. G. *Jung: Letters,* op. cit., vol. 2, p. 289.
26. Edward F. Edinger, *Ego and Archetype.* Baltimore: Penguin Books, 1973, p. 220.
27. C. G. *Jung: Letters,* op. cit., vol. 2, p. 548.
28. *Memories, Dreams, Reflections,* op. cit., p. 319.
29. Ibid., p. 318.
30. Ibid., p. 317.
31. Ibid., p. 318.
32. Ibid., p. 319.
33. Ibid.
34. Ibid., pp. 321-322.
35. Ibid., p. 322.
36. Ibid., p. 323.
37. Ibid., p. 325.
38. See for example, Paul Tillich, *The Protestant Era.* Chicago: University of Chicago Press, 1957, p. xix.
39. *Memories, Dreams, Reflections,* op. cit., p. 319.
40. Ian Stevenson, "The Explanatory Value of the Idea of Reincarnation" in *The Journal of Nervous and Mental Disease, 164,* pp. 305-326.
41. C. G. Jung, *Mysterium Coniunctionis, C.W.* 14, p. 225.
42. Charles T. Tart (ed.) *Transpersonal Psychologies.* New York: Harper Colophon, 1977.
43. Lucy Bregman, "The Interpreter/Experiencer Split: Three Models in the Psychology of Religion." *Journal of the American Academy of Religion, 56,* (Supplement), pp. 115-149.
44. T. S. Kuhn, *The Structure of Scientific Revolutions.* Chicago: University of Chicago Press, 1962.
45. K. R. Pellitier and C. Garfield, *Consciousness: East and West.* New York: Harper and Row, 1976, p. 5.
46. In Patañjali's *Yoga Sūtras,* for example, *karma* obscures reality. The purpose of yoga is to purge off the *karma* until bare reality stands fully revealed. *See Yoga Sūtras* I: 1 & 2.
47. See for example, C. E. Osgood, *Method and Theory in Experimental Psychology.* New York: Oxford University Press, 1960.
48. Aldous Huxley, *The Doors of Perception and Heaven and Hell.* Harmondsworth Middlesex: Penguin, 1960, p. 21.
49. Ibid.
50. Some pertinent experimental studies are summarized by Robert Ornstein, *On the Psychology of Meditation.* New York: Viking Press, 1973, pp. 174-175.

51. Karl H. Pribram, "The Neurophysiology of Remembering," *Scientific American*, January, 1969, pp. 73-86.
52. Jerome Bruner, "On Perceptual Readiness," *Psychological Review, 64*, 1957, pp. 123-152.
53. *The Yoga-System of Patañjali* translated by J. H. Woods. Delhi: Motilal Banarsidass, 1966, *sutra* II: 52, p. 196.
54. Ibid., *Yoga Sutra* II:53, pp. 197-198.
55. See Cp. 11 "An Extended Concept of Human Consciousness" in Robert E. Ornstein, *The Psychology of Consciousness*, New York: Harcourt Brace Jovanovich, 1977, pp. 214-233.
56. *The Nature of Human Consciousness* ed. by R. E. Ornstein, San Francisco: W. H. Freeman, 1973.
57. See for example, *The Psychology of Consciousness*, op. cit., p. 216; and *Transpersonal Psychologies*, op. cit., p. 7.

13
Psychic Scars

ROGER J. WOOLGER

In India the psychophysical discipline known as Yoga has long recognized past life compulsions as a fundamental aspect of every individual's makeup. Everything that happens to us or which we initiate creates impressions within the mental stuff (*citta*) of the experiencer or doer in such a way that a disposition or tendency to repeat or reexperience the action is laid down. The good or evil acts we perform create what Yoga masters call karmic residues (*karmaskaya*), literally the residues of past actions (*karma* = action).

A modern scholar of Indian philosophy, Dr. Karl H. Potter, has summarized the doctrine for us very clearly:

> This karmic residue has or is accompanied by dispositional tendencies (*samskara*) of more than one sort, including at least two kinds of traces (*vasana*), one kind of which, if and when it is activated, produces a memory of the originating act, the other which, if and when it is activated, produces certain afflictions (*klesa*). These *klesas* are erroneous conceptions which characterize the thinking of those engaged in purposive activity and it is they which are responsible for the person being in bondage, that is, continually creating karmic residues.[1]

Vasanas in Sanskrit usage are analogous to the traces or fragrances left behind by perfume on a cloth or smoke from a fire, but in the context of past life memories this trace is conceived as psychic rather than physical. The klesas are the wounds or afflictions that are passed on from life to life in the form of negative and emotionally laden thoughts and attitudes. We have met many examples of these klesas in the various examples: "I'll never get enough," "It's all my fault," "It's not safe to risk my feelings," "I've always got to do it alone," "I'll get back at them," "My life is too short," "He/she is bound to hurt/leave/betray me," "I deserve to suffer," "I am not good enough/worthy," "No one could ever love me." It is the klesas which are aroused by identifying with the symbolic resonances that we have talked of.

Many other psychotherapies have, of course, identified such thoughts as these, calling them "negative laws," "patterning," "life scripts," "dominant myths," etc., but what has not been proposed until recently is that these scripts are actually inherited as part of our psychic makeup at birth. In the words of the celebrated Indologist Heinrich Zimmer, "These vasanas tend to cause samskaras, permanent scars that go from life to life."[2]

The samskara, then, is like psychic scar tissue, or like a "furrow in the psyche" (Zimmer) that leads us to precisely the repetition compulsion Freud observed. We repeat the same old failure one life after another; we are repeatedly attracted to lovers and spouses who hurt and betray us, or we end up with bosses and especially parents who bully and tyrannize us; we contract diseases and undergo pains that other bodies have suffered before and so on. Depressing as this picture may appear to some, I can find no better one to encompass the extraordinary variety and uniqueness of each person's allotment of what Hamlet called "the heart-ache and the thousand natural shocks that flesh is heir to" in any one lifetime.

In discussing the samskaras both Potter and Zimmer emphasize that they are dispositions, propensities, or "tendencies to act according to patterns established by reactions in the past" (Zimmer). The samskara is like a scratch on a phonograph record; every time the record is played, the needle jumps in the same place and there are the same predictable "clicks."

The closest the Western tradition of psychology has come to the Yogic notion of samskaras is Jung's theory of the archetypes of the collective unconscious. Rather than adopt Yogic terminology, he preferred his own theory that the archetypes are responsible for "psychic heredity" . . . such as predisposition to disease, traits of character, special gifts, and so on. He insisted that archetypes are simply formative principles, devoid of actual content, in contrast to the vasanas and samskaras. "An archetype," Jung wrote, "is like a watercourse along which the water of life has formed for centuries, digging a deep channel for itself."[3]

At the time of Jung's death in 1961, both the world of professional psychology and the general public in the West were still skeptical, if not downright hostile, to the idea of past lives and reincarnation. The Bridey Murphy case had been effectively demolished, it seemed, in the late fifties and Edgar Cayce's readings were still only known to a relatively small number of readers. Today, as Gallup polls, TV talk shows, and magazine articles amply demonstrate, the climate surrounding the issue of reincarnation and past lives has markedly changed. There are now thousands of past life memories accumulating in the files of therapists and researchers in Europe and North and South America.

As for prenatal memory, we now have the internationally known work of Dr. Thomas Verney. Verney has garnered the research of many experts around the world who have demonstrated experimentally the existence of in utero patterning laid down in the fetal consciousness. Verney's important book, *The Secret Life of the Unborn Child*, summarizes many of these findings. Interestingly, more and more of his researchers who began with a strictly medical and material standpoint are reporting past life memories mixed in with in utero memories.

I believe that the samskara, which I propose to translate as a past life or karmic complex, offers the missing keystone in the overarching bridge between Eastern and Western psychologies. Conceptually a karmic complex can be seen to lie midway between an archetype, which has no personal memory traces, and a complex, which derives directly from personal experience in this life. In short, I would propose the following extension of Jung's original terms:

ARCHETYPE	SAMSKARA (Karmic Complex)	COMPLEX
Contents: Mythological images; universal forms	Past life memory traces (vasanas, klesas)	Current life memory traces

The immense importance of the samskara for understanding the structure and evolution of the nascent personality was seen clearly by Heinrich Zimmer in his unpublished meditations on the Sanskrit term "samskara":

> Samskara is a rich and highly suggestive term. Its connotations cluster about a concept of "that which has been wrought, cultivated, brought to form." But this, in the case of the individual, is the personality—with all its characteristic adornments, scars, and quirks—which for years, indeed for lifetimes, has been in the process of concoction.[4]

With our characteristic bias in favor of material rather than spiritual causes, the West has long accepted the genetic inheritance of physical and temperamental traits, but lacking the sophistication of Eastern psychology and wary of the excesses of reincarnationalism we have shied away from the notion of psychic inheritance—the claims of astrology being seen as so much arbitrary nonsense. Yet now it would appear that the tide is turning. Increasingly, the evidence is that all the major complexes that structure our lives and determine our personal interactions are already laid down at birth and before. Even though the costumes, the scenery, and the stage set may be different in this lifetime, it is nevertheless a dimly familiar part that we act out, some old unfinished "play of passion" that we find ourselves drawn into by the archetypes and our karmic complexes. But once we bring this to awareness we may find that we need no longer stay stuck in the unconscious compulsion of the samskaras but that finally we can be the true director of our own destiny. What Nietzsche wished for—"thus I willed it"—is within our grasp with the help of our past life awareness.

References

1. Wendy Doniger O'Flaherty, ed., *Karma and Rebirth in Classical Indian Traditions* (Berkeley, CA: U. of Calif. Press, 1980), p. 243.
2. Henrich Zimmer, *The Philosophies of India* (Princeton: Princeton U. Press, Bollingen Series, Vol. 26, 1951), p. 324.
3. C. G. Jung, *Psychological Reflections* (Princeton: Princeton U. Press, Bollingen Series, Vol. 31, 1970), p. 220.
4. Zimmer, *The Philosophies of India*, p. 325.

14
Karma and the Birth-Chart*

STEPHEN ARROYO

*What happens to a person is characteristic of him. He represents
a pattern and all the pieces fit. One by one, as his life proceeds,
they fall into place according to some pre-destined design.*
                                                    C. G. Jung

The word "karma" is used in so many ways by occultists,
astrologers, and others concerned with the universal laws
that guide our lives that, in considering the relation of
astrology to karma, we should first of all clarify the meaning
of the term. Basically, it refers to the universal law of cause
and effect, identical with the biblical idea that "Whatsoever
a man soweth, that shall he also reap." This law is merely
the broader application of our earthly ideas of cause and
effect; it is obvious that no one who plants thistles can
expect to harvest roses. The law of karma is similar to the
law of Newtonian mechanics that states: "For each action,
there is an equal and opposite reaction." The only difference
between the universal law of karma and the mundane
physical law of cause and effect is the scope of existence
that each embraces. The law of karma assumes that life
is a continuous experience, not by any means limited to
one incarnation in the material world. The universal law
of karma, then, can be seen as a way of achieving and maintaining universal justice and equilibrium. It is, in fact, one

*From the book *Astrology, Karma and Transformation*. Published by CRCS
Publications, P. O. Box 1460, Sebastopol, CA 95473.

of the most simple, all-encompassing laws of life. It is inseparable from what some have called the "law of opportunity" —i.e., a universal law that places each of us in the conditions which provide the exact spiritual lessons we need in order to become more god-like.

The concept of karma is based upon the phenomenon of polarity by which the universe maintains a state of balance. This is not to say a state of inertia, but rather a dynamic, constantly changing equilibrium. Inherent in this concept is the assumption that an individual "soul" (or "entity" in some schools of thought) has within itself the causal power which eventually bears fruit, the "effects." The faculty which initiates this process is the "will," and the whole structure of the causal phenomenon is called "desire." "Desire" can be seen as the application of the will in such a way as to direct the person's energy toward the manifestation of an impulse or idea.

The whole idea of karma is, of course, inseparable from the theory (or law) of reincarnation. Although some authors have considered karma and reincarnation to be metaphors or symbols of a cosmic process far more subtle than is apparent in the popular conception of the terms, most people who have accepted the teachings of reincarnation and karma as a living reality are satisfied with the traditional, even obvious, meaning of the words. For most people, the process of reincarnation simply refers to the periodic manifestation of immortal beings, souls, or spirits through the medium of the physical world in order to learn certain lessons and to develop specific ways of being as a preparation for a higher state of being (or consciousness). According to the reincarnation theory set forth in the psychic readings of the great clairvoyant Edgar Cayce (now often called "The Sleeping Prophet," after the title of Jess Stern's best-selling book), all "entities" were created "in the beginning" and periodically incarnate in order to learn the fundamental spiritual lessons: love, patience, moderation, balance, faith, devotion, etc. According to Cayce, it is often an aid to spiritual development to have a knowledge of basic universal laws, such as reincarnation,

karma, grace, "like begets like," and "mind is the builder."
The "law of grace" is the most important in the Cayce
psychic readings.

Like Newtonian mechanics compared to modern nuclear
physics, the law of karma seems to operate at a rather gross
level compared to the law of grace, which, according to
Cayce, supersedes the law of karma when one opens oneself
to the "Christ Consciousness" within. This "Christ Consciousness" is the human experience of *oneness* which has
no *reaction* because it does not take place at the level where
the law of polarity (or opposites) operates. Hence, if we
accept Cayce's concept of the law of grace, we find that
the law of karma is not the ultimate force underlying our
lives. Still, it can be helpful to understand karma, what
it is, and how it works. Cayce himself has stated that "each
lifetime is the sum total of all previous incarnated selves"
and that "everything which has been previously built, both
good and bad, is contained in that opportunity" (i.e., the
present incarnation). Throughout his thousands of recorded psychic readings, Cayce repeatedly stressed that,
when a person was experiencing a specific kind of problem
or a stressful phase of life, he was simply "meeting self,"—
in other words, that the individual was now having to confront the very experience that he had created in the past.

The law of karma at its grossest level is expressed in the
biblical axiom "an eye for an eye and a tooth for a tooth."*
One cannot overestimate the power of desire as the deepest
force initiating karma. Only the separate ego can desire,
for the essential self (or soul) is already one with everything
and so desires nothing. In essence, the law of karma tells
us, "You get what you want—eventually." But, of course,
we may not understand the ramifications of our desires
until we experience them. For example, a man may desire
material wealth. So, in a future time, he is born into a family

---

*For those who care to investigate how widely references to karma and
reincarnation appear in the Bible, see: Job 14:14; Eccles. 1:11; Jer. 1:5;
Matt. 17:9-13 & 16:13-14; Mark 6:15; Luke 9:8; John 3:7 & 1:21, 25; Col. 3:3;
Jude 1:4; and Rev. 3:12.

of astounding wealth and luxury. He now has what he wanted, but is he satisfied? No. Other desires arise immediately, for the nature of the restless mind is to produce desires. In fact, the man may come to realize that his new-found wealth is not only unsatisfying, but even a horrible burden! At least when he was poor, he had nothing to lose; so he was free. Now wealthy, he continually worries about losing what he in fact no longer wants but yet is attached to. The question then becomes: How can one release (or be released from) his desire-forged attachments in order that he can again be free? (The great English poet William Blake called these attachments "mind-forged manacles.") This freedom is the sought-after goal of all paths of liberation and techniques of self-realization.

The greatest wealth of insight about the nature and workings of karmic law is found in the writings and teachings of various spiritual teachers, most of whom are from the Orient and whose teachings therefore are rooted in Buddhist or Hindu traditions. Paramahansa Yogananda, one of the first Eastern spiritual masters to spread his teachings widely in the Western world, wrote a beautiful and inspiring book entitled *Autobiography of a Yogi*, in which we find the following quotation:

> Fate, karma, destiny—call it what you will—there is a law of justice which somehow, but not by chance, determines our race, our physical structure and some of our mental and emotional traits. The important thing to realize is that while we may not escape our own basic pattern, we can work in conformity with it. That is where free will comes in. We are free to choose and discriminate to the limits of our understanding, and, as we rightly exercise our power of choice, our understanding grows. Then, once having chosen, a man has to accept the consequences of his choice and go on from there.

Yogananda further explains how to deal effectively with one's karma and what the proper attitude should be toward one's destiny:

> Seeds of past karma cannot germinate if they are roasted in the divine fires of wisdom.... The deeper the self-realization of a man, the more he influences the whole universe by

his subtle spiritual vibrations, and the less he himself is affected by the phenomenal flux (karma).

Yogananda was also intimately familiar with astrology, since his *guru* was a master of all the ancient arts and sciences. His comments on astrology and the scope of its relevance are therefore worth considering:

> A child is born on that day and at that hour when the celestial rays are in mathematical harmony with his individual karma. His horoscope is a challenging portrait, revealing his unalterable past and its probable future results. But the natal chart can be rightly interpreted only by men of intuitive wisdom; these are few.

> Occasionally I told astrologers to select my worst periods, according to planetary indications, and I would still accomplish whatever task I set myself. It is true that my success at such time has been accompanied by extraordinary difficulties. But my conviction has always been justified; faith in the divine protection, and the right use of man's God-given will, are forces formidable beyond any other.

In Buddhist tradition, the goal of liberation techniques and spiritual practices is called "nirvana," a term which has not been correctly interpreted by many Westerners seeking to penetrate the depths of Buddhist wisdom. The literal meaning of the term "*nirvana*" is "where the wind of karma doesn't blow." In other words, the only way to achieve spiritual progress is to awaken ("*Buddha*" means simply "one who is awake") to a level of awareness beyond the domain of karma and beyond the planes of illusion. One can gather from these teachings that the only way to deal with karma, *ultimately*, is to rise above it. However, as long as we are incarnate in the physical form, the law of karma affects us in one way or another; and it would thus be extremely useful if we could achieve an understanding of the karmic patterns with which we have to deal in this lifetime, if for no other reason than that it would enable us to face our destiny with grace, acceptance, and fortitude.

An ancient tradition in India goes into great depths in its analysis of karmic law, dividing types of karma into three groups. *Pralabd karma* is considered the fate, or destiny, karma which must be met in the present lifetime. This basic destiny pattern is considered to be fundamentally unalterable, simply a pattern and sequence of experiences which the individual has to deal with in this incarnation. It is stated, however, that a spiritual approach to life, the help of a spiritual master, or simply the Lord's grace may occasionally intervene to lessen the impact of particularly heavy karma, thus making "a sword thrust" into a "pinprick." *Kriyaman karma* is that karma which we are now making in this very lifetime, the effects of which we will have to face at a later time. The primary reason for the sometimes severe disciplines of various spiritual paths is that such control on behavior can help the traveler on the path to refrain from making more karma which would inhibit his spiritual progress in the future. Other than practicing such disciplines, the primary way to avoid creating karma in the present is to refrain from intense desires and attachments, while simultaneously cultivating the proper spirit and detached attitude in carrying out our daily duties. Naturally, maintaining the proper spirit and detachment is very difficult, and it is considered in most spiritual teachings to be absolutely impossible without the aid of meditation. Lastly, *Sinchit karma* is the term given to the reserve of karma that we have accumulated over many lifetimes but which is not specifically active in this incarnation. According to these teachings, we have, over thousands of incarnations, accumulated such vast karmic entanglements that it would be impossible to encounter all the results of past thoughts and actions in one lifetime. We would simply be overwhelmed, physically, psychically, and emotionally. Hence, that portion of our karma which is not allotted to our present lifetime's fate, or *pralabd*, karma is held in reserve. We will, according to these teachings, have to face all of that karma also, sometime in the future, unless a Perfect Spiritual Master relieves us of some of that burden.

A spiritual teacher with a large following in the USA, Meher Baba, likewise elucidates the workings of karma:

You, as a gross body, are born again and again until you realize your Real Self. You, as mind, are born only once; and die only once; in this sense, you do not reincarnate. The gross body keeps changing, but mind (mental body) remains the same throughout. All impressions (*sanskaras*) are stored in the mind. The impressions are either to be spent or counteracted through fresh karma in successive incarnations. You are born male, female; rich, poor; brilliant, dull; . . . to have that richness of experience which helps to transcend all forms of duality.

I doubt whether anyone who is familiar with the accuracy and profound usefulness of astrology would deny that the natal birth-chart reveals in symbolic form the individual's primary life pattern: the potentials, talents, attachments, problems, and dominant mental characteristics. If this is so, then the birth-chart obviously reveals a blueprint, or X-ray, of the soul's present *pralabd*, or fate, karma. As I showed in great detail in my book *Astrology, Psychology, and the Four Elements*, the birth-chart can be viewed as revealing the individual's pattern of energy which manifests on all levels simultaneously: physical, mental, emotional, and inspirational corresponding with the four elements *earth, air, water,* and *fire*. The *sinchit*, or reserve, karma is not indicated in the birth-chart, since it is not allotted to this lifetime. Likewise, the *kriyaman* karma is not indicated either, since we seem to have some degree of freedom, limited though it may be, in determining what karma we will create in the present. Hence, I do not want to give the impression, by speaking of "fate," "destiny," and similar terms, that there is nothing we can do *or be* in response to our karma that will change our lives in a positive way. On the contrary, although the birth-chart shows the karma and hence the restrictions that bind us and prevent our feeling free, the chart is also a tool that enables us to see clearly in what areas of life we need to work toward transmuting our current mode of expression. As Edgar Cayce says repeatedly in his readings, "Mind is the builder." We become what our mind dwells upon. If therefore we can subtly alter our attitudes and modes of thought, if we can attune our consciousness to some higher frequency by meditation, by not only *having* but also by *living* an ideal, then we can begin to be liberated from bondage and to breathe freely with the rhythm of life.

Indeed, as one of the twentieth century's greatest astrologers, Dane Rudhyar, has emphasized in his extensive writings, events don't happen to people in nearly as important a way as *people happen to events*. These four words sum up the possibilities of our spiritual-psychological development as we meet our karma, whether pleasant or distressing. In other words, our attitude toward experience is the crucial factor. Our attitude alone will determine whether, in meeting difficult experiences, we will suffer (and curse our "fate") or whether we will grow by learning the lessons that life is teaching us.

The chart therefore shows our mind patterns, our past conditioning, the mental impressions and patterns referred to by Meher Baba as *sanskaras*. The chart shows what we are now *because* of what we have thought and done in the past. These age-old, deeply-entrenched patterns are not easily changed. Let this be said without qualification! It is not a simple matter to change powerful habit patterns merely through the application of a bit of old-fashioned "will power." Neither do these patterns essentially change by glossing them over with the faddish jargon of some of the "New Age" psychotherapies or philosophies that inflate the ego by encouraging people to assert: "I'm taking charge of my life; I make everything happen; I now know that I'm making myself suffer; etc." Human spiritual evolution is much subtler than that. The old "where there's a will, there's a way" approach to dealing with one's problems collapses when the challenge is too intense. And the attempt to rationalize one's conflicts and spiritual crises out of existence will only dam the flow of the life energies for a short while, quickly followed by a torrential release of power that starkly reveals the shallowness of pseudo-spiritual escapism. The karmic patterns are real and powerful. Those habits are not going to fade away overnight following a short positive-thinking pep-talk. These life forces must be accepted, acknowledged, and paid due attention.

Self-knowledge and self-realization is a necessary prelude to God-realization; but—in the early stages—a student of spiritual truths or a student of higher forms of astrology often becomes discouraged when his or her new insights into the self reveal so many negative traits, emotions, and habit patterns. It is at this point in the individual's development that great care must be exercised both by that person and by any person—astrologer or otherwise—who attempts to counsel or guide the student. It should be explained that, just as opening a door a small crack and allowing a beam of light into a dark room reveals all kinds of dust in the air and perhaps other dirt that was not previously apparent in the room, so when the first steps toward self-knowledge are taken, whether utilizing the beam of light known as astrology or another illuminating method, the student very often quickly develops a negative attitude toward his or her self, destiny, birth-chart, etc. It should be further explained that, as the intensity of light increases, the student will become even more immediately aware of his or her faults, weaknesses, or negative qualities, but that such awareness is to be welcomed as an indication of greater self-knowledge and definite developmental progress. The student should be encouraged to use such insight as a prod toward taking definite constructive action in the positive transformation of the individual life, rather than as a reason or excuse for fear or anxiety. Further, it can be pointed out to the student that, as the level of self-knowledge increases, the person's karma often begins to manifest on a subtler level since he or she is now open to learning what must be learnt about the self, and hence, there is no longer the need for shocks or dramatic events to awaken the individual from the slumber of spiritual lethargy. As Jung points out,

> The psychological rule says that when an inner situation is not made conscious, it happens outside, as fate. That is to say, when the individual . . . does not become conscious of his inner contradictions, the world must perforce act out the conflict and be torn into opposite halves. (*Aion*, p. 71)

Hence, it seems safe to say that a commitment to self-development and self-knowledge not only holds out the promise
of aiding the individual to be a more whole, happy, and
illuminated soul in the future, but also that such a step
often begins to alleviate a great deal of suffering in the
present, once the initial confusion and discouragement is
overcome.

We can thus see that we all have certain karmic influences
that we must meet: we all must reap the fruits of what we
have sown. Astrology, by providing us with a blueprint of
our attachments, problems, talents, and mental tendencies,
offers us a way—an initial step—of not only realizing in a
specific sense exactly what our karma is and helping us
to work with these confrontations within and without, but
also a way of beginning to rise above and gain a perspective
on this karma. The idea that the individual birth-chart
reflects what we have done in the past is confirmed in Edgar
Cayce's psychic reading #5124-L-1:

> For, as given from the beginning: the planets, the stars are
> given for signs and for seasons and for years; that many
> may indeed find their closer relationship in the contempla-
> tion of the universe. For man has been made a co-creator
> with the Godhead. Not that man is good or bad according
> to the position of the stars; but *the position of the stars indicate
> what the individual entity has done about God's plan in earth
> activities*, during the periods when man has been given the
> opportunity to enter into material manifestations.

The birth-chart shows, therefore, the past *creative use* or the
misuse of our powers. If we accept the idea of the power of
the individual's mind and will, then we must also accept
the idea that we are responsible for our fate, destiny, and
problems as shown in the natal chart. In an important
sense, we could then even say that the birth-chart shows
nothing but karma. Everything in the chart can then be
assumed to stem directly from our past actions, achievements, and desires. Although Saturn alone has been called
the "planet of karma" in many writings, this is an over-
simplification. Indeed, astrology could legitimately be
called a "science of karma"—that is, a way of realizing

and accepting one's responsibilities in a precise way.

In concluding this chapter, we can say that each of us has the opportunity to harmonize within ourselves the diverse manifestations of the universe; and we have the opportunity to accept all other human beings, even those with whom we strike a discordant note on the personality level. Can we live without demanding that all experiences and all human beings harmonize with our attunement? Can we evolve a mature, detached consciousness that enables us to watch ourselves play our allotted role in the cosmic drama? Can we laugh at our complexity, our conflicts, and our inconsistencies? Most importantly, can we have faith that the universe is harmonious and that it is only our narrow vision that sees discord? The answers to these questions will determine to a great extent how we face our karma in this life and what sort of karma we are creating now.

15

The Ancient Shape of Fate

LIZ GREENE

What is ordained is master of the gods and thee.

Euripides

Once upon a time, it is said, there lived in Isfahan a young man who spent his days as servant to a wealthy merchant. On a fine morning the young man rode to market, carefree and with his purse jingling with coins from the merchant's coffers to buy meat and fruit and wine; and there in the market-place he saw Death, who beckoned to him as though about to speak. In terror the young man turned his horse about and fled, taking the road that led to Samara. By nightfall, filthy and exhausted, he had reached an inn there, and with the merchant's money procured a room, and collapsed upon the bed with mingled fatigue and relief, for it seemed he had outwitted Death. But in the middle of the night there came a knock at the chamber door, and in the doorway stood Death, smiling affably. 'How come you to be here?' demanded the young man, white-faced and trembling; 'I saw you only this morning in the market-place in Isfahan.' And Death replied: 'Why, I have come to collect you, as it is written. For when I saw you this morning in the market-place in Isfahan, I tried to say that you and I had an appointment tonight in Samara. But you would not let me speak, and only ran away.'

This is a short, sweet folktale, and one might read many themes into it. But among its deceptively simple lines is

150

surely embedded a comment about fate: its irrevocability
and yet, paradoxically, its dependence upon the will of
man for its fruition. Such a tale, because it is paradoxical,
invites all manner of philosophical and metaphysical
speculation, of the sort with which sensible people do
not occupy themselves. For example: If the servant had
stayed and spoken with Death, would he have still had to
die in Samara? What if he had taken another road? *Could*
he have taken another road? If not, then what power, inner
or outer, directed him to the appointed place? What if,
like the knight in Bergmann's *The Seventh Seal*, he had
challenged Death? Or, in short, that queer conundrum
which the East has always treated with such subtlety, yet
which the West has persisted in reducing to an either-or,
black-and-white choice: are we fated, or are we free?

I have found that the word fate is often quite offensive
to many people in this enlightened twentieth century.
Death has at last been separated from its original unity
with fate, and has been transformed into a clinical, rather
than a metaphysical, phenomenon. But this was not always
so. Fate was called *Moira* by the Greeks, and was from
earliest times a *daimon* of doom and death, a great power
older than the oldest gods. Greek philosophy had quite
a lot to say about fate, which we shall explore in due course.
But mentioning fate now seems to imply a loss of control,
a sense of powerlessness, impotence and humiliation.
When Cromwell told his Parliament that they should not
speak of fate, he gave voice to a sentiment that has pervaded
our social and religious outlook ever since. The history
of philosophy hinges upon the profound issue of man's
fate and freedom; yet modern philosophical writers such
as Bertrand Russell see 'fatalism' and its inevitable creative
children—the mantic or divinatory arts—as a kind of taint
spawned by Pythagoras and Plato on pure rational thought,
a stain which discoloured the otherwise brilliant fabric
of the classical Greek mind. Wherever there is a concern
with fate, there is also a concern with astrology, for the
concept of Moira evolves from the vision of an orderly,
interconnected cosmos; and astrology in particular finds

disfavour with the modern school of philosophy embodied by Russell. As Professor Gilbert Murray says, 'Astrology fell upon the Hellenistic mind as a new disease falls upon some remote island people.' Russell quotes this passage in his *History of Western Philosophy*, and caps it with one of his own:

> The majority of even the best philosophers fell in with the belief in astrology. It involved, since it thought the future predictable, a belief in necessity or fate.[1]

Christian theology too found this subject of fate a great problem. The denial of Moira, or *Heimarmenê* as it is sometimes called in early astrological texts, has been a popular Christian theme for many centuries, and it does not require a mind of great brilliance to suspect that this denial rests on grounds somewhat subtler than the argument that fate is paganish. Although medieval Christians from Boethius to Dante acknowledged the pagan tradition of the goddess of fate side by side with the omnipotence of the Trinity, the Reformation brought with it a conviction that the very idea of such a figure was an insult to God's sovereignty. God sometimes works with a grace which nullifies the influence of the heavens, says Calvin hopefully, and people are often made new by the experience of conversion. Just as the Reformation threw out the 'cult' of Mary, it likewise threw out the other numinous feminine power in the cosmos. And as Cromwell bade us, since the seventeenth century we have not spoken of fate.

The theological argument which replaced the ancient goddess and which is still viable today is the doctrine of God's Providence. Even Calvin's gloomy children will argue if one calls by the name of fate the predestined salvation of the elect in which they believe. Those of a more scientific bent revert to the terminology of 'natural law'; but the irony of this is that Moira, as she emerged in the thought of Anaximander and the more 'scientific' Ionian school of Greek philosophy which Russell favours over those gullible and mystical Platonists, is nothing more nor less than natural law, raised to the status of deity.

Moira, it is true, was a moral power; but no one had to
pretend that she was exclusively benevolent, or that she
had any respect for the parochial interests and wishes of
mankind. Further—and this is the most important point—
she was not credited with foresight, purpose, design; these
belong to man and the humanised gods. Moira is the blind,
automatic force which leaves their subordinate purposes
and wills free play within their own legitimate spheres,
but recoils in certain vengeance upon them the moment
that they cross her boundaries. . . . She is a representation
which states a truth about the disposition of Nature, and
to the statement of that truth adds nothing except that the
disposition is both necessary and just.[2]

Anaximander and his fellows envisioned the universe
as portioned out into a general scheme of allotted provinces
or spheres of power. The word Moira itself means 'share'
or 'allotment.' The universe was first a primary and undifferentiated mass; when the four elements came into
being, they received their 'allotment' not from a personified
goddess, but from the eternal motion within the cosmos,
which was considered no less divine. But interpreting
natural law as a *numen* does not appeal to us today. And
when we consider other aspects of natural law such as
heredity and the phylogenesis of disease, we are scarcely
prone to see these processes as anything to do with fate.

It has even become acceptable, in some circles, to speak
of *karma*, while avoiding the word fate. Karma, it would
appear, is a nicer term because it implies a chain of cause
and effect, with some importance given to the individual's
choices in a given incarnation. Fate, on the other hand,
seems, in popular conception, to be random, and the individual possesses no choices at all. But this was never
the philosophical conception of fate, not even in the eyes
of the Stoics, who were as their name suggests exceedingly
stoical about the lack of freedom in the cosmos. Stoicism,
the most fatalistic of philosophies, acknowledged fate as
a cause and effect principle; it merely postulated that we
humans are generally too blind and stupid to see the results
implicit in our actions. According to the Indian formula,
man sows his seed and pays no attention to its growth. It

then sprouts and eventually ripens, and each individual must eat of the fruit of his own field. This is the law of karma. It is no different from Heimarmenê, which is eloquently described below by Professor Murray:

> Heimarmenê, in the striking simile of Zeno [the founder of Stoicism], is like a fine thread running through the whole of existence—the world, we must remember, was to the Stoics a live thing—like the invisible thread of life which, in heredity, passes on from generation to generation of living species and keeps the type alive; it runs causing, causing forever, both the infinitesimal and the infinite . . . rather difficult to distinguish from the Pronoia or Providence, which is the work of God and indeed the very essence of God.[3]

It is not only difficult to distinguish fate from Providence; it is equally difficult to distinguish it from karma and from natural law.

Psychology too has found other, more attractive terminology when confronting issues of fate. It speaks of hereditary predisposition, conditioning patterns, complexes and archetypes. All these are useful terms, and no doubt more appropriate for the twentieth century; it is probably fitting that our view of fate should have evolved, over three or four millennia, from a personified goddess to a property of the unconscious psyche. But I am struck over and over by the repugnance those in the helping professions seem to feel—in particular the psychiatrist, who ought to be able to see the connection when he pronounces the prognosis of schizophrenia incurable and declares it to be hereditary —when the word fate is served up cold upon a plate without sauce or garnish. It is not surprising that the modern astrologer, who must sup with fate each time he considers a horoscope, is made uncomfortable and attempts to formulate some other way of putting it, speaking instead, with elegant ambiguity, of potentials and seed plans and blueprints. Or he may seek refuge in the old Neoplatonic argument that while there *may* be a fate represented by the planets and signs, the spirit of man is free and can

make its choices regardless. Margaret Hone is a typical
voice on the subject:

> Synchronisation with a planetary pattern *apparently* denies
> free-will entirely. . . . Inasmuch as a man identifies himself
> with his physical self and the physical world about him, so
> he is indissolubly part of it and subject to its changing
> pattern as formed by the planets in their orbits. Only by
> the recognition of that which he senses as greater than
> himself can he attune himself to what is beyond the ter-
> restrial pattern. In this way, though he may not escape
> terrestrial happenings, by the doctrine of free and willing
> 'acceptance' he can 'will' that his real self is free in its reac-
> tion to them.[4]

Jeff Mayo, on the other hand, appears to belong to the
'blueprint' school:

> You may think that if the future can be foretold we have
> no free-will, we are enmeshed in an irrevocable fate we
> cannot escape. The astrologer *cannot* predict every event. . . .
> An astrological aspect with regard to the future can cor-
> respond with any one of a variety of possibilities, mostly
> dependent upon the 'freedom of choice' of the individual
> concerned, yet the aspect still foretells the actual *trend* of
> circumstances, or the *nature* of the individual's reaction
> to the situation.[5]

These two voices are characteristic of astrology's current
reaction to the problem of fate. Either fate is merely a trend,
a set of possibilities, rather than something more definite,
or it is indeed definite but only applies to the corporeal
or 'lower' nature of man and does not contaminate his
spirit. One is a pragmatic approach; the other, a mystical
one which can be traced all the way back to Plato. Both,
however, are open to challenge. On the one hand, it would
seem, in my experience, that some very specific events
in life are fated and unavoidable, and can hardly be called
a trend or attributed to the individual's active choice. Some
of the case histories in this book illustrate this rather pain-
fully. On the other hand, it would seem that the inner life
of man—the spirit of which Margaret Hone writes—is as

coloured by fate as his outer life, in the form of unconscious complexes which even influence the nature of the God he worships, and which shape his choices far more powerfully than any act of conscious volition. In fact, the concurrence of inner complexes and outer circumstances suggests that the division into 'physical' and 'spiritual' which Hone is making is an arbitrary one. I do not pretend to have an answer to these dilemmas, and I would not suggest that either of these two very accomplished and experienced authors is 'wrong.' But I am left with the feeling that something is being avoided.

Fate means: it has been written. For something to be written with such immovability by an utterly unseen hand is a terrifying thought. It implies not only powerlessness, but the dark machinery of some vast impersonal Wheel or highly ambiguous God which takes less account than we would like of our hopes, dreams, desires, loves, merits or even our sins. Of what value are the individual's efforts, his moral struggles, his humble acts of love and courage, his strivings for the betterment of himself and his family and his world, if all is ultimately rendered pointless by what has already been written? We have been fed, for the last two centuries, on a highly questionable pabulum of rational self-determination, and such a vision of fate threatens an experience of real despair, or a chaotic abreaction where the spinal column of the moral and ethical man collapses. There is equally a difficulty with the more mystical approach to fate, for by severing the unity of body and spirit in order to seek refuge from the strictures of fate, the individual creates an artificial dissociation from his own natural law, and may invoke in the outer world what he is avoiding in the inner.

Yet to the Greek mind, as to the mind of the Renaissance, the vision of fate did not destroy the dignity of human morality or human soul. If anything, it was the reverse. The first religious poet of Greece, Hesiod, states simply that the course of Nature is anything but careless of right and wrong. He implies that there is a definite and sympathetic connection between human conduct and the ordered law of Nature. When a sin has been committed—such as the unconscious incest of Oedipus—all Nature is poisoned by the offence of man, and Moira retaliates with immediate catastrophe brought down upon the head of the offender. Fate, to Hesiod, is the guardian of justice and law, rather than the random predetermining force that dictates a man's every action. This guardian has set the bounds of the original elemental order, within which man must live because he is part of Nature; and it waits to exact the penalty of every transgression. And death, because it is the final statement of Moira, the 'allotment' or circumscribed limit beyond which mortal creatures cannot pass, is not an indignity, but a necessity, issuing from a divine source.

It would appear that since the Reformation we have lost much of this sense of connection with Nature and natural law; we have forgotten what we knew of the meaning of fate, and so the vicissitudes of life, including death, are to us in the West an offence and a humiliation. When an old person dies, we no longer speak of 'natural causes' or a death due to old age, but rather, written on the death certificate, 'cardio-respiratory failure,' thereby implying that, had it not been for this failure or mistake, death would never have taken place. But I do not think we have lost our fear of fate, although we mock it; for if the modern individual were so truly enlightened beyond this 'paganish' concept, he would not surreptitiously read astrology columns in the newspaper, nor evidence the compulsion to ridicule whenever possible the spokesmen of fate. Nor would he be so fascinated by prophecy, which is fate's handmaiden. Nostradamus' *Centuries*, those bizarre visions of the future of the world, have never been out of print, and each new translation sells in astronomical figures. As for the ridicule, it is my feeling that fear, when unadmitted, is often cloaked with aggressive contempt, and rather stringent attempts to disprove or denigrate the thing which threatens. Every palmist, astrologer, card reader and clairvoyant has met this peculiar but unmistakable onslaught from the 'skeptic.' And it occurs, sadly, not least within the field of astrology itself. The outlines of this spectre can be glimpsed in the more determinedly 'scientific' astrologer's attempts to prove his study solely through a tidal wave of statistics, ignoring or refusing to recognise those mysteries which elude his computations, pleading shamelessly for recognition of his science (if that is what it is) from an obdurate scientific community, and ultimately apologising for even calling astrology by its own name, replacing this with such tongue-twisters as 'cosmobiology' in the hope that it will render him more respectable. I am not insulting valid research in pursuit of clarity or truth by this observation, but am rather calling attention to an attitude of what seems to me fanatical overcompensation that throws the baby out with the bath water. The community of modern astrological practitioners often seem terribly ashamed that they must traffick with fate.

Astrology, in company with the Tarot, palmistry, scrying, and perhaps also the *I Ching* which has now firmly entrenched itself in the West, are the modern carriers of the ancient and honourable role of seership. This has been, from time immemorial, the art of interpreting the clouded and ambiguous intentions of the gods, although we might now call it the clouded and ambiguous intentions of the unconscious; and it is directed towards the apprehension of *kairos*, the 'right moment.' Jung used the term synchronicity in connection with these things, as a way of attempting to shed light on the mystery of meaningful coincidence—whether it is the coincidence of an apparently unrelated external event with a dream or inner state, or an event with the pattern of cards, planets, coins. But whatever language we use, psychological or mythic, religious or 'scientific,' at the heart of divination is the effort to read what is being, or has been, written, whether we explain this mystery by the psychological concept of synchronicity or the much older belief in fate. For the uninitiated layman with no experience of such things in their enormous multi-levelled subtlety, acquaintance with Moira is limited to predictions in sun sign columns, and occasional visits to the funny old lady in Neasden who lives with seventeen cats and was *actually right* about my mother's operation.

In these expressions our typically concrete Western interpretations of fate are evidenced in all their schizoid glory. Either we believe wholeheartedly that next week will indeed bring the unlooked-for windfall, the new lover, the bad news by post, the promotion; or, sometimes at the same time, we jeer cruelly at the friend who is stupid, ignorant, gullible enough to think he or she could actually get help from that sort of ridiculous mumbo-jumbo. Novalis' statement that fate and soul are two names for the same principle is, of course, incomprehensible in the face of such concretisation. Yet the astrologer, who ought to know better, may still be found making his concrete pronouncements, and not only about the new lover and the bad news by post: zodiacal signs and planetary aspects mean behaviour and behaviour only from this literal perspective, with not a thought to the inner 'soul' of which Novalis speaks.

It is not my object to convince the layman of either the mantic arts or of fate. What concerns me is the approach of the astrological practitioner. I am not happy with either the 'trend' approach to the horoscope, or the Neoplatonic 'fate affects the body but not the soul' approach. For me, the former evades the issue of the mysteriously meaningful events that provoke individual development, and the latter evades the issue of individual responsibility. From what I have observed in my analysands and my astrological clients, there is certainly something—whether one calls it fate, Providence, natural law, karma or the unconscious—that retaliates when its boundaries are transgressed or when it receives no respect or effort at relationship, and which seems to possess a kind of 'absolute knowledge' not only of what the individual needs, but of what he is *going* to need for his unfolding in life. It appears to make arrangements of the most particular and astonishing kind, bringing a person together with another person or an external situation at precisely the right moment, and it appears to be as much part of the inner man as the outer. It also appears to be both psychic and physical, personal and collective, 'higher' and 'lower,' and can wear the mask of Mephistopheles as readily as it can present itself as God. I make no pretence of knowing what 'it' is, but I am unashamedly prepared to call it fate. And I feel that if we understood this thing better we might be of far greater assistance to our clients, not to mention ourselves.

We need to confront and question the issue of fate in some detail. I have no answers to the fundamental problem of whether we are fated or free; no such conclusion is ever definitively reached in this exploration. I am inclined, when faced with such an enormity, to feebly answer, Both. I do not know what fate is in a defined metaphysical sense, or a theological one; philosophy and religion concern themselves with this problem in far more erudite terms than I am capable of. When Apuleius of Madaura speaks with certainty of dual fate—fate as energy and fate as substance—or when Chrysippos proposes that even our thoughts are fated, I am hardly in a position to challenge them. There have been many attempts to define fate over the centuries, and sometimes the conclusions differ. I do not know with any certainty whether it is possible to alter fate, or whether fate itself alters, or what 'altering' might mean, although I have raised some questions about just what it is that 'transforms' during processes such as psychotherapy. Nor do I know whether some people are more fated than others, although it would certainly seem so on a literal outer level. But sometimes it is the asking of the question that opens doors, rather than the determined search for an unambiguous answer.

Questions that deal with such bottomless issues as man's freedom or lack thereof, however, have a tendency, if taken seriously, to invoke in the questioner a rather uncomfortable ambivalence. It seems as though it is safer not to ask, but merely to ignore or mock; for, having asked, one has, in the act of composing the question, torn the protective skin off a deep and mysterious human dilemma and source of suffering. Once conscious of that dilemma, if no immediate answer is forthcoming, one is suspended between the opposites like someone hanging on a cross. This problem translates itself in human terms in a deceptively simple question: if one is struck powerfully by impulses or desires which erupt from the psyche, does one act them out because they are fated, or does one try to repress or control them? Or might there be a third possibility, which grants the inevitability of the experience but also tests the whole man in terms of his moral choices? This is no easy question, as any psychotherapist knows, for sometimes an individual cannot help himself, and sometimes he can; and sometimes he ought not to help himself, and sometimes he must. This very dilemma in fact permeates the story of Christ's betrayal and crucifixion. Such a suspension may deepen and enrich, but it can also paralyse. Deepening and stretching are not for everyone; otherwise we would probably not, as a collective, shy away so obviously from the question. Suspension robs us of certainty, whether it is on the side of morality or amorality, fate or freedom. And how many of us would dare, like Socrates, to acknowledge the root of all wisdom in the knowledge that we do not know?

The second attempt we need to make is to understand the repugnance and even anger which the subject of fate invokes, particularly in my fellow astrological students and practitioners and in my fellow analysts. There is no modern profession which brings an individual closer to the experience of fate than the practice of the horoscopic art, save that of the psychotherapist. The discussion of 'blueprints' and 'trends' is valid enough for the individual whose life has not been violently touched by fate: the healthy person, physically and psychically, who is 'at a crossroads' or wants vocational guidance or is 'seeking direction' or wants to 'learn more' about himself. But these are not the only clients who come for astrological advice. If they were, our work would always be pleasurable, and never challenge us. Yet there are the people tormented by some inner *daimon* or compulsion, struggling futilely against what they experience as their own evil; who have been twisted almost beyond recognition by childhood experiences which they did not choose; who have been broken open by some numinous or transpersonal experience which demands a sacrifice of something they hold most dear; who have been physically maimed by accident or illness or congenital defect; who have suffered unjust losses and unearned separations, or have been caught up in collective horrors like wartime Germany or post-war Czechoslavakia or Northern Ireland; who have been raped, robbed, pillaged and used; who have gone, are going or will go mad because their mad families have elected them as symptom-bearers and scapegoats. Nor is the gifted individual free of suffering, for the possession of talents and insights and even what we call 'luck' marks a man as surely as deformity does, and separates him from the community into an isolation of the spirit which equally demands an answer of some kind. I do not find it easy to come up with specious phrases when facing this catalogue of apparently unmerited human vicissitudes. I was once told during a workshop, by a woman with a voice of smug certainty, that people are never given more than they can bear. A brief visit to a hospital or a psychiatric ward tends to render this sort of pronouncement nonsensical. I cannot talk glibly about karma as many astrologers do, and imply that it was something to do with one's previous incarnations so not to worry, just close your eyes and think of England; nor can I imply that the individual 'made' these things happen out of what was merely a 'trend,' because he is personally stupider or more culpable than most. I must admit honestly that I do not know, and because I do not know I have engaged in an attempt to understand more deeply the nature of whatever 'it' is. As with many people, the presence of extreme suffering invokes in me the question of meaning. But for me, the roads of human perversity and catastrophe do not ultimately lead to the comforting paternal arms of a benign Judaeo-Christian God whom we must not question; nor do they lead to the indictment of society as the source of all ills. Rather, they lead to fate.

It is my feeling that all genuine vocations or 'callings' have about them, shadowy and often unseen, an archetypal or mythic figure, in itself fascinating and compelling although unconscious, which in some way is the symbol of the inner meaning or 'rightness' of that vocation. Or it could be put another way: the human imagination formulates these figures spontaneously as a means of articulating some mysterious sacredness or numinosity about a particular function in life which the intellect cannot fully comprehend. Jung thought that these figures were archetypal images, perceptions of innate human patterns or ordering processes the source of which remains a mystery and the experience of which conveys a sense of the divine. Take, for example, the doctor. We may know perfectly well that he is fallible, that he has a habit of not answering his telephone at weekends, that he overcharges (if he is in private practice), that he too falls ill, that he cannot cure the incurable. Yet we resonate not to the individual doctor when we panic over an illness, but to the Shaman, the Priest-Healer, the lame Asklepios who has received his wisdom from the gods and is himself a god, and who is holy priest to the desperate cries of both the body and the soul. It has been suggested by Jung and others that the Healer is an inner figure, who may be met in dreams and who embodies that profound mystery of the psyche's and the body's capacity to heal itself. But we do not think in terms of inner archetypal figures; we reach for the telephone to get the doctor. The rather callous playboy recently and barely graduated from medical school, with a disastrous marriage and neglected children and a myriad sexual, financial and emotional problems is not the face we see in the consulting room: but something shining, powerful, able to instil hope in the face of hopelessness, offering calm acceptance even of imminent death.

The more perceptive doctor knows about this Doctor too, and is well aware that healing, in many instances, depends upon the inner image being constellated; for if it is not, the patient will not get better, despite the technical skills and knowledge of the practitioner. Inner Doctor and outer doctor thus work hand in hand, although often no one, in particular the doctor and the patient, is the wiser. If we did not place this divinely, or archetypally, inspired trust in our medical practitioners, it is doubtful that we would ever visit them, save for the broken bones and minor bruises of everyday life. And the doctor himself? Granted, he may acquire handsome financial remuneration in America, and in England if he manages to acquire a Middle Eastern practice in Harley Street; and he obtains also the status which his credential offers, and a place in the community, and a sense of security in the 'network' of his colleagues. But the moral as well as the technical standards of the medical profession are demanding to an excessive degree, and it is no joy to deal with necrotic tissue and disintegration and death every day; not to mention what the Prince of Wales, in his address to the British Medical Association, referred to as 'the stricken spirit who comes . . . with his sick soul disguised as an ailment of the body.' What justification can the doctor offer to his own soul, when he must finally confront it, if there were not some Other glimmering behind his often genuine but frequently insufficient dedication and desire to help, whether he calls it compassion, or integrity, or service, or a need to live a meaningful life?

Analytical psychology speaks with justification of the dangers of identification with an archetype. The doctor is not the Doctor and is better off remembering this, lest he run the risk of inflation and even potential psychosis if the divine image overwhelms the conscious ego's sense of human fallibility and limitation. But these archetypal figures, when approached with consciousness and humility, nevertheless demand an offering from their children. To eat of godly flesh requires a return, which those who pursue 'jobs' rather than the inspiration of calling do not have to make. It is perhaps the sense of this which forms the inner logic of the Hippocratic oath in medicine. This act of returning something to the god—the act of recognising something sacred for which one is a vessel of some kind—differentiates the vocation from the job, or differentiates the individual's feeling about his job. The nervousness felt in esoteric circles about charging money for horoscopes or 'spiritual teaching' is a valid intuition, albeit sometimes grossly misplaced, that somewhere Someone is owed something. And what figure stands behind the astrologer, if not fate?

> The finished shape of our fate, the line drawn round it. It is the task the gods allot us, and the share of glory they

allow; the limits we must not pass; and our appointed end. Moira is all these.[6]

All the scientific knowledge in the world will not erase that which has been there from the beginning, older than the oldest of gods. Science too carries a mythic background which exercises numinous power; otherwise we astrologers would not be so intimidated by it, nor the scientific community so ready to use the word as though it were a religious truth any doubt of which constituted heresy. And, paradoxically, the mythic backgrounds of both astrology and science are united in the same figure:

> Such genuine religious feeling as is to be found in Homer is less concerned with the gods of Olympus than with more shadowy beings such as Fate or Necessity or Destiny, to whom even Zeus is subject. Fate exercised a great influence on all Greek thought, and perhaps was one of the sources from which science derived the belief in natural law.[7]

The same mythic background indeed, though clothed in a new gown. I sometimes wonder whether astrologers, when they can no longer trust anything but statistics, are not in part merely changing the Old Harlot's dress to assuage their own insecurities, as well as offering valuable contributions to a rational understanding of their study. Yet deeply disturbing though it may be to confront these ancient forms while still retaining our twentieth-century's hard-won knowledge of the physical universe and of man's greater choices within it, nevertheless it is this very conflict which I believe to be the modern astrologer's fate, if you like: the conflict with which he must struggle, full of ambivalence yet with Parsifal's question forever on his lips. Whom do we truly serve? Fate or freedom? The passively fatalistic astrologer and his opposite, the self-satisfied rationalist who looks no further than mechanical cause and effect and talks about 'mastering' the chart, perhaps miss the point—and, sooner or later, may betray the gods, the client and themselves.

So we need to try to bring into clearer perspective that figure with which we must deal, which seems to provoke such ambivalence: the ancient shape of fate, from which we have become estranged. In order to facilitate this effort, I have found it useful to draw from a very old past to trace man's images and stories about fate. Much of this may seem irrelevant to the modern astrologer. Yet myths, as Jung was at great pains to point out, are the eternal patterns of man's soul. They are alive and well in our dreams, in our fantasies, in our loves and hates, in the fabric of our lives; and not least in the more sensitive astrologer's consulting room, where the practitioner with any receptivity to the unseen and unspoken psyche may sense the white-gowned forms of Clotho the Spinner, Lachesis the Measurer, and Atropos the Cutter hovering dimly over the zodiacal wheel. . . .

I have found that fate is as liquid and elusive a word as love. Plato thought they were the same; and it is worth noting in passing that in Old Norse, the word for the fates is identical with the word for the sexual organs. Novalis wrote that fate and soul are two names for the same principle. Man's oldest image of fate is the image of a woman; so let us look for her.

References

1. Bertrand Russell, *History of Western Philosophy*, George Allen & Unwin, London, 1946, p. 237.
2. F. M. Cornford, *From Religion to Philosophy*, Harvester Press, London, 1980, p. 20.
3. Gilbert Murray, *Four Stages of Greek Religion*, Oxford University Press, London, 1912, p. 115.
4. Margaret Hone, *The Modern Textbook of Astrology*, L. N. Fowler & Co. Ltd., London, 1951, p. 17.
5. Jeff Mayo, *Astrology*, Teach Yourself Books, London, 1964, p. 6.
6. Mary Renault, *The King Must Die*, Longmans, Green & Co. Ltd, London, 1958, p. 16.
7. Russell, p. 32.

IV

Social Dimensions
of Karma

While we may experience karma most directly on the personal level, we cannot fully understand it until we see its collective dimensions as well, for like individuals, groups incur karma and develop karmic patterns. Individual karma is played out within the larger context of group karma and may at times even be severely modified by it.

Diana Dunningham Chapotin addresses ways we are affected by our cultural environment and explores the question of whether there can ever be unmerited suffering in the life of an individual. William Metzger explores ways karma functions as we make choices on social questions such as abortion and medical intervention for those near death, stressing that consideration of the good of the collective whole naturally arises from recognizing one's intrinsic link with the One Life. Anna Freifeld Lemkow discusses the implications for personal and collective karma arising from recent advances in modern physics and systems theory. Alfred Taylor, noting the almost miraculous advances in the health field in recent decades, examines the question of whether karmic debts can ever truly be eliminated, and suggests that the only genuinely effective means of lessening the karmic suffering of others is through a deep spiritual empowerment. George Linton discusses various aspects of karmic theory and concludes by asking that we consider more closely the implications of aligning ourselves with various groups and their respective karmas.

16

Karma Re-Examined: Do We Ever Suffer Undeservedly?

DIANA DUNNINGHAM CHAPOTIN

[Karma] has not involved its decrees in darkness purposely to perplex man; nor shall it punish him who dares to scrutinize its mysteries. On the contrary, he who unveils through study and meditation its intricate paths, and throws light on those dark ways, in the windings of which so many perish owing to their ignorance of the labyrinth of life, is working for the good of his fellowmen.

H. P. Blavatsky

Of all the Eastern ideas that have become popular in the West, karma is one of the best known. The basic idea is that everything we think, say or do has a result whether we see it or not and will rebound on us inevitably in this life or another.

Go beyond this and confusion can arise. There are some tricky questions which can frustrate us yet push us to a deeper understanding: Do I reap the consequences of my acts or the consequences of the motives of my acts—or both? Is everything that happens to me a consequence of a past action? Am I able to modify my karma? Is a child karmically responsible? If so, from what age? How can one explain the suffering of animals? Does what has traditionally been called "national karma" allow justice for every individual in the nation? What is the connection between earthquakes, volcanoes, and humanity's doings?

It is largely thanks to early Theosophists of the last century that the word "karma" appears in the dictionary and is in popular usage today. One has a reasonable chance of receiving this response from the person on the street: "What goes around comes around!" or "What you put out comes back, man!" For Theosophists, Anthroposophists, Alice Bailey students, Hare Krishna devotees, Buddhists, Bhakti Vedantans, Edgar Cayce students and many Unity Church members, the general idea is that if you put out positive energy, you will attract positive experiences in this life-time or in another; if you put out negative energy, life has its way of bringing you back into line. Typical ideas prevailing in the West, and which we would do well to examine critically, are as follows:

- Whatever I do will be adjusted in this life or another. It is not a question of punishment but of education.
- Whatever lesson I need to learn will come to me, e.g. if I am wealthy and hoard and cheat, I'll be drawn to a position of want where I'll learn. If I'm generous now, I will generate positive opportunities for growth in the future.
- A lot of our present relationship ties are from the past. We are drawn into relationships because of unresolved karma.
- A difficulty we are going through is sometimes a "karmic" one—something we "had" to go through.
- When we enter the spiritual path seriously, a lot of negative karma is intensified, is sped up so that we can clear away karmic baggage quickly. We are burning up karma to purify ourselves for service.
- If we change our ways, we can modify our karma or neutralize it. We are never given more than we can take.
- We choose our parents and our early environment.
- Someone who misses a plane crash because she cancelled her ticket at the last minute was guided away because it wasn't her time.

The central idea here is that whatever misfortunes overtake us in this life are the results of our misdeeds of past lives and likewise present good fortune is the result of past good deeds. However we word it, we seem to conceive of it like a credit and debit balance in the cosmic bank: a debit listing is bad karma in store for us. When we have exhausted our bad karma, we can then be secure from any evil befalling us.

Now if we study all the myriad variations of the doctrine of karma expounded in the East throughout the centuries, we see that this version of karma is really but one variation among scores. It might be called the Western popular version of an age-old doctrine that has as many expressions as there are religions, sects, cults, spiritual philosophies, and mythologies. There are endless schools of karma, all persuasive, detailed and powerful.

The Western popular version seems to presuppose that events in themselves are karmic, are lesson-bringers. Yet the way two people respond to the same event can be entirely different. An event might be traumatic for one and a matter of indifference or even joy for another. Imprisonment in a concentration camp proved to be transformative for psychotherapist and philosopher Viktor Frankl while for others the experience was crushing. The terms "good" and "bad" karma are obviously entirely subjective. The event is in itself neutral but our response to it is the truly karmic factor, i.e., entirely dependent on our past. In a series of talks published under the title *No Other Path To Go*, Radha Burnier says, "External conditions are accidental. We are not born in India, China, Russia or the U.S.A. because of some particular merit." Inner attitude is much more central to the operation of karma than outer circumstance. It is in our attitude that our real freedom exists.

Of course most of what happens to us we bring on ourselves. In looking at our own lives we can see character tendencies that propel us into choices and situations. But if our house is swept away in a flood, is it because of the operation of natural law resulting from a previous life?

There are behavior patterns we learn from cultural conditioning. Distinct characteristics—our sense of etiquette, of social morality, the forms we use to express love, our values and priorities—are shaped by the prevailing world-view of the society in which we live. There is also family conditioning—guilt feelings, fear, the ability to express emotion, to communicate, the prejudices we inherit, etc. These, then, form the personal baggage we carry which we cannot assume reflects our evolutionary status and which, dare it be speculated, we possibly did not earn.

We need to look deeper—at the fundamental traits of character expressing themselves as a life pattern, the seed qualities which are carried from incarnation to incarnation. Here we are looking beyond family and cultural conditioning, beyond the personal baggage visited upon us for better or for worse, to deeper traits. The higher self, the reincarnating self faces the outer circumstances, as it were, and does with them what it can. In this truly karmic struggle, growth takes place, in the meeting ground between inner attitude and outer circumstance. Parents can often easily discern in their children the unique, deeper traits with which they have been born; we can usually see in ourselves the interaction of seed qualities and outer conditions.

H. P. Blavatsky talks of unmerited suffering in *The Key to Theosophy*. In a footnote she explains what she means by the term: "Some Theosophists have taken exception to the phrase but the words are those of Master.... The essential idea was that men often suffer from the effects of the actions done by others, effects which thus do not strictly belong to their own karma."[1] In *The Mahatma Letters To A. P. Sinnett* we find this remark: "Our chelas [disciples]are helped but when they are innocent of the causes that lead them into trouble; when such causes are generated by foreign, outside influences."[2] Further on in *The Key*, Blavatsky formulates a question and answer thus:

> Enquirer: But, surely all these evils which seem to fall upon the masses somewhat indiscriminately are not actual merited and INDIVIDUAL karma?
> Theosophist: No, they cannot be so strictly defined in their effects as to show that each individual environment, and the particular conditions of life in which each person finds himself, are nothing more than the retributive Karma

which the individual generated in a previous life . . . it is upon
this broad line of human interdependence that the law of
Karma finds its legitimate and equable issue.
Enquirer: Do I, then, understand that the law of Karma
is not necessarily an individual law?
Theosophist: That is just what I mean. It is impossible
that Karma could readjust the balance of power in the world's
life and progress unless it had a broad and general line
of action.[3]

A third interesting remark of Blavatsky's is worth noting:
"Every transgression in the private life of a mortal, according
to Occult philosophy, is a double edged sword in the hand
of Karma; one edge for the transgressor, the other for the
family, nation and sometimes even for the race, that produced him."[4]

All this implies that we cannot just work off our karmic
debts and then be immune amidst planetary chaos. And
that's logical. Ultimately at the highest level of our being
we are not separate from others, and so we share the collective karma. It is not a question of personal merit but
of shouldering responsibility together. Freedom from
karma or karmalessness, remember, is not the elimination
or suppression of action or events but mastery of our inner
attitude towards them.

Now let us return to the ideas about karma in the popular
Western view and review some of them in the light of the
above suggestions.

Sometimes we are perhaps too literal, too simplistic.

It has been said that if someone is wealthy and cheats
people instead of managing his or her money fairly, this
person may be impoverished in some future life; or if one
is poor now and cannot hold onto money, it is because he
or she has had immense wealth in the past and mishandled
it. Can such one-to-one correspondences be drawn?

We may be confusing the outer circumstances of the
field of the personality with a soul lesson at the level of
the higher self. If we are suffering from heart disease and
seeking a deeper implication, it is surely unreasonable
to assume that we have stabbed someone in the chest in
a past life. It is more logical to look at character tendencies,

psychological patterns or lifestyle which may be contributing to the present condition.

Sometimes we overpersonalize the workings of karma.

Exactly how many of our present relationships can be linked with past ones? Do we not sometimes jump too quickly to past lives to explain connections with people before we look at the level of the personality within this lifetime? We may try to justify a present relationship by talking of past life links rather than looking at present psychological dependencies, e.g., "I cannot give up this love affair because I am finishing up past karma. I must follow my intuition with this married woman/man because I have a karmic debt to discharge." There may well be links from the past, but it is important that we look at the immediate present level of the personality and at our psychological dependencies before we assert deeper links to explain a tie.

Or we allow a fatalistic note to creep in.

"This is something I HAVE to go through." Perhaps we are actually in a destructive situation where it is time to invoke our spiritual will in order to move into a new phase of our life. Or when we hear statements like "May she be healed if it is within her karma," we can ask why it is necessary to put the conditional into our effort to help someone. Karma is not an outside force that makes us do things independent of our volition. We do not so much *have* karma as we *are* karma. It is woven into our psychological makeup and habit patterns. We have the power to take hold of our lives and actively shape the future.

Sometimes we fail to extend genuine love and sympathy to someone.

"Why did you *choose* to have this happen to you?" "Don't worry, we are never given more than we can take." When we say this hoping to help someone in distress, we may be mixing levels. We may be applying a truth appropriate at the soul level but patently untrue for the crushed and tortured personality. Here is another example of a confusion of levels: "I don't know why Joan Brown is so upset about losing her husband. Surely she knows he is an immortal being and that all this works in accordance with the law of cause and effect?" But Mrs. Brown is grieving quite naturally at the personal level—for the color of her husband's eyes, for his broad shoulders, for the unspoken communion between them. The field of the personality cannot be ignored.

Sometimes we lean on karma in a way which inflates our ego. "As spiritual aspirants, we are being tested. We are having our karma accelerated to prepare us for special service." The apparent intensification of karma may be a subjective impression brought about by increased awareness and lifestyle changes as we enter a more spiritual way of life.

Another possible confusion of levels may arise in response to tragedies we read about in the paper: "Gosh, what about those two or three thousand Indians who died of poisoning near the Union Carbide factory in Bhopal? It's a good thing we know about karma. They must really have been paying off something big!" From another perspective, perhaps we could see the event as a NEW karmic chain of cause and effect, the responsibility for it being a collective one. The consequences of that disaster will belong to us all. The people who died perhaps assumed responsibility at the collective level and did not personally merit the horrible death that came to them in the face of the negligence and exploitation of the industrial world.

Some students think that collective karma is "national" or "group" karma, i.e., that individuals transgressing nature's laws are drawn together to receive group discipline, as in an earthquake or volcano. This is not, it is suggested, what is meant by collective karma. What is meant is that we cannot paddle our karmic canoe. If the river becomes clogged with other people's pollution and I can't advance, there is no point in my leaning on my oars and shouting sulkily, "This is unmerited! I have never thrown one Coke can into the river!"

Being vegetarian will not save us from the ecological repercussions of the unspeakable exploitation of animals. As members of the human race and inhabitants sharing this planet, we are all going to reap the consequences of that totally unmerited suffering. We literally cannot separate our personal karma from the karma of others. Cut a branch off a tree and the whole tree is affected. Prick the finger and the whole body is affected via the sympathetic nervous system. The deforestation of the planet affects us all, the most innocent and the most guilty alike.

It is therefore tremendously important that we involve ourselves in helping the world now, if only because at any time we can be affected by the acts of others, acts unrelated to our own circumstances. In fact, choosing to serve the world in order to advance ourselves spiritually as individuals is a nonsense. All this changes our attitude at the practical level. When we see a severely deformed child, we need not automatically think, "Poor thing, he must be paying back a heavy karmic debt" and then simply extend our sympathy to him. Perhaps we could also consider that his mother might have taken thalidomide and that she and the doctors and the researchers and the manufacturers of thalidomide and the taxpayers, and therefore all of us, are involved in his care and nurture.

In addition to looking backward somewhat passively or focusing on the individual karmic circumstance, we might do well to look also at the whole community and the planet's involvement and try to understand the implications from that angle first. This might be put another way. Let us imagine a primitive tribe whose group or religious life is centered in its village temple. On the great central altar is a huge earthenware urn that the villagers treat with great reverence, as though it were representing Mother Earth in her receptive, nurturing, womb-like aspect. In looking further, we find that these people believe that their future is held in this great vessel, that the gods watch them ceaselessly and distill the good and evil of their souls into an invisible potion contained in the pot. Whatever happens to the villagers—good crops, earthquakes, abundant births, healthy children—comes from the great urn, "ladled out" by the gods.

The villagers are an advanced group. They know in their hearts that there are no personally whimsical gods and that the potion is symbolic of their future; it is brewed out of their ignorance and efforts, their sorrows, their loves, their prayers and their quarrels. They do not seek to identify the fate, the past, the responsibility, the guilt or merits of individuals in the community. They know that, however good individuals are, they are subject to the nourishment or poison of the great urn because they are of that community and spiritually one with it. They acknowledge several kinds of karma but choose to focus on the collective or distributive kind, since they feel that focusing on the individual, personal levels alone can be separative rather than unifying.

What, however, is the meaning of suffering? However individually unmerited, neither suffering nor great joy is necessarily meaningless. Suffering forces members of a community to care for one another, and this leads to discipline, to habit which eventually becomes second nature, and finally to spiritual nature. Joy inspires us to share joy. Suffering can awaken us from a general condition of ignorance or mediocrity. We may be guilty of inertia or lukewarmness rather than cruelty or malice. Suffering and joy personally merited or unmerited, can bring us to a greater feeling of compassion for others, to a greater sensitivity.

A rather Zen or Krishnamurti-like comment on the question of meaning comes from J. J. van der Leeuw in a 1930 lecture entitled, "Revelation or Realization—The Conflict in Theosophy":

> It is curious to see how man dreads the thought of life being beyond explanation. . . . These attempts at explanations, however, blind him to the true meaning of things that happen to him; they tempt his attention away from the event itself, which again is the here and now, and lead it to some imaginary cause or result. Thus the meaning of the event which lies in the actual experience, escapes him and he is no richer, no wiser for his suffering.

There is a catch phrase prevalent in the West these days: "You create your own reality." Indeed it must be repeated that most of what happens to us—at least in the spoiled,

secure environment of many Western lives—is quite clearly
"ready cash karma" i.e., brought on by ourselves right in
the here and now, individually. Spontaneous soul-searching
to find the deeper reason for something is a very human
and salutory activity, which often helps us see limiting
patterns and behaviors that can be changed, affording us
greater freedom in our lives. However, there seems to be a
tendency today to take responsibility in this sense too far.
The psychological issues we are looking at in ourselves
may be genuine but not necessarily causative of external
events. In fact to say that an event—such as the death of
a loved one—took place *in order to* teach us a certain lesson,
or that those gunned down by a madman at the supermarket
brought it on themselves and "chose" to be there, is surely
going too far. Such an attitude may be an attempt to prove
that we can avoid harm by perfecting ourselves.

Why the emphasis on unmerited suffering in this paper?
Because it teaches us unity and compassion. It shows that
ultimately our fates are wrapped up together, that we actually
carry within us tens of thousands of Ethiopians, Kam-
pucheans and Romanians, but also the joy of mothers
holding their newborn, the calm and peace of highly developed meditators, the strength of great reformers, the
constancy of Mother Teresa's sisters.

The discussion of unmerited suffering is not intended to
deny cosmic justice and harmony but rather to show that
such justice is only perceivable ultimately at the broadest
level, from the perspective of the one, in terms of complete
identification with others. Any justice at the personal,
immediate, practical, or socio-political levels has got to be
fought for by humanity and by humanity alone.

A student once related the experience of taking a child
to the beach for a picnic. The wind and waves were un-
expectedly high; the whole atmosphere was unpleasant,
with flying sand, shells, and seaweed, and a heavy sky.
The two huddled under a blanket for a while and then
decided to drive to a hill overlooking the coast. High up,
all was calm. The shoreline stretched unbroken and glorious
below, with great patterns of waves looping unbroken

along the coast for miles. None of the turbulence below was evident, only a harmony afforded by the wider picture. This gave the student an insight into the workings of spiritual evolution. At the level of everyday life, things appear chaotic at times. No justice or order seems to be in place. But from the distant perspective, a wider vision is obtained. Pattern and harmony can appear. The total lives of an evolving soul must surely reveal order and justice viewed from afar, as indeed must humanity's life and progress in its broad evolutionary arc.

What needs to be emphasized above all is that there are thousands of people, animals, trees in the world suffering. It is not possible to sit back and say, "Oh well, that is their karma. They brought it on themselves." IT IS OUR KARMA. We cannot paddle our own karmic canoe. We cannot be like the Bishop of Grenoble in France during the last war. When France was occupied, he is reported to have advised his congregation to accept Nazi rule because it was clearly God's will—their karma, we might say. Along with saying, "This is our karma," we have to say, "This was avoidable, all this pain is avoidable if we work hard enough to avoid it." We have got to be out there helping, hands on. However busy we are, we must reserve some of our time for helping others, and not just our friends or those we find it is actually fun to help.

In her message to American Theosophists in 1889, Helena Blavatsky quoted one of the Mahatmas: "The universe groans under the weight of karma and none other than self-sacrificial karma relieves it. How many of you have helped humanity to carry its smallest burden? . . . Do as the gods when incarnated do. Feel yourselves as vehicles of the whole humanity, mankind as part of yourselves, and act accordingly."[5]

Let us not say, "That's karma!" or "That's her karma," but instead say, "This is OUR karma."

Note to the reader: This article is based partially on the ideas of Arthur Robson in *Human Nature, The Eternal*

Truths of Life, and *Look At Your Karma* (Theosophical Publishing House, Adyar).

References

1. H. P. Blavatsky, *The Key To Theosophy* (Wheaton, Illinois: Quest, 1972), p. 101.
2. *The Mahatma Letters to A. P. Sinnett* (Adyar: Theosophical Publishing House, 3rd ed.), p. 305.
3. H. P. Blavatsky, *The Key To Theosophy* (Wheaton, Illinois: Quest, 1972), p. 122/123.
4. H. P. Blavatsky, *Collected Writings*, Vol. 12, (Wheaton, Illinois: Theosophical Publishing House), p. 385.
5. *Five Messages from H. P. Blavatsky to The American Theosophists* (Los Angeles: The Theosophy Co., 1922), pamphlet, pp. 19-20.

17

Choosing: Karma & Dharma in the 21st Century

WILLIAM METZGER

Karma is a word of many meanings and shadings. As it has been picked up by the so-called "New Age," however, there has been a tendency to squeeze out its subtleties, and in the personalistic way of so much of "New Age" thought, it has been reduced to a concept applying only to individuals and not to the One Life of which we are all part.

In fairness to "New Agers," much that has been written on karma does seem to be focused on individual lives in a horizontal line of pattern and development. A personalistic interpretation, therefore, has been problematical throughout the history of the concept. It is not inherent in the concept, however, and in this essay I attempt to show a broader meaning of karma grounded in social responsibility. In particular we will consider karma in relation to several perplexing issues of our own time and place in history, such as reproductive rights and medical technology.

To do so, it is necessary to consider karma and a related concept known as *dharma* together. Karma and dharma interact in our life choices moment by moment. We are conditioned by the sum total of past experiences, thoughts, and actions, and this is our karma. We say, then, that karma is the universal law of cause and effect. This means that every action has a reaction, every human act has consequences.

We say, furthermore, that one is conditioned by one's personal history, and this leads to the common understanding of karma, which states that if something dreadful happens to you, then surely you must have brought it on yourself by some past action, in this or in some previous life.

This personalistic application of karma is entirely too simplistic, however, and we all know persons who have dreadful things happen to them who so far as we can ascertain are living good and exemplary lives. And surely to suggest that the abused child is a "victim" of his or her own karma must be rejected. It is too easy to wash one's hands of problems on the grounds that whatever happens is a matter of karmic inevitability.

We also know people who have broken past patterns— their "conditioning"—and transformed their own lives and the lives of others. Therefore, our understanding of karma must be combined with our understanding of dharma.

Though we are surely conditioned by our past, by our

karma, we also have a responsibility to our particular time and situation, and this is our dharma, our duty, or inner obligation. Distinguishing our conditioning from our responsibility to act beyond the boundaries of that conditioning is the task of a lifetime, or several lifetimes.

There are many different models by which persons can consider their own life situations and act to make the most of their existences. Some of these models are psychological, some spiritual, but all in one way or another are directed at enabling a person to take charge of his or her life situation, and make the most of it. Karma suggests more than this, however, for it is not just *my* life situation I affect by my actions, but others as well. The choices we make have effects far beyond ourselves. We have a social responsibility as well as a responsibility to make our own personal life situations better.

That social responsibility may manifest itself in a concern for a neighbor who is known to be a victim of abuse. It also manifests in a concern for the social impact of one's own actions. A further aspect of our social responsibility, beyond personal actions, is the part we play in the making of social policy, as is the case with the issues of reproductive choice and medical care.

One way to interpret the relationship between karma and dharma, as stated by Dane Rudhyar elsewhere in this anthology, is that karma defines "what is possible" based on experience, history, and conditioning, and dharma is defined by the "need of the new existential situation."

This may suggest that karma somehow is a set of limits on one's capacity to respond to a situation. Another way of considering this, however, is to say that in expressing one's dharma, one may in fact "breakthrough" one's seeming limits. Such an interpretation explains the sense one gets when a particular person or event seems to transform a situation in a new way, or when a person seems to achieve what his or her own seeming limits appear to prohibit.

Using this approach to an understanding of karma and dharma, we may find a Western analogy in Paul Tillich's theological model, in which destiny and freedom may be seen to take the place of karma and dharma as terms for limits and breakthrough.

Tillich himself might argue with this, for he was critical of the concept of karma, on the grounds that it is strictly personal, and that in it history has no aim. He argued that there is no impulse to transform history in the concept of karma, and the consequence of this lack is that the ambiguities of history are unconquerable (*ST*, 3:351-352).

When karma is interpreted in this narrow personalistic way, it lacks a basis for social action and for human and social betterment. We have an obligation, as Tillich would put it, to "liberate the positive from ambiguous existence" (3:398).

However, I would contend that karma and dharma together are very similar to Tillich's concepts of destiny and freedom. If in reading Tillich we think "karma" when he says "destiny," and "dharma" when he says "freedom," we will gain a different understanding of karma and dharma.

But we do not need to depend on Tillich for our "new" interpretation of karma, for it is not a new interpretation at all. In the *Bhagavad Gita*, Arjuna's existential crisis was resolved by Krishna teaching him how he could do his duty (dharma) without being bound by karma (Eliade, 2:238-239). Krishna emphasizes action over inaction, and selfless action in service to humankind. "Strive constantly to serve the welfare of the world," Krishna tells Arjuna. "By devotion to selfless work one attains the supreme goal of life. Do your work with the welfare of others always in mind" (Easwaran, *Gita*, 77). Arjuna is advised to act without selfish attachment, for to do so is to act in freedom.

Nevertheless, "Even a wise man acts within the limitations of his own nature," said Krishna. The point is that despite one's natural limitations, if one acts without selfish attachment, one frees oneself from the "karmic groove."

It should be noted here that karma is not a "moral law." It is an impersonal law, and does not make clear and unambiguous statements about what is "good" and what is "evil" by the consequences it provides. Life is not so clear-cut. Karma only balances actions; for each action there is a reaction, and accumulations of actions have their own sets of reactions, and those reactions may be good or bad. Karma provides a "balance," but it does not guarantee a happy ending.

One might say that dharma, or "duty," offers a moral aspect to our considerations. Duty implies obedience, but the dharmic obedience is to a higher responsibility, and this is its moral dimension. But that responsibility is driven from within rather than by outer authority. As Annie Besant expressed it, karma "pushes us from the past," but dharma "pulls us from the future."

A detailed consideration of moral questions must be left for another essay, though our consideration of karma and dharma will surely suggest to us some possible solutions to the moral questions that perplex us.

Of the moral dimension of karma and dharma we may say this much: that the purpose of the moral life is to promote overall good, the good of the One Life of which we are all part. This concept means that moral choices are never made on behalf of what seems best for oneself alone.

Still we all make expedient choices, and we make them often without a moment's contemplation of the effect of our choice on the One Life. But these are not moral choices, rather they are expedient and personal ones. Moral choices are those we make with others in mind, and indeed, at their most profound level, moral choices are made on behalf of all of life, what we refer to here as the One Life.

From a moral perspective, dharma is our duty to the One Life. It is not our duty to our self, our family, our employer, or our country isolated from others; it is our duty to all of life. Also, it is a duty that transcends inherited karmic patterns.

Eliade described dharma as the "theoretical body" and labeled it as "good" in the struggle with "evil." Thus we see that our duty is to do what in our best understanding we perceive to be good, and this frequently will require a break from patterns of life in which we are moving.

A visual metaphor may be helpful. If we think of karma as the horizontal, the predetermined, the impulse toward fixity, we see that karma operates in a straight line of action and reaction. It is "in a groove." On the other hand, dharma is the vertical, the developmental and expressive. It breaks the groove, it breaks the pattern of the straight line, and it is responsible for all the dramatic turning points in history, the "breakthroughs" and the "breakups" alike.

It has been said that history is the history of groups, and that historically significant people are significant in terms of their groups. Nevertheless, individuals do stand out—for example Mahatma Gandhi, whose concept of passive resistance influenced the civil rights movement in the United States. Such people created turning points through individual breakthroughs, frequently moving against the forces of their times.

Also, of course, individuals pick up on each other's cues, and create movements, and so we have historically significant turning points such as the Renaissance, the industrial revolution, the computer revolution, the spread of communism from its revolutionary birth at the beginning of this century or its dissolution in the final decade.

"As every historical situation contains trends, so it contains chances," said Tillich. "Chances are occasions to change the determining power of a trend." (3:327) Not all chances are taken, but the exercise of "chance-giving occasions" can break patterns and trends, setting off a series of new events, and new trends may develop. And indeed human nature itself changes in the historical process.

The fundamental point in considering the history-making role of karma and dharma is that we are both free and destined, and history is a mixture of both horizontal and vertical movement. At times we seem to be in grooves, and at other times we embark on dramatic changes in direction. These two aspects of human experience interact at every moment in time.

Perennial debates about "nature or nurture," about the influence of one's genes or one's environment, seem to beg that we make a choice as to whether the animal is one or the other, rather than to arrive at a deeper notion of how it is neither this nor that, but both/and (and indeed also that other as well), and the balance of one or the other is decided again and again as one moves through life.

One's dharma cannot be attained if one is *only* fixed by karmic necessity. But neither can one's dharma be attained without a bow to what one's experienced destiny has "dictated." Dictated is not really the word for it, however; destiny may *seem* to dictate, but human beings in their freedom break from seeming destiny all the time.

There are pitfalls along the way, of course. A common pitfall is at the outset to "condition" oneself to "being conditioned." Too often persons will just begin to get an understanding of who they are, only to lock themselves into a sense of choicelessness based on "karma." "It is my karma" in effect dismisses any notion of having the ability—indeed the responsibility—to make changes in one's patterns of life. This is the danger in all psychological and spiritual paths, and especially in the practice of astrology and other divinatory methods: that one gets a fixed notion of what one is, and then fulfills that notion in a self-limiting way.

The examples of Stephen Hawking, who has had a brilliant career as a physicist despite extraordinary physical odds, or that of the Irish artist and writer Christy Brown, whose story is told in his book and the film *My Left Foot*, demonstrate something of the presence of freedom to overcome enormous odds given by destiny. Hawking must use mechanical means to communicate his insights to students as he suffers progressive paralysis due to Lou Gehrig's disease. Brown, because of the limitations imposed by cerebral palsy, paints and writes with his left foot. One could of course offer examples in the other direction of persons with seeming "golden paths" set by their destiny who somehow go awry and fail to achieve what is expected.

One could, indeed, find an "example" to "prove" either point of view—one is totally pre-destined or one is totally free. The point is that neither of these absolute views is correct. One can accept one's destiny or break from it, day by day, decision by decision.

Two large areas of human choice in our time that can be contemplated in terms of karma and dharma are clusters of issues which can be grouped under the headings of reproductive choice and medical intervention.

Reproductive choice. This includes increasing options for birth control, including pills or other preventive measures, and the option of abortion after an unintended or unwanted pregnancy. Given the knowledge now available through modern medical technology (such as amniocentesis and sonograms) one is enabled to choose to terminate a pregnancy because of genetic damage discovered early.

Any number of social issues are relevant to weighing the questions raised by such choices: a family's economic and emotional capacity to support another child; society's ability to afford the costs to maintain, say, genetically damaged lives and to cope with the lifelong educational and social costs of these impaired human beings; the problem of unwanted and unadoptable children; increasing child and spouse abuse in stressed homes; and the frequently related problems of unemployment, underemployment, and homelessness.

Medical interventions. The increasing medical capability to maintain life in situations not previously treatable brings with it more "choice" challenges. How do we decide when to continue life-prolonging efforts and when to stop? When is the high cost of medical intervention justified, and when does it represent a misallocation of resources? Heart-rending stories could be told of families ruined spiritually and economically by too-long-drawn-out deaths, of "human vegetables" kept "alive" by machine, first because the technology was there, and then because authorities were afraid to terminate the technological intervention once it had been initiated.

These are not only personal moral questions, but questions of social and global concern. We are, simply because we are human, faced with having to make choices, and we do so out of several considerations: a mixture of destiny-given attitudes, moral choices in the situation, and the human impulse to change destiny.

When vast resources are marshalled in the task of enabling one-pound babies to survive, one must ask the question, What is best for the One Life?

The choices offered in these areas are interrelated, and have implications far beyond the lives of the individuals involved in making decisions about pregnancy and birth. There are concerns about population and resources, about the allocation of medical resources, about the availability and cost of health care. There are questions about the quality of the life that we are bringing into the world or that we are preserving against incredible odds, and there are questions about the eventual social costs of celebrated "miracle babies."

When choices are made, of course, other choices are denied. Competition for limited research funds pits causes against one another. We make choices, and we make them again and again.

We cannot fool ourselves into thinking we can move in our karmic grooves toward a universal harmony. It is essential that we exercise our dharmic responsibility, and that we do so on behalf of the One Life, with a concern for all of life, and not for personal or emotional reasons alone.

To change "destiny" is not fundamentally wrong, and we do so every day. Nevertheless, decisions to change destiny are never to be taken lightly. This includes a doctor's decision to place a patient on life-support systems just as surely as it does the doctor's decision to take a patient off life-support. Neither decision is clearly right or clearly wrong, for there is no consensus on such matters, and there probably can be no consensus. Whenever we are at a given moment in history, any seeming "consensus" will have its proponents and its detractors. Any seeming consensus will be a consensus for the "moment" in history, a consensus waiting to be shattered by expanding knowledge and technical capability.

Nevertheless, being human, we tend to opt for human freedom, even when we may seem to be speaking for destiny. Even when a person argues, as some have, that karmic destiny makes human choices for abortion unjust (let us say) to "reincarnating egos," one is, in fact, making a choice out of a human freedom of belief. That belief (in this instance) is in the rather anthropomorphic existence of reincarnating egos whose right to come into a new physical existence outweighs the right of one already in physical existence to terminate a pregnancy. And what about the global population impact if all reincarnating egos' "needs" to be reincarnated were granted?

Increasingly, however, we need to make our decisions from the larger perspective provided by serving the One Life. The American Indian tradition is an example of such a perspective: decisions were taken only after considering their impact on "the seventh generation." Decisions for the One Life—and for the seventh generation—call for considerations beyond the emotional demands of the moment.

There are moral and logical imperatives which indicate that we can transcend our conditions. We have the power to "deliberate and decide, thus cutting through the mechanisms of stimulus and response," as Tillich expressed it. In the language of karma and dharma, karma is the stimulus and response, and dharma is the power to deliberate and decide.

The metaphor of the horizontal and the vertical, mentioned earlier, is widely used in religious expression. Dane Rudhyar used this imagery in discussing karma and dharma elsewhere in this volume. Karma represents a horizontal demand, and dharma represents a vertical possibility.

One could imagine a horse wearing blinders that prevent it from being distracted in its forward motion. The horse does not possess the freedom to break free from the destiny presented by the blinders. A human being, however, while wearing the "blinders" given by karmic destiny, nevertheless has the possibility of throwing off the karmic limits in favor of free choices.

There is of course a great responsibility imposed on us by the fact that our "maker"—God, Nature, or whatever metaphor you prefer—has given us this opportunity to choose. Those choices should be regarded as a gift, and should not be made lightly or without regard for their consequences.

It is not the purpose of this essay to provide the moral or ethical framework in which such choices can be made. But it is obvious that such a framework is required. One should be aware, however, that whatever our own moral framework, the answers we give to the many perplexing questions raised by (for example) the increasing possibilities for reproductive choice, and the widening range of medical interventions possible in life-threatening situations, are made in the context of the dynamics of karma and dharma, of destiny and freedom, of pre-given inclinations and the possibility of breaking old patterns.

It is not a question of both karma and dharma being *necessary* in every moment; both simply *are* present, and we do well to remember that whenever we take a moral stance on any issue.

There are, as Mircea Eliade said, "historical moments." These "moments of cosmic becoming... do not *create* doctrine but merely bring to birth *appropriate formulas* for the timeless message" (2:239).

We live in such moments, and because we are free to choose, we must choose. We cannot simply defer choice by opting always for the pull of our karmic history. We must seize the moment, express our dharma, and thereby advance the cause of the One Life.

In Tillich's expression, "What happens in time and space, in the smallest particle of matter as well as in the greatest personality, is significant for the eternal life" (3:398).

References

Eknath Easwaran, trans., *The Bhagavad Gita*, Nilgiri Press, 1985.

Mircea Eliade, *A History of Religious Ideas*, Vol. 2: *From Gautauma Buddha to the Triumph of Christianity*, trans. by Willard Trask; University of Chicago Press, 1982.

Paul Tillich, *Systematic Theology*, Vol. 3, University of Chicago Press, 1967.

18
Karmic Process in Science and Society

ANNA FREIFELD LEMKOW

*Humankind is on the move, emerging from a chain
reaction of cause and effect that stretches back for
billions of years. Now this species has the power to
affect its own evolution by conscious choice . . . the
capacity . . . to be responsible, the will . . . to do right
when to do so is required to survive . . . the love of the
human for home, and the recognition . . . that this
whole planet is now home.*

Breakthrough, Anatoly Gromyko and
Martin Hellman (editors)

Introduction

To probe the profound concept known as karma, I believe
it is necessary to invoke a holistic and synoptic philosophical
system, such as theosophy—a version of what is often called
"perennial philosophy." I adopt it here because it specifically
incorporates and develops the idea of karma.[1] Indeed, the
theosophical movement was instrumental, in the past
century, in introducing this Eastern concept in the West.

According to the theosophical perspective, the universe
is one—living, intelligent and intelligible, multilevelled,
and comprised of beings that, together with the universe

---

1. The related principle of reincarnation which gives karma added
depth is also developed, but I will not have occasion in this essay to
discuss this principle.

itself, co-evolve toward a higher life. Essential to this philosophy is the proposition that the numinous Reality or the Absolute is inseparable from the manifested world— that It pervades the world and reveals Itself in the order, purposiveness, and meaning of world processes.

Our central concern in considering karma is with *process* since karma is the pre-eminent cosmic process-principle-law that brings about the dynamic co-evolution. It is *the* process of processes, *the* holistic law of laws, and it sub-sumes all other dynamics.

Different dynamics obtain at different levels of our multi-levelled existence. For example, physical dynamics are not the same as emotional dynamics, and the process of reasoning is not the same as the process of intuiting. Yet, because of the impartible wholeness of existence, no process or type of order can fall outside the one, all-embracing karmic process. Moreover, the disciplines we employ to investigate different types of order and process are also essentially a dynamic unity. Notably, though science and spirituality are very different modes of knowing, in principle they are complementary and intimately and beneficially interrelated. Albert Einstein noted this relationship: Science without religion is blind; religion without science is lame.

Dynamic nondualism illuminates the means for recon-ciling all differences, whether in knowledge, religion, or political ideology. It permits understanding the dualities of existence as interactive or mutually defining polarities. These pervasive dualities are not irreconcilable opposites but *necessary* and *indispensable* to every constructive and creative happening, including the process of evolution itself. This applies to such fundamental dualities as spirit and matter, masculine and feminine, particular and universal, necessity and freedom, one and many, finite and infinite, temporal and timeless. For the human psyche, the ideal held out by holism and karma is to integrate these poles of self in terms of the all-embracing wholeness of existence.

If individuals achieved this spiritual integration, it would necessarily be reflected in human society. Indeed, world understanding and world peace *depend* on individuals achieving of an adequate degree of inner unity. More than that, holism and karma imply that man (employing that word in a generic sense) is responsible for his own and the world's transformation, a sublimely creative assignment of healing the world and making it whole. It should be apparent that the perspective we are invoking speaks cogently to the situation in the world today wherein nations (and ethnic and other groups) are tied together in numerous ways but are far from unified.

A fundamental function of karmic process is to maintain balance and harmony in the world. Karma re-establishes these wherever they are disrupted. Obviously, a prime arena of disruption is that of human relations. In that realm, karma may be viewed as an *ethical* principle-process-law. Karma presupposes the wholeness of the flow of existence. That flow is disrupted whenever we think or act inharmoniously with it—that is, contrary to the good of individuals, living nature, or human society. Moreover, although we may not realize it, when we hurt others we also hurt ourselves, we enmesh ourselves in karmic bonds.

Karma implies that everything that is happening to us or in our midst is dynamically intertwined. Where balance is impaired, it will sooner or later be restored by karmic dynamics. Karmic process is ineluctably brought into operation by all our thoughts, values, motives, and actions. This applies to the unfoldment of scientific theory and knowledge as well as to the way we use that knowledge. It equally applies to our individual and societal relationships, which in turn, again by virtue of karmic process, determine our individual and societal conditions and developments.

I would like to explore karmic process in the unfoldment of science and karmic dynamics in the realm of society. Not surprisingly, these two are not unrelated. What follows is but a brief sketch of this large dual theme.[2]

---

2. For an exploration in more depth, see my book, *The Wholeness Principle* (Wheaton, IL: Theosophical Publishing House, 1990).

On Science in the Context of Karma

Of the modern empirical sciences, physics is the most influential. Because of its extraordinary achievements, it has exerted a tremendous influence on modern thought. Specifically, emulating Newtonian-Cartesian physics, a mechanistic or deterministic orientation became widespread; this is the orientation of Marxism, of Freudian psychology (Freud was however both a determinist and a libertarian, apparently never having reconciled these opposites), of neo-Darwinist evolutionary theory, of genetics, of conventional medicine, of capitalist economics and political science. Mechanism, it will be recalled, is a form of materialism. It sees the universe as a dead machine, a wound-up clockwork ticking away in a predictable manner. Human beings are cogs in this vast machine and equally predetermined.

I suggest that the way materialism/mechanism is now attenuating at the leading edge of science in favor of a more holistic orientation is a telling example of karmic rebalancing in the realm of human thought.

Hindsight shows that the mechanistic approach was a fruitful one for its time, especially for physics, in which it reigned supreme for several centuries. But eventually physics came up against the *limitations* of mechanism, and in fact, in the early twentieth century, physics found itself involuntarily refuting the mechanistic model of physical reality. It no longer claims that the universe is a clockwork, but has not as yet found a substitute for the machine image, though different physicists have employed their own metaphors. For instance, Sir James Jeans said that the universe is more like a thought than a machine— the thought of a mathematician; Sir Arthur Eddington used the phrase "mind-stuff" in relation to the composition of the universe; the eminent contemporary physicist David Bohm likens the universe to a flowing wholeness.

Of course the refutation of mechanism as a model of reality does *not* imply that nature is devoid of machine-like aspects and deterministic or cause-and-effect types of operation. As I sit here writing at my word processor, the obvious examples are my own hands. Ironically for mechanists, if they only realized it, the superb engineering designs found throughout nature bespeak not a dead, blindly mechanical world but a world pervaded by intelligence— a living, dynamic, self-organizing, purposive world. At any rate, Newtonian-Cartesian physics remains valid and powerful for its particular range of data, and we possess no substitute for it. But it is inapplicable in the range of the very small, the very large, and the very fast-moving phenomena studied by high-energy physics and astrophysics. It has become a subset of modern physics.

Modern physics, comprised of quantum mechanics and relativity theory, radically modified the earlier understanding of such fundamentals of physical science as time, space, causality, and matter itself. (Linear or time-conditioned causality or determinism, for instance, which is found in Newtonian science, is entirely inapplicable in quantum physics and in relativity theory.) By the same token, the erstwhile certainties that went with determinism do not apply in the new physics; the predictive powers of the new physics are excellent, but they are couched in terms of statistical probabilities, not certainties.

The concept of physical matter itself has become ambiguous; physics still uses measurement as its chief tool, but physicists have to concede that what they measure may not be physical at all.

The limits of the mechanistic approach have made themselves felt in different disciplines. Let us glance at these limits in a holistic or karmic context.

In psychology/philosophy, mechanism gave rise to the vexing freedom-determinism controversy. According to mechanism, our voluntary or involuntary acts, like the behavior of all other things, are conditioned; given particular conditions, no other behavior is possible. Now, the notion that we are conditioned by our cultural milieu and by our upbringing remains valid and accepted by all schools of psychology and equally finds an important place in the doctrine of karma. But *strict* determinism—which implies that humans are automatons with no freedom of will and therefore with none of its corollaries such as responsibility and creativity—is a *perversion* of truth. By contrast, karma states that whenever we merely react to others or to events, we are not being free agents; we are further enslaving ourselves to the bonds of conditioning. It teaches further that we can *win* freedom from conditioning by self-effort.

Furthermore, karma views the epitome of freedom non-dualistically—as the union of freedom and necessity. (This is the state of consciousness known as mystical union of which the various religious traditions speak, variously designating it as enlightenment, liberation, *mokshi, satori, nirvana.*) Just as scientists may freely choose what they investigate but must obey nature's laws to achieve results —for example, getting to the moon—so must the individual obey spiritual laws to achieve the objective of a measure of inner freedom. Paradoxically, the more one obeys the laws of one's higher nature—the more one identifies with others—the freer and more creative one becomes (Lemkow, 1981). The relatively new school of transpersonal psychology, which recognizes the human being's potentials for self-transcendence, accords very well with this phase of karma. Its advent reflects a trend away from mechanism toward a more holistic worldview.

One science after another is encountering the limits of mechanism—from biology to medicine, from economics to political science. Scientists are forced to look for alternative approaches. Biology, for example, has focused for some decades on molecular biology of a mechanistic character. This approach yielded spectacular successes—such as the discovery of the structure of DNA, the discovery of the mechanism of protein synthesis, and the cracking of the genetic code. But today not a few scientists doubt that mechanism could ever explain such large and still unsolved problems of biology as the origin of species, differentiation and development, regulation and regeneration, behavior of organisms, embryological functioning, and brain functioning. They are exploring alternative approaches such as the systems approach and the (somewhat older) organismic orientation.

The systems orientation is indeed a significant development

vis-à-vis the postulates of karma. It goes to the heart of the
basic reorientation that is under way in science—the change
which, I suggest, is a karmic re-balancing: a change from
a mechanistic, reductionistic outlook and values to a holistic
outlook and values—wherein nature and human beings
and human society are perceived in their organic, dynamic,
interconnectedness, their living wholeness. For, according to
the systems approach, the world is not a fortuitous organization of atoms but an intelligent and intelligible organization
or system, itself comprised of a myriad subsystems—of
wholes within larger, more encompassing wholes, or lives
within lives. This condition means that every system or
unit—whether an atomic nucleus, a living organism, or a
society of human beings—should be understood not in
isolation but as integral to an organic, dynamic process.
It implies that the myriad existents are a unity-in-diversity.
It accommodates the notion of many different types of
order and relationship; for example, linear and multilinear,
causal and acausal or synchronistic, and mutual interpenetration (for instance, the way I and the cells in my
body interpenetrate each other) (Bohm and Peat, 1987;
Laszlo, 1987).

It is instructive to compare the expanded view of causality
implied by the systems approach to that found in theosophy.
Recall, for example, the term for the universe used by H. P.
Blavatsky, the principal founder of the Theosophical Society.
She called it a "web" of infinite relations "spun out of the
two substances made in one," the two being spirit and
matter. For Blavatsky the livingness of the universe and
its ubiquitous psychic content result from the inseparability
of spirit and matter. Such is the universe that at every moment
everywhere it manifests living psychic power, akin to such
powers as we exhibit in imagination, will, sympathy, and
the like (Prem and Ashish, 1969).

Systems theory led to the birth of a number of new sciences
that as a group are called the "sciences of complexity."
These sciences imply the primacy of the whole over its
parts and of dynamic process over form or structure (a
telling example in nature: the caterpillar and the butterfly).
Chaos science is especially pertinent to our theme.

As already made clear, the processes of existence and of karma are not dead and mechanically predetermined, but living, intelligent, orderly, innovative or creative, and meaningful. Necessity and creativity are mutually defining polarities. As Blavatsky put it, change is constant and ubiquitous, but it is never random: it never contravenes law. Even seeming disorder is, paradoxically, a form of order. (This insight is also found in ancient Chinese thought, notably in the *I Ching*.) The same insight has recently come to us by a different route—from the new science called "chaos."

Chaos science investigates the irregularities in nature. It finds that even seemingly chaotic processes, such as weather patterns and turbulence in fluids, exhibit on detailed analysis subtle strands of order. Chaos science in fact discovers universal laws governing chaos or disorder and also pattern formation; it employs for this purpose nonlinear mathematical equations (Gleick, 1988). The advent of chaos science is cogent for our present theme in two ways: (1) it is a striking example of the reorientation in science which I am interpreting as a karmic rebalancing —the swing of the pendulum in science from mechanistic to holistic approaches; and (2) it illustrates the truth of the karmic dictum that the world process is intelligent, orderly, and creative.

Science and Holism

As already said, karma implies and flows from the fundamental holism of existence. A further word might be added about the relation of science to holism.

Science is a magnificent enterprise of the human mind. However, as presently constituted it is not itself concerned with philosophical or spiritual questions and values. Consonant with its methodology, it looks outward, it measures. It bypasses all immeasurable or metaphysical experiences and qualities, including love, compassion, beauty, goodness. This makes it a limited form of knowledge. A person wishing to attain to a fuller vision, which karma implies we all need, must supplement scientific knowledge with the insights of philosophy and spiritual modes of understanding.

Put differently, science, while it cannot make philosophical statements, can arouse and stimulate philosophical thought by what it discovers. More precisely, its findings and data have holistic *implications*. The latter suggest themselves to one's intuitive and spiritual faculties. (It is noteworthy that many of the greatest scientists have engaged in mystical writings.[3]) For, science's findings and their interpretation have philosophical import. In fact, much that science has revealed about the cosmos and about terrestrial life, including our own constitution, points beyond science to transcendent questions and insights. Quantum physics, for example, can be interpreted as pointing to a higher-dimensional reality behind the subatomic world. (David Bohm, for one, so interprets it.) Biological data on the organization of "inanimate and animate matter" reveal the interdependence and mutual penetration of all terrestrial life. Physics, biology, medicine, psychology, parapsychology (which many today regard as a genuine science), neuroscience, to name but a few disciplines, uncover, if often unintentionally, abundant evidence that consciousness and mind pervade the phenomena being investigated. Mainstream science (because of long mechanistic indoctrination) still resists admitting the presence of consciousness and mind in natural phenomena. But many individual scientists, including some of the most distinguished, are unequivocally asserting the primacy of consciousness and mind. (I have documented this trend in *The Wholeness Principle*.)

Karma and the Societal Realm

Let us turn now to society. This vast and complex domain is obviously determined by relationships—the relationships of individuals, groups, and nations with each other, with nature, and of course with Reality, however defined. By the same token, society's processes are karmic. The principle

---

3. See Ken Wilber, ed., 1984, *Quantum Questions—Mystical Writings of the World's Great Physicists*. Boston & London: Shambhala.

of wholeness is here again the key principle. The crucial problems we witness today may be understood as acute problems of relationship, such as those between industry and the environment, between governments and the governed, between rich and poor, among individual nations, among blocs of nations. In the context of karma, the problems stem from our acting contrary to the good of the greater whole. They stem largely from the prevailing materialistic worldview.

Today we are all necessarily participants in a world of global connections. The degree of interdependence among nations and peoples is unprecedented. We can no longer do without a global co-ordinating agency such as the United Nations. The new situation has also called into existence many other international governmental and non-governmental organizations. (The nongovernmental organizations, which work in widely ranging fields, are especially numerous, having grown from 176 in 1909 to some 18,000 in 1988.) It has become amply evident that the major concerns of society—political, economic, social, ecological, security, human rights—are interrelated and global in their implications. Thus, for example, human rights infringed in one place affect all of us; an act of terrorism in one place threatens all of us; air pollution knows no territorial boundaries; by their nature, shrinking forests, expanding deserts, and eroding soils have global implications as well as common roots; environmental degradation threatens security no less than nuclear weaponry. Everything affects everything else. Every commission and omission of ours—whether in agriculture, oil drilling, telecommunications, economic policy-making, political organization, militarization or war-making, and in any locality—sooner or later impacts to some degree all domains and localities. We can no longer deny responsibility for our acts and for each other.

Our situation illustrates in a new way the truth of the karmic dictum: the different dimensions of existence—spiritual and moral, mental, emotional and physical—are interconnected and interdependent. However, we have far to go in living by this truth. For while nations and peoples are sewn into the web of connections, they are far from united. The fact is that human society is in crisis.

The problem of how to live together and how even to survive on a planet with finite resources, with the added factor of nuclear weaponry, has given rise to a good deal of soul-searching. The diagnosis of many thoughtful people is that we need a fundamental change of consciousness—and hence of values to live by—at least on the part of a critical number of people. The present widespread materialism must give way to a new era.

Let us glance at materialism. This will reveal the relationship between science and society, or more generally between what we know and what we do.

Mechanism, which is a form of materialism, though refuted by physics as a model of reality, is still entrenched. It is predominant among a very influential segment of human society: scientists and educators in various fields. It regards nature and mind as at bottom nothing but the motion of atoms in space (a naive view if only from the vantage point of science, since atoms are somewhat mysterious). Mechanists pride themselves on their rationality, but they contradict themselves by depicting existence as blind and mechanical—therefore *devoid* of rationality. They admire instrumental values but contradict themselves by insisting on "value neutrality." Mechanists discount traditional values and wisdom itself as "merely subjective." These are held as less than real simply because they are not locatable and measurable. Many mechanists go further: they believe that what science does not know does not exist, a stance known as "scientism," which is a perversion of science. The mechanistic idea of self is that the mind is reducible to nothing but physics and chemistry, that we are the physical brain only, and the brain is nothing but an unusually complex computer. This view naturally discourages recognition of our own higher faculties and the corresponding higher values. It deprives people of the basis for a serious commitment to higher ideals and consigns them to a spiritual vacuum.

Elsewhere I have written the following about the consequences of mechanism:

[Mechanism] has fostered dichotomies, schisms, fragmentations, alienations: alienation from self . . . and hence from others as well, alienation from nature (automatons cannot feel much for other automatons—if we are only machines, we may as well grab for ourselves as much as we can, conquer and exploit nature to the hilt), the dichotomy between knowledge and values, between ends and means, between mind and matter, between the universe of matter and the universe of life, between the sciences and the humanities, between the rich and the poor, between industrialized countries and what is called the third world, between the present and future generations (Lemkow, 1990, p. 11).

Let us glance now at materialist values in a few specific contexts.

In market-oriented countries, industry and the related school of economics rely on the maximization of (money) profits by individual enterprises. Industry has been exempt from concern for the social costs of its operations. It has not been required to consider its impact either on the natural support system or the welfare of future generations. As the new age economist Hazel Henderson has enumerated, these costs include "efforts to co-ordinate anarchistic economic activities and conflicting technological applications; to clean up the mess left by mass production and consumption; to ameliorate social problems and care for dropouts, addicts, disabled workers and other social casualties; to mediate conflicts and sustain even larger security forces against theft and crime; to keep the air breathable and the water drinkable" (Kumar, 1981, p. 166).

Economists generally preach the pursuit of growth as the panacea for economic difficulties. They do not ask growth of what and for whom and at what cost to the physical and social environment; they simply urge indiscriminate growth. Capitalist economics, as one writer put it, makes a virtue of covetousness and ambition, both in individuals and in society. The market respects only the bottom line, the net commercial value that can be obtained for a product. That is the criterion which outweighs all other considerations:

Thus, environmental catastrophes that kill hundreds or thousands are not seen as crimes or signs of moral failure;

they are simply part of the costs of doing business (Power, 1988, pp. 201-202).

Perhaps the most telling feature of today's societal system —showing the fruits of materialism—is elitism. Elitism holds sway alike under capitalism and socialism and in the third world. The "haves" of the world become ever more advantaged and the "have-nots" become ever more marginalized. In the United States, we see in recent years a geometrical growth in the number of both billionaires and homeless people. Elitism prevailed, as we know, under the communist regimes of Eastern Europe that fell in 1989. (One need scarcely emphasize that here we saw remarkable instances of the power of collective human will to bring about changes, as well as of effects sooner or later following cumulative, pent-up causes.) Both the capitalist and the socialist economic systems contributed to the mass poverty in the third world. Capitalist culture "legitimizes, encourages, and even glorifies the unlimited acquisition of wealth by an individual. . . . Comparable results inevitably come from a misnamed socialist culture that legitimates, encourages, and glorifies the unlimited acquisition of power by the state" (Gran, 1983, p. 7).

The third world labors under a disadvantage vis-à-vis the industrialized world. Notably, the terms of trade are inequitable, due both to the lower wage levels and prices being determined less by supply and demand than by those countries' relatively weak political and economic position. At the same time, the third world is far from free of its own elitist tendencies. In many instances, land tenure patterns are grossly inequitable. Large landowners export cash crops, including food, while the rural poor are landless and hungry.

The biblical phrase "By their fruits ye shall know them" is equally a karmic one. Materialism has brought about a world system with the two extremes of the advantaged and powerful and the disenfranchised, destitute, and powerless. The gulf between the two ends of the spectrum is widening. It threatens nature's support system and the very survival of both the rich and the poor of the world, and indeed of all life on this planet.

A succinct and authoritative statement of today's global dilemma was made by the World Commission on Environment and Development,[4] in its first report, entitled, *Our Common Future* (1987, p. 22):

> [The poorer countries] face ... life-threatening ... desertification, deforestation, and pollution, and endure most of the poverty associated with environmental degradation. The entire human family of nations would suffer from the disappearance of rain forests in the tropics, the loss of plant and animal species, and changes in rainfall patterns. Industrial nations face the life-threatening challenges of toxic chemicals, toxic wastes, and acidification. All nations may suffer from the releases by industrialized countries of carbon dioxide and of gases that react with the ozone layer, and from any future war fought with the nuclear arsenals controlled by those nations. All nations will have a role to play in changing trends, and in righting an international economic system that increases rather than decreases inequality, that increases rather than decreases numbers of poor and hungry.

Now in this connection, karma states or implies a number of interrelated things. Individuals and societies are the authors of their own (desirable and undesirable) circumstances or conditions. Moreover, in coping with their self-created problems, they learn and further deepen their consciousness, and they may in effect correct imbalances in their outlook and values. An extraordinary case in point is the effect of unprecedented interdependence of nations and peoples. We ourselves—that is, human thought, knowledge, values and action—have brought about this new global situation. In turn, the situation impels us to learn greater tolerance.

Indeed, the deepest significance of the industrial era may be an evolutionary one. Karma implies progressive development toward universalism and human unity

---

4. The Commision was established by the United Nations in 1983. It is charged with the task of proposing long-term environmental strategies for achieving sustainable development by the year 2000.

beyond all differences, whether of color, sex, culture, or creed. Our present situation impels us to re-examine our premises, values, and relationships. We are led progressively to integrate the particular with the universal in us. We are human beings before we are men or women or members of a particular locale, culture, or religion. There is arising today, albeit among a minority of us as yet, a veritable new form of spirituality: wholeness (some might say holiness or healing) is emerging as the primary meaning and guiding principle of life.

Societal Chaos and Order

According to karma (and likewise chaos science), the chaos and anarchy we witness today must, paradoxically, express an underlying or inner order. If so, we ignore it at our peril.

Extraordinary evidence for this inner order is at hand. Major problems—notably, poverty, hunger, disease, population explosion in the poorest quarters of the world, threat of nuclear war, environmental degradation, depletion of natural resources, international debt, inflation—are of a paradoxical nature. Outwardly they are distinct or disparate, yet inwardly they are connected. They arise in different circumstances and parts of the world, yet their impact is global. Mass poverty is intimately related to the way the affluent segments of the population pursue power and wealth. Environmental degradation is connected with resources-and-energy-intensive industrial production. Equally related are poverty and environmental degradation (something made clear in the aforementioned report, *Our Common Future*). The global threat of nuclear war is closely tied to the turmoil caused by economic and social injustice and abject poverty. Interlinked equally are poverty, international debt, and inflation. One of the main causes of hunger is war, and hunger is both the cause and effect of war. One could give further examples. The point is simply that the inner connectedness of the many disparate problems and their globality attest to an ineluctible inner order.

Self-aggrandizement, greed, corruption, and exploitation of the weaker are only too apparent today. But also evident is a growing revulsion against inequality, injustice, and oppression. A strong and vigorous new impulse has arisen among people in many places around the globe to reassert their voice in their own destiny and also to help others regain their self-reliance. In the past two or three years we have repeatedly witnessed on television scenes of extraordinary mass rallies in the streets and central squares of cities in far-flung parts of the world—in communist countries, in third world countries, and sometimes in capitalist countries. In the capitalist world we have seen the advent of the remarkable grassroots movements for social change—spiritual, environmental, feminist, simple living, appropriate-technology, nonviolent action, and other movements. These are directed at reconstructing values, communities, and political participation. The activists concerned believe they can make a difference, and there is ample evidence that they *do* make a difference (Cf. Mendlovitz and Walker, eds., 1987).

All these developments attest to the new struggle against society's moral and practical failures. We find ourselves having to rethink and to deepen our understanding of the meaning of all the political ideologies, including democracy, liberalism, socialism, communism, and capitalism. We shall be further challenged to integrate such polarities as self-determination and pluralism, and decentralization and global responsibility.

We have violated the principle and, by virtue of karma, have precipitated a global crisis. This crisis compels us to try to grasp what we are doing and what we *need* to do to resolve our impasse and avert further disaster. As Teilhard de Chardin wrote some decades ago, there is a general direction to the transcendent evolutionary process which will evidence itself, above all, in the human realm: we will progress in attaining self-knowledge and in our capacity to situate ourselves in space and time, to the point of becoming conscious of our place and responsibilities in relation to the Universe (Teilhard de Chardin, 1964).

The present planetary crisis serves at once as a warning, as a corrective compass, and as a tremendous opportunity. As Christopher Fry wrote in *A Sleep of Prisoners:*

> *Thank God our time is now*
> *When wrong comes up to meet us everywhere*
> *Never to leave us till we take*
> *The greatest stride of soul*
> *Men ever took.*

References

Bohm, David and F. David Peat. 1987. *Science, Order and Creativity.* New York and Toronto: Bantam.

Gleick, James. 1988. *Chaos.* New York: Penguin.

Gran, Guy. 1983. *Development By People.* New York: Praeger Publishers.

Gromyko, Anatoly, and Martin Hellman (eds.). 1988. *Breakthrough.* New York: Walker and Company.

Kumar, Satish (ed.). 1981. *The Schumacher Lectures.* Harper & Row.

Laszlo, Ervin. 1987. *Evolution, the Grand Synthesis.* Boston & London: Shambhala, New Science Library.

Lemkow, Anna Freifeld. 1990. *The Wholeness Principle: Dynamics of Unity within Science, Religion and Society.* Wheaton, IL: Theosophical Publishing House.

———— 1981. "Of Holism, Freedom, and the Creative Meeting of Opposites," *Revision,* vol. 4, 2.

Mendovitz, Saul H. and R. B. J. Walker (eds.). 1987. *Towards a Just World Peace.* London: Butterworths in association with the Committee for a Just World Peace.

Power, Thomas Michael. 1988. *The Economic Pursuit of Quality.* Armonk, New York and London: M. E. Sharpe, Inc.

Prem, Shri Krishna and Sri Madhava Ashish. 1969. *Man the Measure of All Things.* Wheaton, IL: Theosophical Publishing House.

Teilhard de Chardin, Pierre. 1964. *The Future of Man.* New York: Harper & Row.

Wilber, Ken (ed.). 1984. *Quantum Questions—Mystical Writings of the World's Great Physicists.* Boston & London: Shambhala.

World Commission on Environment and Development. 1987. *Our Common Future.* New York: Oxford University Press.

19

Can We Avoid Karmic Debts?

ALFRED TAYLOR

If all that we are is the result of past karma, how can we help another person? Are not his or her troubles those which have been earned, so that to remove them would be against karmic law? This problem has been raised with respect to healing procedures as well as to other aspects of relieving human suffering.

For example, there is the idea of personal responsibility, and yet a scientific discovery, such as the pasteurization of milk, or the discovery of the need for certain trace minerals and vitamins in foods, can eliminate much ill health. Other even more spectacular research has made such great killer diseases as small pox, yellow fever, bubonic plague, comparatively rare. Did these discoveries eliminate the karma of great numbers of people so that they were no longer forced to endure the suffering and death associated with these illnesses? With the aid of the knowledge arising from biological research, the average life span in the West has been greatly increased in the last century. What are some of the possible answers to this problem?

In this materialistic age, there is, of course, much emphasis on survival. Even the addition of a few years, or even a few months, is considered to be of great value, since supposedly this is all the life a person will have. An existence of great suffering is preferable to final and complete extinction. Therefore, when the average life span is increased ten years, people are thrilled with the achievement.

Certainly we are supposed to make the most of our life here. It can be a great opportunity, but to the great mass of people, a few extra years of life are not so important. Many individuals work with some zest and are alive to the values around them, but as the number of years accumulate, their enthusiasm fades away. It is quite common for people to spend the last part of their lives in a retracted, depressed condition. The body wears out and the temptation is to coast through the final period of a lifetime on the momentum gained in the earlier years. Under such circumstances it may not be too important whether life continues on the physical plane.

There is no elimination of karmic debts because some scientific discovery leads to the control of a disease. Whatever we have earned will come to us whether for good or for bad. But there are various ways our karmic debts can be satisfied. The individual saved from suffering and death from a childhood disease will nevertheless work out karmic obligations. It must be remembered, too, that in the days before medical techniques were discovered that have helped to control many diseases of childhood, the great majority of children either failed to become infected or survived the illnesses that caused the death of so many others.

It is interesting to note that certain diseases have grown less serious in countries where medicine was not concerned. Deaths from tuberculosis declined in the Western countries, and it might have been considered to be the result of increased medical knowledge, but there was the same decline of mortality in the other countries in the absence of medical intervention. Also, we do not know the complete effects of the various treatments used in modern medicine. Since we are living in a materialistic, body-minded civilization, everything is assessed in terms of giving the individual a few years or even a few months of extra life. But if we could view these affairs from the occult viewpoint and note their effects through several lives, we might be surprised to learn that much that is emphasized is of comparatively little significance. Health in this country is not good in spite of all the wonder drugs. Even among young people, it has been reported that the number of draftees rejected because of physical defects has increased progressively since World War II. Also, while some diseases have been controlled, others such as cancer, heart and circulatory ailments have become more serious, and new diseases such as AIDS and Alzheimer's have arisen. Mental diseases have increased markedly.

The approach to health must be through right living, which includes harmonious thoughts and emotions as well as words and actions. Well-being comes from within. In this age of materialism, we assume the problem of disease can be solved by physical means. Illness is generally treated by efforts to remove effects rather than removing causes. Even psychosomatic medicine still works on effects, since, while it is concerned with mental and emotional states and their effects on health, it is still oriented towards materialism. There is an array of drugs used in the treatment of psychosomatic diseases.

What is the use then of trying to help people to overcome their health and other problems? The answer to this question involves some deep aspects of occult science. In the first place, help given another when motivated by sympathy, by impersonal love, increases the strength, the resistance of the one in trouble. Also, it is a tribute to the oneness of life, since we cannot really help others without becoming in some way one with them. In other words, the real healer of illnesses and other troubles clears the channels that connect the personality with the inner Spiritual Self. The result is a flow of power that adds to strength and well-being. Also, as we assist others we can often clear away the ignorance that has been the cause of the trouble. The main asset, then, to helping others is to bring more of the power of the spirit into the personality, and secondly, to awaken the lower mind to a recognition of the laws of nature that bring the person to a better level of life and well-being.

We can certainly help others, not in the sense of avoiding karmic debts, but rather by increasing the person's capacity to meet and solve the problems of life more effectively. Real aid leads to a strengthening of the spiritual nature of the one aided. We are all one and through that oneness we should share the harmony, the beauty, the well-being which is a normal asset of humanity. Individuals through ignorance become detached from the main stream of the human spirit, and other individuals can pool their resources with these unfortunates to bring them back to their natural state.

We all need some help at times, and it comes to us as a part of our birthright. It comes to us from other human beings, and it also comes to us from nature. We can, as our understanding permits, draw on many sources for assistance, and we balance the debt by passing on what we have gained to others. The world is naturally beautiful, radiant, harmonious, blissful. As we bring ourselves into closer alignment with the Divine Plan, all that we need flows into us as our heritage. We do not pay rent on the planet we use, and are not charged for the air we breathe or for the sunshine that is so vital to our existence. Likewise, with the problem of healing, we can assist others to come back into right orientation to the world and to themselves. Health and well-being are not earned, they belong to us already. We cut ourselves off from them by our behavior. The cutting off is the karmic consequence, but the turning on is the re-alignment to the natural state of things.

In this age of materialism, there are relatively few who consciously seek spiritual development, and a still lesser number who aspire to help in the spiritual development of humanity. Most people are in pursuit of objectives that turn out to be worthless when attained. But this is all part of the long, arduous work of evolvement. Whether or not our goals prove to be of value, the effort to achieve them carries us forward in consciousness and understanding.

In spite of individual differences, there are certain assets and limitations that affect us all. The Secret Doctrine contains principles or truths that apply to all of us in varying degrees. Also, at any time in human affairs, there are misconceptions or kinds of ignorance, that inevitably doom us to lives of frustration, suffering, uncertainty, fear, illness, and death. We all know this to be so, but it is difficult to point out specifically the nature of these misconceptions. The great religions have always been concerned with this problem. They have offered teachings, such as those given by Christ or the Buddha along with many others, which contained the wisdom required to enter our real heritage. At this stage in human evolution, few are able to take advantage of that which is offered to them.

Human behavior, as reflected in thought, feeling and action, is influenced by ideas that are innate in the civilization in which we live. There are certain principles taken for granted that are so embedded in people's consciousness and subconsciousness that they act like hypnotic commands. As a result it is extremely difficult to remove them from a person's heart and mind. They may be recognized intellectually as untrue, but nevertheless their influence is revealed in the person's evaluations and standards of behavior.

Table 1 summarizes some of these assumptions and the alternatives given in *The Secret Doctrine*. These assumptions motivate and underlie much of human behavior in our modern civilization. Generally, the individual is not conscious of their presence in the mind and emotions. This fact tends to make them more potent in their effects on our evaluations and outlook on life. Most people, if they gave these assumptions careful thought, would recognize them to be contrary to our deepest and truest experience.

TABLE 1

COMMON ASSUMPTION	THE SECRET DOCTRINE
1. A person is the physical body. This belief is revealed in our constant identification with the physical form and by our attitude towards age, illness, disposal of the dead, and many other events in our lives.	1. A person is a spiritual being and utilizes a series of physical bodies while going forward in evolutionary development.
2. There is no conscious existence before or after life in the physical body.	2. A person, as a spiritual being, gains experience in the physical world and in the after-

death state assimilates the lessons learned in the physical body, then again incarnates in a new physical form.

3. Each person is separate and apart from other human beings and from nature. Competition, the effort to out-do others is a normal and necessary part of life.

3. Each person is a manifestation of the One Life, or Spirit, and so is one not only with his fellow human beings but with all nature.

4. Law-breakers, or those who commit crimes against humanity or nature are punished only as they are discovered and brought to trial.

4. The Law of Karma unerringly brings to every individual that which has been earned, whether good or bad.

5. A person can think with malice and hate, but as long as these thoughts are not revealed in words or actions, no wrong has been committed against others.

5. What we think can affect the minds of others for good or for ill.

6. The success or failure of a lifetime is based mainly in terms of material gains.

6. The success of a lifetime is measured in terms of spiritual development that has been attained.

7. Chance determines whether we are born with a good body and are endowed with latent or special capacities. Also, chance is a big factor in the degree of our success in life.

7. The universe is a universe of law and order. There is no place for chance in human affairs or nature.

In addition to these beliefs that characterize a whole civilization, we all have family and individual beliefs that have accumulated in the course of time. One of the values in studies of such works as *The Secret Doctrine* is that it helps to awaken us to the presence in us of these hidden influences. As we recognize them we can begin to erase them from our beings. But until we are aware of their presence, their power over our behavior continues.

Common sense is enough to tell us that any kind of belief that is not in accord with truth will be associated with adverse consequences. Otherwise, we would never be stimulated into discovering our mistake. As it is, untrue assumptions, such as those listed above, inevitably bring to the individual some degree of suffering and ineffectiveness in life. Human progress or evolution is essentially a process of coming nearer to the light of truth. Untruths may appear to flourish and to be permanently established in a civilization, or in the thinking of individual men and women, but sooner or later truth must prevail. The pressure of life forces us finally to give up our most cherished delusions, and the parting with them is often painful.

Karmic law is a guiding light for us in our difficult journey towards enlightenment. If we are to evolve in freedom, then we cannot be led around by a more advanced being, but must learn the way ourselves through our own experience. Actually, experience is a record of what has brought happiness or suffering. In the millions of years human beings have been going through this learning process, it would seem that experience should be ample to enable us to live happily and effectively. But some lessons have to be repeated many times before they become part of us. For one thing, there are so many kinds of behavior that initially bring much satisfaction and enthusiasm, and it is only in later years that the individual learns he or she has made a serious mistake. Many people repeat the same error through several lives before that particular lesson is learned. One thing is certain, karma is impartial and impersonal, and through it we develop and grow into the truth, the reality of ourselves and the world.

20
The Side Blows of Karma

GEORGE E. LINTON

> . . . you know nothing of the ins and outs of the
> work of Karma—of the 'side blows' of this ter-
> rible law.
>
> The Mahatma Letters

The quotation is from a letter to A. P. Sinnett, received by
him in London in 1884, from the Mahatma Koot Hoomi.
The Mahatma is discussing with Sinnett the failure of an
endeavor to establish in India a newspaper under the latter's
management. The previous year, the owners of the Allahabad
Pioneer had terminated Sinnett's editorship of that paper,
and he and his friends had been endeavoring to raise sufficient funds from the Indians to start a new paper which
would be sympathetic to the Indian viewpoint. The endeavor
had failed, due to the lack of support by the Indian financiers.
The Mahatma asks Sinnett if he ever had any idea as to
the *real reason* why the venture had failed, and then he intimates that it was a karmic "side blow" occasioned by
the fact that in his earlier years in India, Sinnett had looked
upon the Indians as an inferior race and had felt a profound
contempt for them at that time. So at this later date, when
he wanted to help the Indians and could have done much
useful work for their betterment, his past karma denied
him the opportunity.

The short study which follows is an endeavor to consider
some of the ways in which karma appears to operate, based
on information which is available, together with some

added observations. Many events occur which to our limited observation are seemingly accidental or without adequate explanation; some are pleasant and some are tragic. Yet if we could see the entire picture, we would probably find that they are all the direct or indirect results of past actions, emotions, or thoughts. Take for example the large number of fatalities that occur each year on our highways. From a superficial point of view, there appears to be no logical moral reason why a particular accident occurs at a particular time and place, involving certain specific individuals. There is no apparent reason why "X" should be the one to run into "Y," a total stranger, and kill him. But perhaps they are not such total strangers as it appears at first thought. This is where the theory of reincarnation comes into the picture and adds the missing parts of the story which enable one to see that there may be some link that will explain the reason for this particular "accident." Perhaps the two entities who are the real beings who are at the present time functioning on the physical plane as "X" and "Y" have met before, in some previous incarnation; perhaps "X" is settling some past action in which "Y" has been involved and has to account for. But whatever the reason, there must have been some antecedent cause for the occurrence if one is to believe in a moral law of universal justice operating in the world. To the occultist, nothing can happen by accident.

Or again, some chance meeting may bring about a life-long friendship or some other good fortune for no apparent reason. Again appearance may be deceiving, and what appears to be accidental may be really the fulfillment of some cause set in motion earlier.

First, perhaps it would be advisable to review briefly the general concept of the law of karma and how it operates. A general outline can be found in many theosophical books, so there is no need to discuss the subject at length here, but a few basic considerations may be helpful. It is considered to be a basic law in nature that when equilibrium is disturbed at any point, a corrective action must take place sooner or later to restore the balance. Since manifestation itself is an action that disturbs the equilibrium of matter in *pralaya* (the state of rest in which exists during periods of inactivity), nature is ever in the process of restoring balances, hence it is stated that karma is action (implying also reaction). Ceaseless eternal motion is the order of the universe, states one of the Mahatmas in a letter to Mr. Sinnett, and affinity or attraction its handmaid of all work.[1]

If karma is a universal law in nature, its operation should and must follow (ultimately) a lawful pattern, and therefore if all the facts regarding a relationship are known it should be possible to accurately predict the results that will follow. In other words, a proper understanding of the law of cause and effect at all levels of being should enable one so to order his life that certain definite results will ensue. In general, however, few people stop to consider the underlying causes of many of the things that happen to them, being content to attribute these to circumstances, chance, or fate. They are content to deal with results rather than to seek for basic causes and deal with these causes. Life in the western world today is so busy and hectic that few take the necessary time to analyze things and find out the why of them. In fact, few would be willing to admit that they are living and operating within moral and spiritual energy fields, the laws governing which are as unerring, impersonal, and predictable as the laws governing the gravitational and electromagnetic fields. Many in fact would be loath to acknowledge that everything that happens to them is the result of actions which they themselves have set in motion at sometime in the past, either in this or in some prior incarnation.

A recognition of the existence of such moral and ethical laws and a search for knowledge as to how best to live in accordance with them would go far toward making life more livable and would enable humanity to progress more swiftly along its evolutionary path. Instead we are content to spend much of our time and energy trying to counter effects without seeking to find the underlying causes, thus bringing upon ourselves much unnecessary trouble, as for instance when we get an acid stomach, we seek to overcome the difficulty by taking some patent medicine, rather than finding out what is wrong with our eating habits and correcting them. Or, again, we raise our taxes in order to provide treatment and care for chronic alcoholics, while at the same time spending uncounted millions of dollars promoting the sale of alcoholic beverages, thus encouraging people to become alcoholics.

The concept of a universal law of justice is a simple one in principle. It is only when we begin to apply it to specific situations that we begin to have difficulty in observing its operation. Comprehension requires an understanding of basic theosophic concepts regarding the planes of nature, the origin and purpose of life, the total human constitution and the various vehicles of consciousness. Unless one has an understanding of the fact that a human being is essentially a spiritual being, rooted in an ultimate reality and expressing on the mental, emotional, and physical planes of nature in vehicles suitable for use on those planes throughout a long series of incarnations in these different vestures of evolutionary experiencing, one will be unable to realize that nature has laws which are operative at these higher levels with as great a degree of certainty as those which are known at the physical level. Without this knowledge of the total picture of man, the idea of karmic law will be difficult to comprehend.

According to Annie Besant,* every event in our lives, at whatever level, is linked to a preceding cause, and generally also to a succeeding result, so that life appears to us to be a continuous flow of events.[2]

In many instances we can perceive, or imagine that we can, the direct action of this law of compensation or balance as it applies to an individual person, provided the balancing effect takes place within a short period of time. If the karma has been accumulated at some earlier time in the life of the person or in some previous incarnation, we are normally unable to make any reasonable connection with the current event, since the whole picture is not available to us in the ordinary conditions of consciousness; but this lack of

---

*A. B. was a lecturer, author, former President of the Theosophical Society.

knowledge does not preclude the existence of the chain of causative events. We are constantly in the process of generating new karma, or balancing up past actions, and the results we think of in terms of good or bad, helpful or harmful, etc. Of course, in reality there is neither good nor bad karma since these are relative terms coined to describe things on the basis of one's judgment. Karma in itself is without attributes of human-made morality.

The intricate network of events impinging upon an individual and producing an offsetting reaction in him or her might be illustrated graphically by analogy to the vector diagrams used in the analysis of mechanical forces in the study of mechanics. In these diagrams the direction of the force is indicated by the direction of the line and the strength of the force by its relative length. The composite action of a group of forces acting through a given point produces a resultant which is of a certain strength and direction. To produce a state of equilibrium, another force equal and opposite to this resultant must be applied. The analogy fits quite well if we consider the individual as the point and the external forces acting upon him or her from differing directions as the vectors, producing a resultant effect which we call karma. To maintain one's state of equilibrium, one must exert a force which will neutralize the external forces, otherwise the person will be pushed about by them until he or she willingly or unwillingly, does something to bring about the balance, i.e., until he has settled the karmic debt.

Karma can be considered under several categories such as personal karma and group karma (national, racial, religious, etc.), or by levels of causation and outworking, or by time sequence. By this last is meant such things as current, earlier in life, or in some past incarnation. It is said that karma which has been accumulated in past incarnations is apportioned to the individual in a particular lifetime by certain intelligent forces in nature (generally referred to as the *Lipika*). The special function of these forces seems to be that of maintaining the integral balance of the universe and therefore of all the separate elements within it. The methods by which this is accomplished are not easily comprehended, except possibly by those who would personalize these forces as agents of an anthropomorphic God.

It is stated by some students that no one is burdened in any one lifetime with an amount of his past karma greater than he or she is able to bear. Some persons might question this assurance when all the "slings and arrows of outrageous fortune" that are heaped upon them seem to be too much for them to cope with; but somehow most people do seem to manage to get through life, even though it isn't always easy. This applies especially to those circumstances which appear to be mostly burdens and misfortunes. Whether or not people have the same capacity to bear excessive good fortune might be questioned, as persons in these circumstances are the ones who seem to fail most often to make the best use of their opportunities. Few indeed seem to be able to withstand the effects of excessive wealth or power without abusing the opportunities and obligations that these offer or require, and thus creating for themselves much new karma of an unfortunate kind that they will be long in working out. As one of the Indian Adepts once remarked to Sinnett, "It is only in adversity that we can discover the true man." History seems to bear out this statement as excessive affluence, either individually or as a nation, is usually followed in a short time by decadence.

If we consider how karma works at the superphysical levels of consciousness, we need to understand how thought and emotion act and react in our lives. The matter of these planes being much more tenuous and rapid in movement than that of the dense physical, it is natural to expect that actions and reactions will occur with greater suddenness and rapidity at those levels. Tensions and disturbances in the emotional and mental planes can discharge themselves suddenly and with violence, as can an electrical discharge or the elements in a thunderstorm.

When the psychic atmosphere thus erupts, we see the results often in physical form, whether natural or human-made as in the case of revolutions, mob violence, or political disturbances. When a group of people or a nation builds up vast clouds of turbulence in the psychic atmosphere, it can seldom be dissipated slowly, but generally takes the form of physical disruption and violence such as we are now witnessing in connection with racial and social problems.

The mechanics by which karmic obligations are carried forward from one incarnation to the next until they are balanced out is something that is not easy to comprehend. During the intermediate periods between incarnations, the experiences of the incarnation just completed are said to be assimilated into the Ego or spiritual nature by a process analagous to digestion, and the valuable parts of such experiences are built into the causal body, the permanent vehicle of the individual consciousness on the plane of abstract mind. The portions not suitable for absorption in the form of traits of character, capacities, talents, etc., are said to be left behind at the threshold of the heaven world, to be picked up again by the entity when it returns to incarnation at the physical level. The amount of this carryover of unfinished business must be considerable, with humanity still at the present stage of imperfection, and so we can probably attribute many things in our lives to actions that we ourselves have generated in prior incarnations. The actual method by which these uncompleted actions (primarily of a less spiritual nature) are brought forward from incarnation to incarnation is not described in theosophical literature except in general terms, and this mostly by analogy. It is indicated that the individuality through the causal body maintains a continuing connection with the lower planes through attachments to certain particular "atoms" of those planes which perform the function of supplying vibratory or harmonic capabilities around which it attracts matter of the lower planes when reincarnating. These "atoms" collect the matter of the astral and physical planes suitable to the requirements of the individuality according to karmic law.

In Buddhist metaphysics, it is stated that the skandhas play an important part in the transmission of the "unfinished business" of one incarnation to the next. The skandhas are said to be the elements of limited existence, the "bundles of attributes" of the personal self, which are ever at work preparing the abstract mold, or "privation" of the future "new being."[3] In Buddhist philosophy these are listed as five in number, and together they make up the personal self with its sense of separate existence. While they disappear at time of death, they form the attributes of the future personality, and although there is no personal recollection of them in the new brain-mind in the ensuing incarnation, nevertheless they appear to be "forwarders" of the results of past action, in part at least. Thus when the individual returns again to the sphere of objective existence, part of the karma embodied in these privations is assumed in the new life (incarnation). The remainder presumably carries over until a still later incarnation. Perhaps we may infer that the "abstract mold" referred to attracts to itself matter of the lower planes that is harmonically attuned to its vibratory rates, and thus we get the type of physical, etheric, and emotional bodies which we deserve and to which we are entitled. "Like attracts like" as we all know, and this should be as applicable to the mental and emotional worlds as it is to the physical. The Mahatma, in another of his letters to Sinnett, asserts that "this law of attraction asserts itself in many seemingly inexplicable incidents in life, into which the entity has been drawn by the preponderating influences of past life actions."[4]

It is indicated by a number of clairvoyant investigators that the outline or characteristics of both the mental and emotional bodies are formed by or for the returning entity prior to the formation of the etheric and dense physical bodies for the projected incarnation. From this it would seem that the course the personality is to take in a particular incarnation is determined to a large extent prior to the birth of the physical body. Some investigators have indicated that some of the specific elements of this coloring process enter into the aura of the child at an early age and become diffused into the aura at the astral and lower levels. Possibly this is part of the method of operation of the skandhas of the Buddhists. The Mahatma writing to Sinnett further corroborates this point when he states that there are no "accidents of birth," as the new personality coming into incarnation is almost entirely the product of the past, and that the circumstances of the new existence have already been determined essentially by ourselves, meaning presumably our higher or spiritual selves. The cholera victim, he says, could not have died from the disease had not the "germs" for the development of the disease existed within him from birth. It would seem that the word "germs" is used here in the sense of latent causes rather than in the medical sense.

In considering further some of the ways in which karma works, it is said that physical acts to another produce reactions of a physical nature, depending in type and effect upon the motive behind the act as well as the act itself. Generosity from an unselfish motive is said to be productive of an agreeable environment in the future, whereas the same act performed from a selfish motive will not produce the same result as regards the future circumstances. Mistaken efforts to help another, performed from a good motive, will produce less reaction than if done from a poor motive, but in either case, the balance of justice must eventually be restored.[5] Deliberate cruelty, whether to a human or animal, is said to result in physical impairment of some appropriate kind in a later incarnation. Persons suffering from congenital handicaps or crippling diseases may wonder why fate has visited such affliction on them for no reason of which they are aware in their own mind, i.e., their present brain consciousness. But perhaps if they could see behind the veil, and gain a more comprehensive view of things, they would see that they are only paying a just debt for something done in some earlier incarnation. At the level of consciousness of the spiritual self, the individual is undoubtedly aware of the reasons for the presently existing situation.

Most every investigator capable of observing at the level of consciousness of the immortal self, and who can trace back the life of an entity through past incarnations, has testified that deliberate cruelty is one of the most terrible of crimes and results in the most severe karmic repayments. Some of these investigators indicate that this situation applies not alone to actions between humans but also to human treatment of the animal kingdom. Unintentional cruelty or cruelty from necessity do not appear to evoke the drastic karmic responses that accrue from intentional cruelty. It may be a long time before the world is free from pain and suffering, but to deliberately add to the existing accumulation is not aiding in the evolution of life on our planet.

Before leaving this point, it should be recognized that cruelty to another human being can be perpetrated at the mental and emotional levels as well as at the physical level. In fact it seems probable that some people generate more suffering and anguish among their families and friends in this manner than by physical means, and oftentimes are quite unaware of it. But regardless of the manner in which the cruelty is manifested, whether intentional or not, the law of compensation will eventually bring about suitable redress.

Neither should we overlook the other side of the ledger, since love as well as hate is a binding force; while its reactions may be much more agreeable to bear, it is still something which binds people together. As to whether this type of link is a help or a hindrance to one's evolutionary advancement is perhaps a matter for individual consideration. Both are creators of karmic ties, and eventually it would seem that a time must come in one's stage of evolution when one should not be bound by either. Action without desire for the results of the action has ever been the attitude of the seeker after liberation from the bondage of the personal self, an attitude ably set forth in the Hindu classic, the *Bhagavad Gita.*

The collective karma of a group or a nation is something to which we probably give much less thought than to our individual karma. This is perhaps due in part to the fact that it is less observable and not as easily understood as our personal situation. The greater the freedom of the individual and the better the educational level, the greater the opportunity to become involved with the larger units of society and thus participate in the collective karma of the nation or group. In times past, when communication was limited—and even in some underdeveloped countries today—interest was and is centered more at the family and group level, and probably the collective karma was much less than in the Western nations of the world today with the worldwide contacts, communication, business problems, and political differences which exist. A public generally enlightened about events on a global scale, with all the problems involved between nations and cultures, must be creating a vast amount of collective karma, not only physically but also emotionally and mentally. Moral and ethical conduct by a nation becomes more and more a responsibility of the individuals in that nation. Considering the violent thoughts and feelings, mostly of a negative kind, which are being aroused both within the nations and on a global scale, the psychic atmosphere of the world today must be full of turbulence and charged to the point of explosiveness. It is little wonder that we are witnessing so much violence and turmoil.

The Christian scripture admonishes us to return good for evil, and while this evokes the heart qualities, it still leaves one tied karmically to the recipient of his meritorious action. Return good for good, for evil, justice, says the Confucian, which would seem to be more in keeping with a philosophical approach to life. This approach would also seem to be more in keeping with the teachings of the Lord Krishna as given in the *Bhagavad Gita*, where a more impersonal attitude toward the results of one's actions is advised.

Justice "makes no difference between the many and the few," says the previously quoted Mahatma,[6] which would seem to indicate that the integrity of a nation or a social group is just as important as one's personal integrity, and that all alike are weighed in the scales of justice. But how often do we find complete honesty and true integrity in the field of international diplomacy, or even in the business world? It would seem that individual citizens should be as much concerned with the honesty and integrity of their country as with their own personal lives, for in the end they have to assume accountability for both.

The subject of group karma has some very interesting aspects which deserve consideration by the individual who is striving to live in accordance with highest understanding. In everyday life, how little thought is given to the karmic aspects of one's group associations or of professions of which one makes use. Does one ever consider that in belonging to a religion or in availing oneself of the services of the medical profession, as examples, one is partaking to some extent in the collective karma of these groups? In joining a religion, do devotees ever consider their vicarious association with the intolerance and persecution which have been perpetrated by that sect? Do persons who avail themselves of the latest developments in medical practice ever stop to think of the suffering and torture that may have accompanied the development of those techniques? Probably not, but it is something deserving serious thought.

As long as minds and emotions continue to generate hatred, jealousy, envy, and greed, whether as individuals or as members of a group, so long will karmic ties be created and karmic debts be balanced out. When will the wheel stop turning? Who knows? But probably not until all humanity has reached perfection.

References

1. *The Mahatma Letters to A. P. Sinnett*, transcribed and compiled by A. T. Barker, 3rd ed., Adyar: Theosophical House, 1962, p. 67.
2. Annie Besant, *The Ancient Wisdom*, Adyar: Theosophical Publishing House, p. 272.
3. Barker, op. cit., p. 109.
4. Ibid., p. 147.
5. Besant, op. cit., p. 286.
6. Barker, op. cit., p. 395.

V
Beyond Karma

As a law of nature, karma affects us all. Spiritual and mythological traditions have long shown that to ignore or defy it is to court disaster. Yet the esoteric traditions also suggest that we can in various ways mitigate or even transcend the binding effects of karmic law. The following set of essays explores this process of transcendence from a variety of viewpoints.

Dane Rudhyar speaks to the relationship of karma and dharma or duty and of the way in which karmic conditions can be transformed through spiritual awareness. Virginia Hanson discusses the principle of grace and how it might be understood within the framework of traditional karmic theory. Christopher Chapple considers the importance of purification, renunciation, and detachment as traditional steps in the practice of yoga that move one toward transcendence. Ray Grasse describes the relationship between karma and the esoteric yogic doctrine of the chakras, and suggests techniques to neutralize karma by working with the chakras and their energies. Laurence Bendit stresses the importance of one's personal reaction to karma and of consciously harmonizing oneself with the cosmic whole, essential steps in the process of moving beyond karmic limitation.

21
Transmutation of Karma into Dharma

DANE RUDHYAR

Everything in the universe enters the field of existence at the place and time to which it 'belongs.' It appears there and then because at that place and time a particular *need* exists which it can meet.

Why can a particular human being fit the need of a particular family, group, or nation—and in general of humanity—at a particular time? Because the sum-total of the series of past experiences, thoughts, and actions which condition what is possible for this human being to accomplish has made of him or her a *potentially* effective answer to the need.

The newborn is conditioned by the past—ancestral, social-historical and/or personal-reincarnational—as the last link in a chain of attempts by the universe (or some may say by God) to successfully meet a particular cosmic need, and thus to perform a specific role on this planet (or any other). This conditioning is the newborn's *karma*. But the task of performing this role in terms of the need of a particular place and time constitutes his or her *dharma*. Thus dharma and karma are the two sides of the coin of individual existence. Karma is constituted by what is *possible* for the newborn by virtue of a long series of past experiences, whether they be successes or failures. Dharma is defined by the precise character and need of the new existential situation in which birth occurred. This dharma requires a human being whose particular karma makes it possible for him or her to perform the dharma.

231

In terms of karma, the performance of the new dharma is, however, only possible. The performer may be so deeply and irrevocably conditioned by a past series of at least relative failures that these have created an irreversible momentum. The child and growing youth may have been born in so difficult an environment or with such a handicapped body that the effort needed to effectually *decondition* himself or herself and perform the necessary act of total severance from the birth-surroundings is too difficult. All spiritual living, at least for the vanguard of human beings today, is a constant warfare between the pull of an often dim realization of what one is born to perform and the ghosts of a long series of past 'sins' of omission as well as commission. The inertia of the past (karma) makes the mind unable to clearly see the new possibilities for action and thought (dharma) which the birth-situation actually contains. The special character of this dharma made necessary the existence of a particular karmic situation. Karma may have meant a serious illness in youth or polio in midlife, but these *seeming* handicaps to further achievements may have been indispensable for the maturing of the individual charged with the performance of a dharma requiring mental concentration or the exercise of a powerful, independent will.

Karma, I repeat, conditions. It sets limits to possibilities and gives them a particular character; but that character is what is required for the performance of the dharma. Conditioning does not mean predetermination. The fact of being a member of a minority group in a city tenement indicates only what the human being *starts from.* It does not determine whether the person will be a heroin peddler, or through a series of barely recognizable opportunities immediately made use of, a political or business leader. Both possibilities are there. If we look at the situation strictly from the point of view of the human being gradually developing under extremely difficult biological, psychological, and social conditions, we can only see karma at work. Ancient causes have produced new effects which *of themselves* will automatically seek to reproduce similar causes whose power normally will increase at each repetition. But is this the only way to consider any human situation, and in general the sequence of events and activities representing the warp and woof of a universe? Is strict causality the only way of interpreting the immensely complex relatedness of everything to everything?

Causality, as understood by the intellectual and rational mind, refers only to what recently has been called 'horizontal' relationships—relationships between entities operating at essentially the same level. If we believe in a strictly individualistic kind of 'reincarnation' according to which one personality succeeds another, the latter inevitably and automatically inheriting the karma of success and/or failure left by the former at death—and the old Hindu would say condensed in "the last thought before death"—we picture in our mind the relationship between the two persons as a strictly horizontal relation. The Mosaic law, "An eye for an eye," etc., refers to the horizontal relationship between two persons operating at the same physical level of existence. At this level, an action is followed by a reaction in the opposite direction. This is the principle of mechanical action-reaction, however formulated. It is the law of the Newtonian physics.

If we interpret the world strictly and exclusively in terms of horizontal relationships, we are logically compelled to accept the concept of absolute determinism. It has therefore been said that if all the causes operating in the past were known, their effects and the future effects of these acting as causes could also be totally known. The chain of karma would be unbreakable. If it can be broken, transformed, and perhaps altogether dissolved, there must be a transcendent power able not only to observe and understand the nature of the series of causes and effects, but also to affect it—thus to intervene in the process. To intervene means to act from an at least symbolically 'higher' level. Such an action implies a non-karmic relation. This relation is 'vertical,' not horizontal.

In the Christian concept of a divine intervention in human affairs, God sent His Son to redeem a mankind

seemingly hopelessly entangled in its not only collective
but generic chain of karma (since the original sin).

A vertical relationship between God and mankind-as-a-
whole is implied. A similar type of relationship is postulated
in the *Bhagavad Gita* when Krishna states that whenever
mankind reaches a state of spiritual darkness and ignorance
He reappears among men to restore the dharma obscured
by the *maya* of horizontal (social and interpersonal) relationship. In Mahayana Buddhism, Gautama, having reached
the supremely transcendent state of Nirvana, returns from
it to bring some of its light to humanity; and his example
is followed by many Boddhisattvas who accept ceaseless
rebirths out of sublime compassion for mankind.

This compassion is essentially a vertical relationship.
The Hindu ascetic returned from Nirvana should not be
considered, strictly speaking, a 'human' being, even if the
outer physical appearance remained that of Gautama. As
he *relates* himself once more to human beings in a radically
transformed way, he acts as an 'agent' of a 'Reality' that
not merely transcends our human and physical planetary
realm of existence but—and this is the essential point—
encompasses it wholly.

The concept that the universe is a 'hierarchy of systems'
has become increasingly acceptable to the modern scientific
mentality. I call the principle of organization operating
in such a hierarchy 'holarchy.' From this holarchic point
of view, existence operates in terms of wholes—in terms of
organized systems of activity and consciousness—which
are all lesser wholes within greater wholes and at the same
time greater wholes encompassing a myriad of lesser units.
At the physical level we see the holarchic series: atoms,
molecules, cells, living organisms, planets, solar systems,
galaxies, etc. Each new class includes a myriad of entities
of the preceding class and is itself one of many components
in a still more inclusive class. Such a hierarchy is one of
containment—the higher class contains all that belongs
to the lower—not (as in the Army or governmental bureauc-
racy) one of rank in which, while the higher gives orders
to the lower, both levels of command are occupied by persons
that are equally human.

According to such a holarchic picture, every whole can, and at times must, consciously and deliberately relate itself to both the lesser wholes it contains and the greater whole in which it 'lives, moves and has its being.' Such inter-relatedness between a greater whole and the lesser units it contains is evident at the level of national operation. The State passes laws that constantly affect its members, and it also fosters and maintains what we call the national spirit and an official type of culture and way of life. Conversely, each member of the society contributes positively or negatively to the society's welfare and growth or decay.

A holarchic relation of containment thus links a single person to his or her family, social class, nation and culture, and to mankind-as-a-whole. Such a hierarchical series operates fundamentally at the level of what I call *collective psychism*. This collective psychism is, in most instances, deeply rooted in biological or generic factors, but it transcends the strictly physical level and operates in terms of collective feelings and mental-emotional attitudes that are taken for granted and therefore are, to a large extent, compulsive.

When a person emerges from this collective realm and becomes a truly self-reliant, autonomous, and responsible 'individual,' he (or she) most often today finds himself under the control of the structural power that had been needed for such an emergence from the collective psychism: the ego. This is a state of transition, the state symbolized by the Great War between the forces that represent the essentially 'open' and 'closed' ways of life. The way of the ego can be considered closed because the ego generally resists vertical relationship with a greater whole and cares mostly for horizontal relationships it can manipulate to ensure its own security, comfort, and aggrandizement. The open way is, by contrast, pervaded by a willingness to accept vertical relationship with the greater whole of which one is a part. The battle between these two approaches to life is inherently tragic and at times the bitter struggle seems not worth pursuing. But he whose deepest nature resonates to the power of the open way finds himself an Arjuna whose psyche-mind is able to receive and assimilate the truth Krishna presents to him before the battle begins.

Krishna may be seen for an illumined yet frightening instant as the centralized and all-encompassing Will and Form of the universal Whole; but in less exalted moments he is more simply the revealer of dharma. He reveals to Arjuna what this troubled individual *had been born for*—thus his place and function in the greater whole, humanity. It was Arjuna's karma to be born in a situation of constant feudal warfare; but this birth made it possible for him to perform a particular dharma as an important factor in the victory of the open way of consciousness and activity, which was also the way of emergence from a confusing medley of metaphysical systems, the way of spiritual individualization. *Spiritual* individualization: because it was the process of becoming an autonomous, self-reliant, and responsible individual in terms of what India and humanity-as-a-whole *needed* at the time. Krishna revealed what this need was; but Krishna should be understood as simply a metaphor giving a concrete form to the active and transformative relationship of humanity to a particular man, Arjuna.

An Avatar, as an 'agent' of humanity and an answer to its acute need, is a metaphor revealing the possibility of the Greater Whole, humanity, intervening in a situation expressing the temporary triumph of karma over dharma. This intervention has nevertheless to be focused *through* a particular human individual. This individual is a lesser whole within the greater whole of humanity. He or she is the lesser whole that could most effectively *resonate* to the impact of the revelation from the greater whole—the revelation of the need and of how essentially to meet it.

A great leader able to move people acts as an avatar of the nation that gave him or her birth. He (or she) acts in terms of a national need to which he seeks to give a constructive or transformative answer. The action is conditioned by the karma of *both* the nation-as-a-whole and the leader as a person born in specific circumstances. The family and environmental circumstances into which any would-be leader was born and educated represent his or her karma.

But his or her dharma is the voice of the nation revealing to him or her the need to which his or her birth provided the necessary requirements making possible an effective answer. It is nevertheless, I repeat, only a potential answer; for the 'called upon' leader may fail. He or she may even refuse to hear the voice or allow the fear it arouses to engender doubts of its authenticity. The mind filled with karmic inertia may initially fasten upon rationalizations to escape the dharma, as did Arjuna's mind. A lesser loyalty may be used by the karma-conditioned consciousness to invalidate the intuitive, yet still dim and uncertain, feeling of what one's 'truth of being' (dharma) is. A poignant feeling of incapacity may arise justifying itself on the basis of the karmic load one has to bear: "Why me, when so many better persons must be available?"

They may not be available. Karmic conditioning is never of itself good or bad for a task. The question is *how to use it*. A well-known and highly creative psychiatrist was once accused by a colleague of being paranoid. He replied, "Of course, I am paranoid. But I have used this paranoia to give power to my determination to make a basic contribution to psychotherapy." Would Franklin D. Roosevelt have been the leader he proved to be, in a time of severe national and world crisis, if he had not accepted the tragedy of his illness as a means to develop willpower and an ineradicable sense of destiny?

The key to the spiritual life is indeed the transmutation of karma into dharma. It is the ability to make of the past, as Franklin Roosevelt said, only a prelude to the future—a 'noble' future. Nobility, in the deepest and truest sense of the word, is the capacity to serve the purpose of a Greater Whole-in-the-making; that is, the exteriorization of a new archetypal system of organization whose time to be concretely manifested has come according to the rhythm of social, planetary, or cosmic evolution.

The truly noble person is aware that he or she is performing a part in a historical drama. He or she is a person, yet the noble performance is *transpersonal*. To live a transpersonal life is to live as a person in terms of the inner directives of a Greater Whole of which one intuitively (or perhaps clearly and objectively), knows oneself to be— potentially—and one wills oneself to become fully and effectively a self-dedicated agent. Such a noble life, which is also an essentially heroic life, is the life of dharma. The individual who lives it is the true 'Aryan,' because the Sanskrit term *Ayra* means 'noble.' It denotes the capacity to make any karmic conditioning serve a creative function; and here to create simply means to allow the pull toward the future to overcome the inertia of the past.

This past has produced the lesser whole; but the future, if it be true to the fulfillment of the historical need—the need of the moment, at any level of existence—is nothing other than the working out of the process of exteriorization and concretization of a new potentiality of being inherent in the life and function of the greater whole to which the lesser whole is able to effectively relate itself according to the limitations of his or her birth-conditioning.

At any time, the future is, in a sense, present as an archetype—that is, as a potentiality which, sooner or later and in one way or another, will be actualized. It *will be* realized, but (except probably in relatively rare cases) *who* will actualize it, and *how* and *when* it will be perfectly actualized is not 'determined.' It cannot be determined existentially— thus, in terms of exact deeds and particular doers—because the war between the inertia of karma and the creative power of dharma does not have an inevitable result insofar as any one person or collectivity of persons is concerned. There will be failure as well as success; but no failure or success can be 'absolute,' for the very fact of existence includes both—and their conflict. And the failure of one person sooner or later paves the way for the eventual success of another person who is then, as it were, offered the task of taking the place of whoever failed to perform his or her dharma effectively.

The conflict between dharma and karma should be experienced as a dance rather than a war. In a dance the dynamic will and imagination of the dancer constantly struggles against gravitation. The dancer also *uses* gravitation as well as the floor to define the field of the joyous or tragic battle. To collapse on the floor is to accept defeat by gravitation. To play with the antinomy of fall and recovery is to train for the great performance when the dancer will accept direction by the divine choreographer who, in turn, will have imagined a scenario that fills the needs of the Greater Whole, humanity.

Existence is relatedness. But to limit the principle of relationship to its 'horizontal' manifestation is to give to the concept of causality a strictly logical and intellectually binding character. It is to accept Newton's mechanistic view of the universe—the view that triumphed through the 19th century—and to ignore the Einsteinian world of relativity and space-curvature, and Heisenberg's principle of indeterminacy. If we isolate one level of activity and relatedness we can indeed refer every effect to a cause, itself the effect of preceding causes. This leads us inevitably to a God that has to be the First Cause, and as such is incomprehensible because there can be no intelligible 'reason' for an original Act setting the infinite line of cause-and-effect into operation. Thus we are faced with the tragic and self-defeating statement of St. Augustine, "*Credo qiua absurdum*" —I believe because it is absurd.

"Because!" Our minds seem always driven by the compulsion to postulate a cause for the deepest belief that controls the essence of our living. We are driven also by our seemingly inescapable dependence upon the feeling-concept that we are separate and unique individuals who can only relate to other external and equally separate individual entities. Again, this is the Newtonian concept of motion, a motion interpretable in terms of push and pull, of the mechanical action and reaction of separate bits of matter.

We have come at last, in this century, to the realization that nothing is separate from anything else, and that every conceivable entity, micro- or macrocosmic, is related to every other entity at all levels. The basic fact of existence, at any level our minds can imagine, is not only the interrelatedness, but the interpenetration of all there is.

Realizing this, if we still use the term 'karma' we are compelled to identify its ultimate cosmic meaning with that of such an interrelatedness and interpenetration. H. P. Blavatsky stated that the keyword of the 'fourth dimension' —which corresponds to the traditional fourth level or state of consciousness, *turiya*—is indeed 'interpenetration.' At that level, effects act upon causes, just as the future acts upon the past, and Greater Wholes act upon lesser wholes.

Every system of spiritual philosophy accepts the idea that the Divine intervenes in the human. God sends His 'grace' to those who believe in and pray or sacrifice to Him. Boddhisattvas bestow their blessings and spiritual guidance upon the aspiring and 'noble' section of humanity. Holy men give their *baraka* to their disciples. Even the great Medieval mystic, Meister Eckart, said that God needs man as much as man needs God. The future needs the past in order to have something to overcome and a concrete foundation for creativity. The past needs the future in order to become the present; and the present has meaning only in terms of the interplay between past and future.

Anything is possible because all there is is a network of multidimensional relationships. But, at any particular level of existence, the infinite potentiality of being finds itself limited by the mere fact of being defined—i.e., of being given a particular form and rhythm. Karma, as usually understood, is the limitation imposed upon beings existing at the level of our present humanity—the level at which we have to speak of 'choice' between alternatives. But from a cosmic point of view, all 'choices' are being made at all times. They are interrelated and interdependent.

Such a statement does *not* mean that for a particular human being all choices are equally valid. What constitutes the individuality of a human being is the fact that, for him or her, certain choices are constructive—thus future-oriented —while others are inherently destructive or regressive. In a world of constant motion and actualization of new potentialities of being, to refuse to move toward the future is to regress. Evil is essentially the refusal to move toward the future. It is to accept the repetitive inertia of past choices as inevitable or too powerful to oppose. It is to succumb to karma, instead of using what the past had produced as a floor against which to rebound, and of investing this rebounding with a creative, future-engendering meaning.

22
The Other Face of Karma

VIRGINIA HANSON

Few people who have given serious thought to the subject of karma would deny that it is one of the most complex, the most profound, and probably the least understood of all the great universal principles. To attempt to touch upon any of its more subtle aspects may seem presumptuous in the extreme. In particular, as one approaches the subject from a Christian background, one may seem to be inviting an impasse, for sooner or later one is confronted with the juxtaposition of karma as an immutable law and grace with its secret and mysterious dynamics which seem to operate independently of law.

In human affairs, both karma and grace may, in a sense, be said to "happen," that is, they are experienced and experienceable. This seems undeniable fact, so that neither can be denied. We feel instinctively that fact cannot be untruth; at the same time, it can never be the whole of truth. It says, in effect, "I am both hiding and revealing truth." Dare one explore what is hidden beneath what is revealed in the action of karma and grace?

The mere placing of these two words together may seem to be drawing lines for an irresolvable conflict. In the dead-letter, literal interpretation of karma as a mechanical process grinding on and on like a locomotive on a single pair of tracks, there can be no such thing as grace. In the sentimental, wishful, unrealistic view of grace as a favor dispensed by a jealous and erratic God, to be gained by flattery and profession of belief, karma is a concept to be rejected vehemently. Yet in any real and earnest search for truth there can be no conflict, for searchers do not begin with rejection; they do not begin with any conditioned attitude at all, but only with eyes and mind open to see what they may find.

What is the nature of the reality of karma? What is the nature of the reality of grace? And what is the nature of the relationship between them? Are they two sides of a coin, or are they totally foreign and antagonistic to each other?

H. P. Blavatsky calls karma "the One Law which governs the World of Being."[1] It has been described as the Absolute in the process of manifestation and as manifestation seeking to restore the harmony of the Absolute. It is spoken of as impersonal, inexorable, immutable—but also as modifiable. It has been called a "mathematical equation."

Sir James Jeans, the British scientist, declared that "the universe appears to have been designed by a pure mathematician"[2] and that ". . . the laws which nature obeys are less suggestive of those which a machine obeys in its motion than of those which a musician obeys in writing a fugue, or a poet in composing a sonnet. The motions of electrons and atoms do not resemble those of the parts of a locomotive so much as those of the dancers in a cotillion."[3] In other words, they seem volitional rather than automatic; they are dependable and observable, yet they hold forever the potential of creative innovation. But, mysteriously, the innovation never creates confusion; rather it seems to grow logically out of the inner meaning of the dance. Such steps as are no longer appropriate become transformed into that which is useful to an ever-expanding synthesis.

In his book *Out of My Later Years*, Albert Einstein comments on the element of unpredictability in atomic behavior and adds: "One need only think of the weather, in which case accurate prediction even for a few days ahead is impossible. Nevertheless, no one doubts that we are confronted with a causal connection. Occurrences in this domain are beyond the reach of exact prediction because of the variety of factors in operation, not because of any lack of order in nature."[4]

In other words, the creative innovations of nature do not mean breaches of law. They simply mean that the law has so many variables within it that no one can claim to have final and conclusive knowledge of all its workings.

So we have a concept of a great mathematician whose nature is law, but with untold reserves of ways in which the law may work out. Even here on our mundane plane of operations, with our limited intellects, it is a commonly known mathematical principle that when we change the relation of the elements within an equation, we change the results. As very simple examples, we can add and get one result; we can subtract, multiply, divide, square a number and carry the process to the nth power; we can extract square root, cube root, and so on; or we may introduce some new element into the equation. In all these ways we get different results. The equation must work out according to mathematical law, but the elements introduced and the relationships in which those elements are arranged determine the nature of the equation itself and what the results will be. It is known also that the solution to any equation, to any mathematical problem, always lies within the problem itself, never outside, although we may find ourselves unable to solve a problem because we are over-looking some element; we are not seeing it whole.

Surely the relationships between the myriad elements of life affect each other and the end results in any situation, in any experience, just as do the elements within a mathematical equation. The law itself makes no exception, but it would be staggeringly brash to say that we know what all the elements are or that we can predict everything that can happen within the operation of the law, particularly since no situation, no experience, is ever exactly duplicated. Although there is but One Law, it has so many facets, so many variables, that it seems to be many laws in operation; and at times we may not even be able to discern law at all because it is operating at a level far beyond our comprehension.

So it would seem that the *mechanical* explanation of karma hardly explains what is taking place. It is particularly inadequate, and holds no key to growth and understanding, if we use it *merely* as an explanation and search no deeper, in ourselves or in nature, for causes—for those elements which will make the problem and thus reveal its true nature.

As karma operates in our own lives, it is undoubtedly the law through which we inherit our own past. But, again, there is a hint of something deeper and more profound. The universe turns as one (which is the root meaning of the word "universe") and we all live in one element. Out of this emerges the principle of relativity. Every part of the universe must therefore be kept, at every moment, in harmony with its own integral balance. This happens, it is suggested, not only at the physical level, but at higher energy levels which are inconceivable to us. We might think of it as a "making perfect" process—or perhaps a more descriptive term would be the invincible divine will to perfection eternally in action. This gets away from the idea of something static and motionless or of something wholly mechanical. Rather it would seem to be perfect rhythm and perfect harmony, or balance, in simultaneity. The will to perfection is conceived of as the Logoic Will, and its operation in maintaining the equilibrium of the universe is, one might say, stretched out in time and space. This might be termed universal or cosmic karma.

As this applies to the individual, it is a mystical energy of inconceivable power which derives from the Logoic Will, is one with it and is—at every moment—in rhythmic balance at the level of the Self. Disturbances (pleasant or unpleasant) take place in the outer circumstances where the fragment, the personality, is focused. The impact of these disturbances is felt—or perhaps a better term is "absorbed"—at the causal level.* But here it does not disturb the integrity and equilibrium because all is immediate and whole; no element is missing, so that everything *is* balanced and perfect at every moment. Perhaps what takes place is a perfectly coordinated operation of centrifugal and centripetal forces at every level of energy. At the mundane level, the action is slowed down so that, to us, it "takes time." It becomes

---

*"Causal level" here refers to the level of the soul or Self.—ED

our world experience. At the causal level it is instantaneous.

Events as cause and effect in space and time, then, must be worked out in the personality. And while the personality cannot escape its responsibility, it would seem that the Ego is the primary "mover." One might even go so far as to suggest the possibility that the Ego initiates the events, that is, it uses the law as a tool for its own growth, for it can develop its powers only through learning to deal with circumstances at the outpost of consciousness which we call the personality.

A concept emerging in depth psychology seems to relate to this possibility. Dr. Edward C. Whitmont comments that it has been customary in his profession to assume that traumatic experiences which might be avoided under "ideal" circumstances are responsible for the later development of neuroses or psychoses. He suggests that it may be of value to examine this assumption, and he advances the theory that these often unhappy experiences "may perhaps be seen as essential landmarks in the actualization of a pattern of wholeness. They may be understood as the 'suffering of the soul' which is needed to engender present and future psychological advance. . . . In following the development of past events into future consequences, we might discover a meaning beyond mere cause and effect in the way the past comes to view when regarded as the first stage and necessary setting for present and future unfoldment." It may be seen, he says, "not just as accident or misfortune, but as a destined emotional impasse essential for the actualization of our own particular pattern of wholeness."[5]

Drawing a parallel with the development of the action in a drama—using the concept of Greek tragedy as a "mirror of the soul"—Dr. Whitmont points out that the sequence of events on the stage works out as cause and effect, but he adds: ". . . while it is true that the staging of the tragic or joyful situation in act two seems to be caused by the 'right' or 'wrong' action which preceded it in act one, it is equally true that this effect of causation is deliberate or destined. Act one has set the scene and built up its consequences or 'effects' in order to reveal the intent or plot of the drama as it unfolds later in actuality.... Although we may understand the play (as) the sequence of cause and effect, unless we are also able to comprehend the dramatic intent or the destined meaning behind the causal sequence, we will not be moved by the inner logic of its timing...."[6] He is making the point that there is an "archetypal destiny" for each individual which is known to the Self and that, while cause and effect are necessary to the outworking of this destiny, the real impulse comes from a much deeper level. This is not determinism, nor does it absolve the personality from its responsibility; it does not preclude the concept of free will. It is the "meaning" of the drama that is destined and must, in some act, be fulfilled. The Ego is indeed the true Actor and the personality is the role through which he deals with the effects of his self-initiated causes. But the Actor *becomes* the role, else it is empty of meaning; it is an extension of himself onto the stage of life. The personality may choose whether to accept this fact and thus move toward the fulfillment of the meaning, or whether to delay that fulfillment by refusing to acknowledge the true nature of the drama.

All this carries the clear implication that what happens to us happens by the secret will of our own innermost being. For the Ego is not separate from the Self (using the word in the theosophical sense); it is indeed that aspect of the Self through which action must take place. In the earlier stages of evolution, this is perhaps a feeble and even fumbling process. But as the Ego develops its capacities and becomes more facile in using them, it comes more and more to direct the process and even to pose for itself greater challenges out of the inexhaustible storehouse of past experience.

Thus, we are always in the process of creating our own drama, our own world action, from within. This creation, which in its outer aspect becomes cause and effect in continual adjustment to the interrelation or interaction between the personality and its environment, is what we ordinarily think of as karma. And because, as personalities, we are mostly unaware that, as Egos, we have brought it all about, even the causes seem to impinge on us from the outside. But surely these can no more be outside ourselves than we can be outside our own hearts and minds. The causes are within us, and so long as they remain they must continually create effects.

Once a disturbance has taken place, it may take time for the balance, the harmony, to be achieved in the outer circumstances. We may even have to wait for act three or even later (here for the moment considering acts as successive incarnations) before the event in act one finds its outworking. As personalities we experience sequentially. But to the Self, the concepts of time and space must be irrelevant. "When" the impulse from the Self comes into our lives, then, it seems from our point of view to come in time and space. But what we experience as adjustment in the personality is part of the archetypal "plot," which is already perfect, whole, at the causal level; it has never been anything but perfect and whole.

The Self is not subject to the working out of personal causality because it is not subject to the personality, although, paradoxically—to take some liberty with Dr. Whitmont's hypothesis—the acting-out on the stage and the underlying theme of the drama "are not mutually exclusive but complementary and mutually in need of each other."[7] But the Self *is* harmony, integrity, perfection. Personal karma cannot affect it, however rigidly and inflexibly it may operate in the space-time world of our everyday experience. It has been pointed out that just as the sky's nature remains the same however black the clouds which pass across it, so the Self's purity is undisturbed by the human thoughts, emotions, and passions which move within its projection, the personality—although in some mysterious manner it descends into the depths with us and teaches us the meaning of the heavenly agony. But we have to remember that, even in this, the Self is still experiencing itself when it sees the myriad personal lives through which it manifests. And since it is perfection, it *experiences* only perfection. This is poetically expressed in the words, "Of purer eyes than to behold evil." Unfortunately, such concepts are too subtle for the blundering uses of language. We are consantly faced with the fact that words are indeed, as someone has called them, the broken wreckage of the reality of thought.

Quite tentatively, then, and at the risk of being misunderstood, it might be said that the Self "cares" beyond measure what happens to the personality, but because it is love in the ultimate it is not "concerned." Worry is a vice which belongs exclusively to the personality, in which love is incomplete and which is therefore insecure.

In this view, presumably, everything is "right," and when we see that which we regard as wrong or evil and attempt to remedy it, that is a part of the rightness. In this view, too, life has a kind of "built-in" integrity and immortality. Everything has an inner balance and truth and harmony; everything, in its true nature, reflects that perfect equilibrium at the core of all creation.

It seems possible, then, that this built-in integrity and immortality can be equated with the element of redemption which has received so much emphasis in the Christian religion and without which, perhaps, no resolution of karma is possible. Redemption, in this view, is not to be thought of as coming about through the sacrifice of God in the person of one son, but mystically through the Logoic sacrifice on the cross of matter, redeeming matter (which seems to resist but in reality is ever "seeking" to be redeemed), the process repeated endlessly, down to the lowliest cells and atoms of our bodies.

The symbol of the cross is of course a universal one, far antedating the Christian era. We find the conception that at the "beginning of time"—that is, of manifestation— the Logos impressed Itself upon creation in the form of a cross, the pattern of all manifestation, repeated at every level. Therefore the symbol implies, if we look deeply enough, that our efforts are divine efforts unrecognized. Or, perhaps more accurately, the cross is a symbol of the mutual sacrifice of spirit and matter in becoming one. It is not, in its profounder meaning, a symbol of death, even death as sacrifice, but of the union of opposites—God and humanity in mutual and simultaneous self-surrender. In every kind of cross known there is a point at which the perpendicular and horizontal shafts become indistinguishable—where they are not opposites at all, each being completely "lost" in the other. This point is at the very heart of the cross. It is what makes the symbol a cross and not some other figure. It is what makes the cross a triumph and not a disaster. It is the pattern throughout life, and it is the inner secret of redemption. Because of it, grace is a reality.

Grace, then, is not something that comes "unearned"; rather is the earning something quite different from what we think it is. It is perhaps not earning at all in the sense of achieving some reward as a result of conscious effort. Grace is unpredictable; it cannot be commanded; it operates when it will and as it will and often in ways which may seem strange to us.

In the biblical story of Joseph, the beloved son who was sold by his jealous brothers into slavery in Egypt, there is a curious statement. It will be recalled that, after his betrayal, Joseph rose from his humble status as a slave to that of the most powerful man in Egypt, second only to Pharoah himself. He was able to interpret Pharoah's dream and to save the country from starvation during the long famine which visited the land. When Joseph's brothers came to Egypt for help, and when he finally made known to them his identity, they were profoundly afraid, for now, they thought, he would revenge himself upon them. But Joseph reassured them and added, "Ye thought evil against me; but God meant it unto good."[8] Thus was grace operating unseen through even a perfidious act. The story of Joseph, whether or not rooted in history, is a marvelous allegory of the universal grace operating in nature and which, we would say, forever makes good come out of evil.

In his book *The Hero With a Thousand Faces*, Joseph Campbell tells the story of Virachocha, a great divinity of prehistoric Peru: "His tiara is the sun; he grasps the thunderbolt in either hand; and from his eyes descend, in the form of tears, the rains that refresh the life of the valleys of the world. . . . The meaning is that the grace that pours into the universe through the sun door is the same as the energy of the bolt that annihilates and is itself indestructible; the delusion-shattering light of the Imperishable is the same as the light that creates."[9] Is this not saying, in effect, that karma and grace, are, in fact, but two aspects of the same law?

Is it not possible that the ultimate resolution of karma is not through an extension of good deeds on the part of humanity, not even through detachment from the fruits of action, but mysteriously through participation in a sovereign state of being in which attachment is meaningless—a total union of the actor with the power that moves him or her to action, a total surrender of self and a simultaneous Self-surrender in an act of grace, the sublime and heavenly gift. The mystical energy which is the will to perfection eternally in operation "moves out" into the personality. This comes inevitably like a "visitation from on high." It is experienced within, yet it *seems* to the personality to come from *outside* because the personality has been isolated in its own zone of awareness. In other words, the Christian would say it comes from God—a God who is generally thought of as completely outside his creation. It is unexpected; it is unpredictable; and it seems totally undeserved.

This "undeserved" aspect is probably because the full flow of grace comes usually—although not always—when the self has been completely surrendered; it comes to the humble and the contrite heart, repentant and earnestly seeking to be filled with the fire and sweetness of divinity. It is the Kingdom of Heaven which "cometh as a thief in the night." It would seem to be identical with the energy, the active will to perfection, which has been termed karma—the most dynamic, the most potent form that karma can take because it brings about the awareness, in the personality, of its real nature, that total fulfillment represented by the perfect equilibrium at the heart of the cross where God and humanity become one. The fulfillment is inherent in the very nature of the law itself. For its nature is ever the nature of the cross. When that realization flows into the personality, it is known as grace.

Grace has its own purposes, not to be discerned or controlled by humanity. Not always does it wait for the surrender of the self; it sometimes forces that surrender. When this happens, it can be devastating. Paul, on the road to Damascus, was blinded by it and was three days without sight or the ability to eat or drink. Yet thereafter he preached, through persecution and trial, "Christ in you, the hope of glory."[10]

Paul spoke of being "above the law, in grace," and this is often taken to mean that in some miraculous manner we can escape the working out of the law in our personal lives. Surely one may assume that Paul was speaking of that total union with the Source of the action, that oneness *with* the law which must be dimensionless and timeless. But individuals must come back again and meet their "everyday"; they may even be faced with a particularly difficult evolutionary assignment, as was Paul. And again they are subject to the operation of the law in space and time; again they are on the stage. But there is a difference. The power of grace to alter circumstances is incalculable because it alters the personality, which is the most important element in the circumstances. The theme has come to a climax. Old causes are "blotted out" and new and powerful causes are initiated. New effects become inevitable. This may be thought of as the "forgiveness of sins."

Such forgiveness can hardly mean, however, that the world experience, the life drama of individuals, will immediately become one long sweet song, or that they will never meet the consequences of the things done in the past. The drama continues, but now instead of being helplessly caught in its action, the actors are participating in the denouement; they are letting the action flow through them. They meet events with an entirely different consciousness, so that the events become something quite different from what they would otherwise have been. It is probably not too much to say that measure of the flow of grace into one's life determines the degree of strength and wisdom with which he or she now meets and deals with experience. "The lamp of knowledge is the perception of truth. The lamp is the passionless heart; its oil is Divine grace; the air that keeps it burning is the breeze of love that blows between man and God; and the boisterous wind from which it is protected is the desire for things perceived by sense of mind."[11] Or, as it was expressed by the seventeenth century mystic, Brother Lawrence: ". . . our sanctification (does not depend upon *changing* our works), but in doing that for God's sake which we commonly do for our own."[12]

As to what brings about the dynamic moment of fulfillment, that moment when the law becomes self-transformed into an act of grace, who can say? Perhaps it is a decision of the Self, that power behind the action of our individual world drama. If so, we cannot know at the personal level why that decision is taken. Perhaps it is not a "decision" at all in our understanding of the term, for choice is the burden—and the gift—of individual consciousness. Perhaps it is a "happening" that takes place when all the elements of a situation have made it inevitable. Paul Brunton calls it "a descent of the Overself into the underself's zone of awareness . . . the voice of the Overself speaking suddenly out of the cosmic silence with which we are environed." And he adds, "Because the Overself exists in every man, grace too exists potentially in every man."[13]

But I think we can say that the Overself violates no law; rather that when it moves "into the underself's zone of awareness" it is its own fulfillment.

References

1. H. P. Blavatsky, *The Secret Doctrine*, Adyar: Theosophical Publishing House, 1938, 4th ed., vol. 2, p. 359.
2. Sir James Jeans, *The Mysterious Universe*, New York: The Macmillan Co., 1930, p. 140.
3. Ibid., p. 146.
4. Albert Einstein, *Out of My Later Years*, New York: Philosophical Library, Inc., 1950, p. 28.
5. Edward C. Whitmont, M.D., "The Destiny Concept in Psychotherapy," a paper read at Zurich, Switzerland, September 1968, before the Fourth Congress of the International Association for Analytical Psychology, *Spring*, 1969, p. 74.
6. Ibid., pp. 78-9.

7. Ibid., p. 79.
8. Gen. 50:20.
9. Joseph Campbell, *The Hero With a Thousand Faces*, Bollingen Series XVII, New York: Pantheon Books, Inc., pp. 145-6.
10. Col. 1:27.
11. Commentary on verse 11, Chapter X, the *Bhagavad Gita*, tr. M. Chatterji.
12. Herman Nicholas (Brother Lawrence), *The Practice of the Presence of God*, New York: Fleming H. Revell Co., 1895, p. 16.
13. Paul Brunton, *The Wisdom of the Overself*, New York: E. P. Dutton & Co., 1969, pp. 236-7.

23
Karma and the Path of Purification

CHRISTOPHER CHAPPLE

The doctrine of *karma*, which is common to the Jaina, Buddhist, and classical Hindu traditions, has been frequently criticized as pessimistic. Furthermore, it has been associated with practices that emphasize exploration of past lives as a basis for spiritual development. In this essay, a reading of karma based on Indian texts will be given that explores its positive aspects and emphasizes the interconnectedness of all life rather than dwelling on personalistic, biographical interpretation. The following primary sources will be used: the *Yoga Sūtra* of Patañjali, a parable describing the nature of karma from the Jaina tradition, and a brief passage from the *Laṅkāvatāra Sūtra*. The efficacy of human effort as explicated in the *Yogavāsiṣṭha* will also be explored. The essay will close with a discussion of a proposed "horizontalist" approach to karma that simultaneously affirms self-power and allows for the empowerment and betterment of others.

The term "karma" is derived from the verbal root $\sqrt{k r}$ and in the strictest sense refers to action. In the Vedic tradition, it is linked to the sort of ritual action that produces desired results. In the Sramanic or renouncer traditions of ancient India, from whence derive Jainism, Buddhism, and Yoga, it is seen as the basis for an overarching psycho-cosmological scheme in which one's actions cause a person to enter repeatedly into the world of *saṃsāra* until one achieves liberation through renunciation. These two traditions come

255

together in classical Hinduism which combines the Vedic affirmation of action with ideas of karma, rebirth, and renouncer values. In the Hindu *Dharmaśāstra* literature, the ultimate goal of freedom from all action is to be pursued only after one's societal duties or *dharma* have been fulfilled. One must perform well one's dharma within *saṃsāra* before seeking release, a process that may take many births. In the *Bhagavad Gītā*, renunciation in action (*karma yoga*) is advocated, with total detachment employed in tandem with the maintenance of societal order. In this model, action is not undertaken because one is compelled by exterior or interior forces; action is performed for the sake of holding the world together (*loka saṃgraha*). When performed in the spirit of detachment and with the intention of purification, action or karma can promote spiritual growth and advance one toward the goal of freedom (*mokṣa*). Impure action binds a person within the morass of afflictive, noneffective, or deleterious action, bereft of either conscience or pure consciousness. It is this latter aspect of karma that the renouncer traditions seek to eliminate.

Whether pure or impure, one aspect of karma is inescapable: that the performance of action leaves a residue and that this residue can be activated at a later time, whether positive or negative. *Saṃskāra* and *vāsanā*, the terms used for these residues of action, spawn a rich variety of English equivalents. The word *saṃskāra*, like karma, derives from the stem *kāra*, originating from the root √*kṛ*, which means to do or act. This then is prefixed with *saṃ*, indicating together or with. Hence, a literal translation and interpretation could be "(that which obtains) with action." *Vāsanā* has as its verbal root √*vas*, which means to dwell, referring to traces of past action that abide within one's psyche. Although both terms are used in treatises of various traditions, *vāsanā* is generally more closely associated with Buddhism. Translations for these terms include latent tendency, habit patterns, habituations, impressions, imprinting, learned response, scar, propensity, proclivity, conditioning, predispositions.

Some *saṃskāras* bear fruit immediately and predictably.

If one does not study for an exam on an utterly unfamiliar subject, one will not likely pass. If a person conditions himself or herself over a period of time to run five miles, it then becomes possible to run five miles. The absence or presence of cultivated *saṃskāras* leaves one incompetent or able. Some persons, however, regardless of effort, seem predisposed to excel effortlessly; others unaccountably fail. A familiar explanation from traditional Indian perspectives is that action before this particular life can bear fruit at any time; one's accumulated propensities propel and follow a being from one embodiment to the next. Hence one is born with certain abilities and/or disabilities.

Regarding the concept of rebirth, early Indian cultures simply could not conceive that death brings an end to life. For Buddhists, Jains, Yogis, and followers of Sāmkhya, existence dates from beginningless time. Due to the pervasiveness and tenacity of desire, beings enter the realm of thought and sensation again and again, even after death. Such a death is merely a pause, a moment of withdrawal before the seeds of action propel one to a new embodiment. This process is fundamentally linear: acts are committed within one life that accrue and are carried over to the next birth. Sleep here can be seen as analogous to death: activities performed within the scope of one day lay the foundation for days that follow. When we awaken each morning, our world is slowly reconstructed and then engaged, building on prior experience. In sleep, however, memory continues to operate; in death, memory is erased, except for those who have cultivated the skill of remembering past lives.[1]

The primary concern of this linear model is personal and ethical well being. "If I do this good act now, I will earn merit which will be rewarded in the future" would be one expression of this approach to karma, as would be "The reason I am so unfortunate now is because of evil

---

1. See Gregory Schopen, "The Generalization of an Old Yogic Attainment in Medieval Mahayana Sutra Literature: Some notes on Jatismara." *Journal of the International Association of Buddhist Studies* 6 (1983): 109-147.

acts I committed in the past." Interpreted mechantistically, this outlook could easily foster passive resignation (if not pessimism) regarding the importance of human behavior. The benefits of virtuous action cannot necessarily be reaped in the near future; seemingly none can plumb the depths of deleterious action that has been committed in the past. Furthermore, this interpretation is essentially self-centered, focusing on one's own pleasure and pain. The role of the human person within society is somewhat neglected, though threats of karmic punishment can be used to motivate socially acceptable behavior. Karma in this view is synonymous with fate.

To the contrary, from the perspective of the Sramanic traditions, the karma doctrine is seen as an incentive to strive for purification. Regardless of the particular configuration of one's *saṃskāric* structure (in other words, regardless of what one has done or has been), the goal lies in the cleaning up of all tendencies. For the person bound by convention, actions are unreflectively undertaken, thus binding one repeatedly to worldly involvement, a sense of self, and consequent pleasure and pain. The goal of the Yogic, Jaina, or Buddhist *śrāmaṇa* is to undo all such compulsions through the process of purification. According to the *Yoga Sūtras* of Patañjali, the action of the one involved in *saṃsāra* is fraught with affliction (*kliṣṭa*, I:5), while that of the yogi is unafflicted (*akliṣṭa*, IV:30).[2] He states that the residues of past action are inseparable from affliction (II:12). The goal is not to explore or explain the particulars of why one engages in compulsive or afflictive activities; the goal is to cease ultimately all such compulsions through progressive purification. To actively pursue cataloguing one's past lives, as some contemporary American spiritual practices advocate, would be seen as a distraction, taking time and energy away from the tasks required to undo negative influences that inhibit one in the present.

---

2. References to the *Yoga Sūtras* are based on the translation and grammatical analysis of the text by Christopher Chapple and Yogi Anand Viraj (Eugene P. Kelly, Jr.) (Delhi: Sri Satguru Publications, 1990).

This work involves the cultivation of opposite behavior (*pratiprakṣabhāvanā*, II:33) through the observance of meticulously ethical behavior.

The root of all afflicted action is said to be ignorance (*avidyā* in Yoga, *mithyādṛṣṭi* in Jainism). Ignorance is defined by Patañjali as attributing eternality to that which is perishable, purity to that which is impure, pleasure to that which ultimately leads to dissatisfaction, and an abiding essence to things when no essence is to be found (II:5). Anything in the realm of the senses, including thoughts and the sense of self, must be seen as fluctuating, evanescent, and unreliable. Every possible object of desire, anything that can be grasped by the body, senses, or mind falls into this category. All such entities are occasions for attachment; the process of becoming attached leads to building more *saṃskāras* and *vāsanās*. This reifies a fixed notion of self, attraction to what one thinks will bring pleasure, aversion for things deemed objectionable, and a desire to keep the whole wheel and world in motion (II:3). Without correction or restraint, karma leads to repeated attachment, impurity, and dissatisfaction.

Within the Jaina tradition, the notion of karma is both graphic and literally colorful. While various Hindu and Buddhist texts speak eloquently of the effects of certain actions, Jainas talk of colors associated with particular activities. The following tale from the Jaina tradition captures the core of this approach, associating degrees of negative action with a spectrum of color:

> A hungry person with the most negative black-*leśya* karma uproots and kills an entire tree to obtain a few mangoes. The person of blue karma fells the tree by chopping the trunk, again merely to gain a handful of fruits. Fraught with grey karma, a third person spares the trunk but cuts off the major limbs of the tree. The one with orangish-red karma carelessly and needlessly lops off several branches to reach the mangoes. The fifth, exhibiting white karma, "merely picks up ripe fruit that has dropped to the foot of the tree."[3]

3. Jagmanderlal Jaini, *The Outlines of Jainism* (Cambridge: at the University Press, 1916), p. 47.

The *Yoga Sūtras* use a simplified color system in describing karma, labeling it black, white, or mixed (IV:7). In both systems, a qualitative analysis is advanced, with white karma seen as conducive for correct living, providing the antidote to negative *saṃskāras*.

The Sramanic tradition developed a number of practices to bring about the purgation of *saṃskāras*. These range from breathing exercises to elaborate forms of visualization and are well documented in virtually all schools of Asian meditation. Regardless of tradition, one practice remains central: the taking on of vows (*vrata*) which form *saṃskāras* opposite to those which bind a person. The earliest historical records for these vows date to the time of Parsvanatha, the Sramanic teacher of the eighth century B.C.E. Parsvanatha taught four ways of purification, interpreted by some to require adherence to nonviolence (*ahiṃsā*), truthfulness (*satya*), not stealing (*asteya*), and nonpossession (*aparigraha*).[4] Chastity (*brahmācarya*) was added to these four at a later time. All five vows, designed for the expulsion of negative karmic influences, are foundational to the practice of Patañjali's Yoga (II:30-45) and are found in Buddhism as well.

Adherence to these vows is an act of restructuring negative or afflicted (*kliṣṭa*) residues of past action. By increasing the authenticity and clarity of one's presence in the world through adherence to principles of nonviolence and the like, negative intrusions and illusions are diminished. The self, rather than imputing highest value to the conventional, rather than asserting its unique identity, and rather than repetitiously being attracted to and repulsed by phenomena, assumes a stature of detachment, a witnessing mode that does not disturb the abiding tranquility. The action thus generated goes beyond even what might be considered good: in the highest form of action (*paravairāgyam*) there remains no concern for reentering the realm of grasping (I:15-16); the karma of the yogi is said

4. See Padmanabh S. Jaini, *The Jaina Path of Purification* (Berkeley: University of California Press, 1979), p. 16.

to be other than black, white, or mixed (*YS* IV:7). In this detachment, there is nothing to be done that one is impelled to do; from this arises the power of higher awareness (*citi-śakti*, IV:34). This highest state of human accomplishment, entered into during states of *samādhi* or absorption, is the goal of the karmic purification.

This purified state clearly sets oneself outside the realm of conventional self-driven behavior. In this moment where grasper, grasping, and grasped dissolve (*YS* I:41), a freedom from limiting self-concept emerges. The non-separability of self from other renders one speechless, thingless, without attributes. Consciousness is swept clean; there remains not even a vestige of self to claim the bliss that can be assumed to present. However, other than those rare times when this flash of insight coincides with the point of death, this poignant moment of purification is of limited duration. Even the wise take up life again: "Desire for continuity, arise even among the wise, is sustained by one's own inclination" (*YS* II:9). This same notion is found in the *Bhagavad Gītā*, where Krishna states that "Indeed, no one can exist, even for a moment, without doing some action" (*BG* III:5).[5]

The return to the flow of life (*ṛtu*) from the equipoise of insight provides one of the great ethical challenges of Indian tradition. Having dispelled all that to which one can cling, how does such a liberated person then act in the undefined that ensues? Echoing statements in the *Bhagavad Gītā, Yogavāsiṣṭha,* and other texts, Vijñānabhikṣu's *Sāṃkhyasāra,* written in the late 16th century, states that such a one "neither rejoices nor hates . . . possesses an even and unshaken mind . . . acts without any attachment . . . (is) the same in honor and dishonor."[6] This last attribute shows that this person is still subject to both positive and

5. Srinivasa Murthy, translator, *The Bhagavad Gita* (Long Beach: Long Beach Publications, 1985), p. 16.
6. Gerald James Larson and Ram Shankar Bhattacharya, *Samkhya: A Dualistic Tradition in Indian Philosophy* (Delhi: Motilal Banarsidas 1987), p. 411.

negative assessment by others, but remains grounded in knowledge that the true self is untouched by either. By reentering the world after having stopped the endless round of compulsive activity, a new perspective on life is gained. Things are not seen as discrete unto themselves but are seen as part of an interconnected web. In the *Laṅkāvatāra Sūtra*, a Sanskrit text of the Mahayana Buddhist tradition, a vision is given that links literally all life forms and all actions:

> In the long course of saṃsāra, there is not one among living beings with form who has not been mother, father, brother, sister, son, or daughter, or some other relative. Being connected with the process of taking birth, one is kin to all wild and domestic animals, birds, and beings born from the womb.[7]

This passage provides an eloquent statement regarding the nature of birth and rebirth. Birth is a sacred gift: it allows us to act within the world, to experience the realm of the senses, and to interact with others. As a life form, we are so ancient that we have entered into relationship with every other life form. Our biography is seen not as the story of an individual life or series of lives but as the story of life itself. The details of one's past life pedigree are utterly insignificant in light of the magnitude of one's accumulated experience. The web of relationships and interrelationships makes it difficult if not impossible for one to do harm to any living creature; no sane person would desire to hurt his or her own relative.

An action must be seen in this light as both sequential and horizontal, stemming from and affecting one's own past and future life, but also impacting on the life of others. Rather than adhering strictly and exclusively to a discrete biographical entity, an action extends its influence throughout the web of one's relationships. If one acts violently, and is imprisoned as a result, many people experience harm: entire families are affected, as well as the whole of

---

7. Translated from the Sanskrit edition, Nanjio Bunyiu (Kyoto: Otani, University Press, 1932).

society. Similarly, actions taken by individual scientists affect the society at large. One's intention and behavior extend outward beyond one's immediate circle into the whole of culture. We do not fundamentally differ from those with whom we interact. The literal interpretation of the interrelatedness of all life provides an urgent call for correct and careful action. The concern for one's own well-being extends horizontally and compassionately to others, who are not seen as different from oneself.

The human person in this broadened interpretation of karma is instantiated within the horizons of all reality and experience. The particular forms and manifestations of karma are endless and inherently interesting to those enmeshed therein; the interconnectedness of things is inexhaustible. However, according to the Sramanic analysis, it is fraught with suffering and dissatisfaction due to the clinging nature of afflicted karma. Although the possible forms of attachment are variegated and infinite, the purgation of karma is always the same. Its stoppage through vows and insight halts the wheel regardless of where or how it has turned. Purified consciousness serves as a leveler, bringing a grounded equilibrium that, regardless of how it was approached, restructures later action with its abiding purity. As stated by Patañjali, "the *saṃskāra* born of it (*samādhi*) obstructs other *saṃskāras*" (I:50).

The termination of impure karma does not mean that nothing remains to be done. Rather, it is the compulsion to do seemingly beyond one's power that ceases. Indeed, this approach provides an urgent call for action, for responsibly holding the world together (*lokasaṃgraha*). The renunciation of the fruits of action, often mistakenly associated with shunning the world, is seen here as a call to unafflicted action (*akliṣṭa karma*). As stated in the *Yogavāsiṣṭha:*

There are some persons who, due to their desire, have incapacitated themselves to such an extent that they cannot squeeze their fingers together sufficiently enough to hold water without scattering several drops.
On the other hand, there are some who, by efficacious

actions, take on the responsibility of seas, mountains, cities, and islands, as well as families, for whom even the earth itself could not be too much (*YV* II:4:20).[8]

Persons bound by impure desire find their actions impeded accordingly. For the one of purified action who has gone beyond the limits of overweening self-concern, great responsibility for action is possible and encouraged; society itself benefits from this purified action.

The goal of freedom in action, which requires transcending egocentric behavior, does not necessarily require retreat from the things of the world. In the texts cited above, it can involve an active embrace of the world, not from the perspective of petty biography, but from a vision of the interconnectedness of all life. When distinctions between doer, doing, and done dissolve, and when self is seen to be not different from other, then action of the highest order may proceed. Karma thus construed and enacted does not bind one self but in fact can help to liberate others, just as one's self has been liberated. Specifically, in countering self-centered behavior through the observance of vows, a model for purified action is held out for others to benefit from and to emulate. As one abides in the high ethical standards required in the taking of vows, others receive the positive effects of purified action: violence, deceit, and possessiveness are minimized wherever the holder of vows appears.

Some early scholars have regarded karma to be a fatalistic doctrine, providing justification for suffering in the human life. By contrast, karma in its original intent must be seen dialectically. It in fact supplies some information regarding the mystery of human suffering. But more importantly it is inextricably linked to a worldview that has as its goal liberation from all binding effects of action. By positively and actively cultivating correct behavior, the effects of past action are mitigated and, depending upon one's resolve, eventually overcome. The *Yogavāsiṣṭha* states that "One is to be released by self power from this abyss of worldly

---

8. Christopher Chapple, *Karma and Creativity* (Albany: SUNY Publishers, 1986), pp. 105-106.

existence. Having resorted to creativity and effort, one is released, just as a lion escapes from his cage" (*YV* II:5:15).

In traditional Indian culture as typified in the *Bhagavad Gītā*, the performance of purified action was socially sanctioned in the concept of dharma. Regardless of what was done, if one performed one's societal role as delineated by caste and culture as described in the *Śāstra* literature, a degree of peacefulness was assured for both oneself and the society at large. Karma, regulated through dharma, stabilized existence; self and society were seen as inseparable from one another. One's social and family function simultaneously served as one's identity. Consequently, as Madeleine Biardeau has noted, virtually any human activity provided access to the sacred.[9] Within the cocoon of village Hinduism, the effects of the karma teaching were immediately perceived within a closely governed microcosm.

How might the model of interpenetrating karma and purification bear relevance outside the confines of traditional Indian society? First, regardless of culture, it provides a rejoinder for the human tendency of holding on to an inflexible self-centeredness that promotes greed in oneself and evokes antagonism in others. By learning not to hold too tightly to things or theories, receptivity to the other opens. It also fosters a deeper understanding of self, seeing one's fundamental being as connected with the life force of others. Rather than fixing on the appropriation of things, the concept of self is broadened, strengthening a sense of dignity based on knowledge of that which is inviolable within oneself. The person holds himself or herself accountable for the worlds that he or she creates. Error requires quick attention because one has learned the deleterious effect of delayed response. With the knowledge that "I am not the doer" repeatedly in mind, and bound by the great ethical vows of nonviolence, truthfulness, not stealing, and nonpossessiveness, the consequences of what is

---

9. See Madeleine Biardeau, *Hinduism: The Anthropology of a Civilization* (Delhi: Oxford University Press, 1989) especially chapter three, "Salvation Through Deeds."

undertaken are carefully attended to, benefitting both self and others. From this purified state of consciousness, acts of true creativity arise. Rather than doing what one is impelled to do by *saṃskāra* and *vāsanā*, the one of purity and insight stands prepared to foster new worlds without compulsive reliance on the past. Action thus construed becomes truly a path of purification and liberation.

24

Karma, the Chakras, and Esoteric Yoga

RAY GRASSE

Over the last several decades, an increasing number of Westerners have become familiar with the Eastern concept of *karma*—the spiritual principle of cause-and-effect. Less understood to many of us in the West is the intricate way this idea is associated in some schools of Eastern thought with the esoteric doctrine of the *chakras*. While not exclusive to any one tradition or lineage, this synthesis of ideas has played an especially important role in the Hindu system of Kriya Yoga—a school of yoga perhaps most familiar to Westerners through the teachings and books of Paramahansa Yogananda. What follows is a brief look at some of the central points developed around these ideas within the Kriyic system. Much of this material has not been written down but rather passed by word of mouth from teachers to their pupils.

The Chakras

Simply described, the chakras may be thought of as the essential psycho-physical centers of awareness located along the length of the spine. For the yogi, these chakric centers constitute the core structure of human personality in much the same way that for a physician the biological organs comprise the greater organism of the human body.

While tradition speaks of many thousands of minor chakras, most systems of yoga emphasize seven or eight *major* chakric centers, each with its own psychological and physical correspondences. Since these associations have already been fully covered in countless other books and articles, I will review here only the names and locations of each chakra:

- Chakra one: Muladhara, at the base of the spine.
- Chakra two: Svadhisthana, at the small of the back.
- Chakra three: Manipura, at the level of the navel.
- Chakra four: Anahata, at the level of the heart.
- Chakra five: Vissudha, at the level of the throat.
- Chakra six: Chandra, at the back of the head, near the medulla oblongata.
- Chakra seven: Ajna (or the "third eye"), at the front of the head.
- Chakra eight: Sahaswara (or "thousand-petaled lotus"), at the top of the head.

It is worth mentioning that for some yogis, such as Yogananda, these last two centers are not regarded as fundamentally separate chakras, but in fact as different aspects of the same spiritual center.[1]

The Chakras as Memory Banks

An essential facet of the Kriya Yogic philosophy of the chakras is the idea that the energy fields of each chakra in part represent a kind of "memory bank" or karmic "storage bin." Each center possesses a uniquely different psychological quality, and each in turn relates to the storage of a distinctively different kind of karma. In acting out any thought or action, one therefore sets up a corresponding karmic "charge" that embeds itself in the related chakric field. In expressing anger, for example, a karmic "seed" is planted within the third (Manipura) chakra. Or, if one engages in an act of unselfish love, a corresponding "seed" is planted at the heart (Anahata) chakra.

Frequently, a given action will express the qualities not only of one isolated chakra but of two or more chakras operating in tandem. For instance, one may be engaged in an act of communication, but in a fiery, argumentative way—a combination that suggests a discordant linking of energies between the throat (communication) chakra and the navel (energy/forcefulness) chakra. In a similar way, one may be moved to express feelings of aesthetic beauty, but through some tangible, concrete medium, such as sculpture. Here, we might expect to find a connecting of energies between the fourth (heart, beauty) chakra and the first (root, earth) chakra. In this manner, karmic patterns of considerable complexity involving several different chakras at once may be constellated through time.

The Chakras and Samskaras

Over the course of several lifetimes, an individual may reinforce certain karmic patterns more than others, thus fixing even more firmly within the chakric memory banks those habitual ways of perceiving and responding. These patterns are referred to in Sanskrit as the *samskaras*. For one individual, that samskaric pattern may consist of a deeply ingrained thirst for power that continues to drive his or her actions from lifetime to lifetime. For another it might manifest as a burning resentment toward religious authority. Yoga also identifies habit patterns of a more constructive nature, termed *moksha samskaras*, resulting from spiritual actions or attitudes reinforced over time. In any case, such deeply rooted patterns bind the individual to rigidly prescribed modes of experiencing, and they become, like a broken record, replayed over and over again.

The effect of the negative samskaras on one's chakric system is ultimately debilitating. According to yogic philosophy, with each breath a person breathes, a subtle spiritual energy (or *prana*) is drawn into the person's vehicle from the universe, which is then processed and modified by the different chakric centers. In the case of any powerful samskaras or karmic blockages within the chakric system, this pranic energy becomes blocked or siphoned off in an especially pronounced way, thus sapping the overall vitality of the individual.

At the same time, it is worth noting that even with the

most seemingly negative chakric patterns/obstructions there always exists the potential for the *transmutation* of these energies into constructive directions. By way of illustration, one might think of the ancient Greek orator Demosthenes, who experienced great frustration early in his life over his difficulty to communicate effectively (a fifth-chakra condition), only to eventually overcome that difficulty and develop into one of history's greatest orators. In both cases, the same chakra was involved, but at different levels of expression.

The Cycles of Karma

As pointed out by Arroyo and Greene elsewhere in this volume, in both Eastern and Western schools of esoteric astrology one's personal karmic patterns are said to be reflected in the configurations of one's astrological horoscope. In the words of Yogananda's teacher, Sri Yukteswar, "A child is born at that hour when the celestial rays are in mathematical harmony with his individual karma."[2] For the Kriya Yogi, this suggests on a deeper level that within the patterns of the planets at one's moment of birth we can symbolically glimpse the inner patterns of the chakras as well. Hence, the greater solar system outside becomes a reflection of the chakric "solar system" within.

In associating the outer planets with the inner chakras in this manner, we encounter another important insight, namely, that both the chakras and karma can be linked with certain discernible *cycles*. Having been born within a given moment of time, every karmic seed will eventually "ripen" at some later point, in alignment with the cyclic rhythms of each chakra. At that time, the corresponding chakric center is activated and the latent karmic energy is released from its dormant state into manifestation. By way of illustration, one might think of the way a seed planted in the ground will grow depending on the cycles of the seasons in which it is planted. A seed planted in the middle of winter will grow in a different way from one planted during the middle of spring. And when the timing is finally right in that seasonal cycle, that seed will be "triggered" into its unfoldment. In a similar way, each of the chakras may be said to have its own "seasonal" cycles of ebb and flow (analogous, for the astrologer, to the orbital rhythms/cycles of the planets in their movements relative to the earth). How a given karmic seed will grow therefore depends on when it has been planted, and when the timing of that chakric cycle is right. Together, the different chakras with their varying cycles combine through time to form a continually shifting chorus of karmic and psychological impulses—what is known in esoteric circles as the true, *inner* "music of the spheres."[3]

As these karmic patterns unfold within the chakric unconscious, one may be experiencing corresponding shifts in the various areas one finds oneself responding to externally. For example, with the opening of the third chakra (associated with energy and forcefulness), one may be drawn to sports, exercise, arguments, or even fields of combat. If one were experiencing an opening of the fourth (heart) chakra, one might be attracted toward any symbols or activities related to love, social interaction, money, or the arts—all in the effort to satisfy the "symbolic hunger" awakened by that chakra. Conversely, the *closing off* of either of these two chakras might produce a marked *aversion* to any of these activities.

In this way, a person might move through an entire lifetime simply responding, with Pavlovian regularity, to the shifting energies choreographed by one's chakric system. Indeed, to the yogi, the condition of the average individual may be best described as one of virtual *enslavement* to the chakras, much in the way an unassertive parent may be overpowered by unruly children.

The Transcendence of Karma

If this describes the state of the average man or woman, the goal of esoteric yoga becomes that of *transcending* this condition. Within Kriya Yoga, this liberation is achieved in one of several ways.

At the simplest level, freedom from the compelling influences of karma may be obtained through *mindfulness:* through the continuous, vigilant observation of one's own thought processes. For the average individual the subtle karmic impulses exert their influence at a level below the threshold of awareness. By becoming more aware of these energies as they initially awaken, one gradually defuses their grip on one's behavior. Through attentiveness, the individual no longer reacts blindly to the karmic impulses.

In a somewhat more esoteric vein, we also find in traditions such as Kriya Yoga techniques specifically designed to mitigate the effects of karma through working directly on the energy fields of the spine. Among these, perhaps the most famous is a practice referred to in both Kriya Yoga and Chinese Taoism as the "circulation of the light."[4] Here, the procedure is to visualize a luminous current of energy ascending and descending along the front and back of the spinal axis, usually in coordination with certain mantras or breathing techniques. (Needless to say, such techniques are invariably prescribed under the close supervision of an experienced teacher, to avoid a premature overloading of the subtle spiritual circuits.) Curiously, while in Kriya Yoga the preferred direction of this circulation is up the front and down the back, in certain other schools of mystical thought (such as Taoism) we find exactly the opposite approach, with the directing of energies *down* the front and *up* the back. In either case, the values associated with such techniques remain largely the same, and are generally described as five-fold in nature:

1) To consciously regenerate and revitalize the energies of the mind/body vehicle.

2) To consciously speed up the pace of spiritual evolution. On their own, the Kriyic currents in the spine are said to rotate around the spinal axis one full cycle every year, in correspondence with the rotation of the sun around the heavenly zodiac. By consciously rotating the spinal currents in deep meditation, one is able to speed this process up enormously. Yogananda states: "One thousand Kriya practiced in eight-and-a-half hours gives the yogi, in one

day, the equivalent of one thousand years of natural evolution: 350,000 years of evolution in one year."[5]

3) To center and balance the scattered energies of one's entire being into the central axis of the spinal column. The underlying principle here is that one's karmic energies lie primarily along the *outer fringes* of the chakric system, within the location of the ascending and descending currents running *adjacent* to the spine (what the yogis have termed the *ida* and *pingali*). As long as one's awareness is directed off to either this right or left channel (as it is in the case of most men and women in their normal waking or sleeping lives), one remains subject to the influences of karma, and to the compelling influences of one's horoscope.[6] But if one is able to balance one's awareness within the very center of the spine (the *sushumnic* channel), one becomes free of those karmic influences. While they may still present themselves to consciousness, one no longer compulsively responds to them.

4) To both neutralize and "roast" the karmic seeds within the spinal system. This is accomplished both through the reversing of what Kriya Yoga claims to be the natural polarity of the spinal currents, as well as through the burning off of karmic seeds by the heat generated through the Kriyic currents.

5) To assist in the lifting of the *kundalini* all the way up through the spinal levels into the primary spiritual centers within the head, ultimately moving through the five-pointed star located at the center of the Ajna chakra, into the domain of pure self-awareness; for while the ascent of kundalini may occur in a purely spontaneous way, yoga asserts that one may gently facilitate this movement through certain techniques.

Conclusion

To summarize, while an individual in the course of an average life may be subject to the influences of karma, through an understanding of the science of karma and the chakras one can not only soften the effects of karma, but ultimately transcend the karmic process itself, thus breaking free of the cycle of compulsory rebirth. Having balanced and ascended the chakric ladder, one becomes fixed in a condition of balanced self-awareness, free to re-enter the world with its myriad forces, neither motivated by karma nor generating new karma.

References

1. As related in a private letter from Yogananda to his student, Shelly Trimmer.
2. *Autobiography of a Yogi*, by Paramahansa Yogananda, Self-Realization Fellowship, Los Angeles, 1971, p. 168.
3. For a slightly different and more elaborate discussion of how karma is activated within the chakras, see Goswami Kriyananda's *The Spiritual Science of Kriya Yoga*, the Temple of Kriya Yoga, Chicago, 1985, p. 240.
4. Yogananda, p. 245. See also, *The Secret of the Golden Flower*, by Richard Wilhelm. Harcourt Brace Jovanovich, 1962. p. 30-35.
5. Ibid., p. 246.
6. As related to the author by Sri Shelly Trimmer.

25
Karma and Cosmos

LAURENCE J. BENDIT

Part One

It is very easy to write or speak glibly about the doctrine of karma, calling it the law of cause and effect, pithily stated in human terms by the Gospel saying that "whatsoever a man soweth, so shall he also reap," and so on. The statements are true. But in order to understand their deeper aspects we need to see the matter against a much wider background, that of the cosmos itself. This cosmos is a whole, including everything from the very greatest to the most minute—remembering too that our own conception of great and small is limited by the horizons of our mental capacities, that is, the mind which perceives, at this present stage of the evolutionary pattern. This, in turn, means a mind only partly developed and operating, as a rule, far short of its latent capabilities.

Thus, before we come to karma itself, we should consider a few points relating to the universe we live in. To begin with, we need to see it as a single unit, in which anything occurring in any part of it influences, in however minute a degree, the rest. A person jumping on the Earth, an electron shifting its orbit around an atomic nucleus, a star or galaxy exploding a thousand lightyears away send a ripple of some kind throughout the physical universe. And, equally, a mental act of thought, feeling, perception affects the whole of the psychic or mental and perhaps also the spiritual world.

This whole, however, operates within its fields as if it

were subdivided—"granulated," to use Teilhard's phrase—
into an infinite, or at least indefinite number of "monads."
A monad can be defined, in line with both Leibnitz, H. P.
Blavatsky, and others, as consisting of a nucleus within a
field of matter or energies, contained by a "semipermeable
membrane" or enclosing skin which at once connects it
and separates it from its surroundings. Such a monad may
be infinitely small (e.g., an electron) or on as vast a spatial
scale as the universe itself. Typically, a single cell such as
one of yeast shows us the basic monadic pattern: the nucleus
is its creative center, holding the genetic material; the
protoplasm is the surrounding field, while the outer membrane allows a controlled circulation of material between
the inner body of the cell and the fluid in which it lives.

In the *Stanzas of Dzyan* in H. P. Blavatsky's *The Secret Doctrine*, the "skin" is called by the picturesque name of "the
Ring Called Pass-Not" or, simply, the "Ring-Pass-Not."
It is evident that each monad, great as a cluster of galaxies,
small as an electron, is related to a hierarchy of other monads
on its own scale or level; greater (as a cell is in an animal
or vegetable body); or itself enclosing a number of smaller
ones (atoms, molecules, etc.). On this pattern the Creation
is built, or so it seems to us.

Before proceeding with our study it will be well if we
establish firmly in the back of our minds that any such
study can only present us with a relatively real picture of
things. Owing to the limitations of our minds, we never
see things as they are, but, at best, build up a picture more
or less closely related to the actual truth. We do not see the
truth itself. The importance of this will become apparent
as we go on and it becomes clear that no understanding
of our subject can arise until we are capable of combining
at least two seemingly divergent forms of mental approach
to it. In these the science of causality, which is our traditional
Western mode of thinking, becomes wedded to another
form of science, where synchronicity—the impact of events
on the immediate here and now—is the basis of another
kind of philosophy. The latter is mainly derived from
Chinese Taoism which, as it were, cuts at right angles across

the linear, time-track habit of the West, adding a new dimension to our way of thinking. This gives a stereoscopic view instead of one that is two-dimensional and flat.

This can best be illustrated when we consider the created and manifested universe which is our present home, even from the level of the physical plane and without going into the less defined and seemingly less organized realm of the psyche or nonphysical. For there are two schools of thought among cosmologists today. One sees Creation as an Act (Latin: *Actus* or *Actum*, something done and achieved) in time, hence as having a beginning and an end. Indian thought tells of a "Day of Brahma" or *Manvantara*, lasting so many million years (presumably earth-years). This follows the time-track and is in line with those modern astronomers who see the universe beginning with a "big bang" and gradually running down. But the other school, observing stars exploding, "black holes" appearing in outer space, nebulae condensing into stars—and that within our own lifetime—conceive the universe as in a state of constant becoming: creation, destruction, re-creation which might go on indefinitely. The latter tunes in with the other kind of science, that of Taoism.

One is tempted to take sides, to accept one theory as true, the other as false. But the occultist needs to develop the kind of mind which is able to see that both approaches are true; since time is part of the *maya* or self-created "illusion" by which we live, there is no fundamental contradiction between the synchronistic, Taoist view and that of India and Western science. Together they can serve us in our search; one alone hides Reality and gives us only a blinkered, partial view of things-as-they-are, in truth.

So we can consider that what we call monads are in a constant state of being created, dissolved, and re-created all the time. They can be looked upon as existing off the line of time, as beginningless and endless, or as permanent entities. They exist, moreover, on every time scale, from the momentary one of certain subatomic particles to the apparent everlastingness of a galaxy, or, if not a galaxy, of the physical universe as a whole. The question is one of our ability to measure time with our mental processes. The same applies to the space-scale as between an electron and a cluster of stars. We do not know in any absolute way what either time or space may be. We know them only as we glimpse them at any NOW and HERE, in the "intersection of the timeless moment."

This, however, is to think only of the physical aspect of a monad, or of those monads which have physical existence. There is also the factor of consciousness, of the fullness or otherwise of the expression of the life within each one. We can, here, speak only in relation to humanity, the nearest kind of monadic unit to ourselves, and here we believe, rightly or wrongly, that on the evolutionary ladder we are the first to have the potentiality of self-identity, both of being a self-monad, and of knowing ourselves as self-monads. Who can say whether the center of a solar system or even a planet—what we call a god if not God—has anything like what we call a Self and is conscious of it-Self? It would be surprising if Selfhood were limited to such cosmic creatures as earthlings, but we do not know directly, even from the deepest mystical experience centering round our own selves; even if it shows us how much more there is beyond that Self, how much of the Divine remains unknown and unknowable so that it is called the Void and, equally aptly, the Plenum—the opposite of Voidness.

I-ness is the center of a human's Being, known in more technical terms as the *Atman* operating through *Manas*, Pure Mind, within the "Ring-Pass-Not" of the physical body during physical incarnation. It is individual at root, yet one has to remember also that it is incorporated in the context of the cosmos as a whole; it is made up of the same material as this cosmos, planned on the same archetypal blueprint as every other monad, though the "protoplasmic" elements within its field will be differently arranged and will differ in their power as against one another, because of the individuality which is its nucleus. Morever, these elements may, at any given time, operate in different patterns from their momentary and passing state outside the "Ring-Pass-Not" of an individuality: from what we call

Nature, or the world outside us. This differential, however embryonic, in some measure alienates each of us from Nature and gives us a new relationship to that world. This in turn brings into being a certain stress, a field of force between the individual and "crude, unaided Nature" which, like any other energy field, is at least potentially creative of new things.

This, at least in the definition I shall adopt, is where karma starts. No self, no karma. Introduce self and that self begins to interact actively with its environment, and that interaction is karma. There are some who speak of animals generating karma but, if this is the case, the term must be further extended to include all forms of action and reaction in any part of the universe. This is logical, but then the idea of karma is equated with the whole field of causality, even if this is entirely mechanical and devoid of any kind of consciousness or self-determination. It seems better to use the word in the narrower sense, as applied to the entity which has at least some degree of identity as a self. At the same time, such an idea has the value of making us realize the total integration of all levels of the world we live in, in terms of universally applicable law. The law of karma is, in the scientific sense, nothing but a "special case" within this universal law.

The idea of humanity being integral with the world in which it lives bring us to a most important consideration, which takes us back to our ideas on cosmology. Here we can find at least three languages in which we can start thinking thoughts about this universe, each of which embraces the seemingly conflicting pictures presented earlier.

First let us look at the statement made in a kind of shorthand in the *Stanzas of Dzyan*. These—said by H. P. Blavatsky to come from what may be the most ancient document in the world still in existence, hidden away in some remote library—are so obscure that either a highly developed intuition, or such immense commentaries as are contained in Blavatsky's major book are necessary to make them explicit.

We then have science where, at least as regards the physical world, vast progress has been made, especially since the day of Einstein. Surprisingly enough, this has resulted in showing us that matter is not really there at all, that at best something *may* be *somewhere in space at a particular moment of time*, but that is not so much certain as *probable*. (Incidentally, this discovery has brought some people back to a religious sense of the numinous which no amount of scriptural reading or theology could do. It has also brought into existence a new sacred language, that of higher mathematics, intelligible only to its initiates.)

More open to us, because closer to the ordinary mind, is the third approach, that which comes through the study of myth. Here we have a pantheon of beings supposedly immortal and superior to humans. These equate with celestial bodies, stars, constellations, and planets, and also with various earth functions or features such as sky, sea, water, earth, and so on. In effect it would seem that when modern science speaks of energy, matter, spin, inertia, mass, gravity, speed, and so on, it really gives new names to the gods. These gods (in the case of the Greeks especially) not only interfere in human affairs, but are often shown in conflict among themselves. In particular there is the strange idea of the displacement of the "old gods" by a new hierarchy, when the Titans, ruled by Kronos, were ousted by Kronos's upstart son Zeus, and relegated to a remote sphere away from earth and its humanity: a story which can be taken to suggest the stresses and strains inevitable when a solar system breaks out of a galaxy, a planet from a central sun— and, it may be added, when a humanity or human monad becomes differentiated from the mass life of the biosphere and is individualized.

The relevance of this to the doctrine of karma is that humans are made up of precisely the same "material"—i.e., forces and energies in one terminology, or of the very same gods in another—as the universe itself. In other words, the pantheon itself is not only outside a human but also within. And, like the external world, it is active and dynamic at all levels from the physical "up" or "inward."

In the external world the gods may be said to be organized

around a center which we call God. In humanity they cluster around the nucleus of Self, where they are governed by the same laws that govern the surrounding realms. But the effect of Self may be strong or weak, and so exerts more, or less, influence on the conflicting gods within its field; and conflicting they certainly are, until we learn how to bring them into order, which is the task of what we know as religion and its disciplines, simple or sophisticated.

Meanwhile, the personality which is made up of these forces interacts with its surroundings and generates karma. Our personal reaction to this is to find some effects pleasant and we call them good, or unpleasant, and we call them bad. In reality, karma is neither good nor bad; it is simply karma and is exactly suited to the causes which created it. Indeed, the working of the karmic law may be likened to that of a celestial computer. There is a tradition of certain agencies known as the *Lipika* or Recording Angels. They do far more than keep ledgers of our acts. They are constantly being programmed with new information which, added to the material stored in their "memory," feeds back on this and alters the resulting impact from moment to moment. This result is in perfect dynamic balance from instant to instant. There is perfect justice throughout the whole universe.

All of this suggests that karma is a somewhat mechanistic process paralleled in Newton's famous law that "to every action there is an equal and opposite reaction." And so it is. Effect follows cause, inevitably. But it is obvious that in many cases a karmic reaction is not immediate, that many "wicked flourish like the green bay tree" and die in full enjoyment of the results of their misdeeds. But karma is not a fixed quantity like the debits or credits entered in an account book. It is made interestingly elastic because of the complexity of factors involved. We have not only the cyclic workings of the mechanical cosmos, we have other and more personal factors less mathematically exact to be placed along the time-track. One can forecast an eclipse or a certain stellar configuration, but one cannot accurately forecast what a living entity such as collective humanity, may do, and so what effects will result, let us say, at the time of some physical or meteorological event.

To a greater or less extent, individuals are involved in wars, revolutions, earthquakes so long as they are human: they seem to have no more free will or ability to choose their fate than the animals have to act of their own volition in the face of a cataclysmic storm or drought. But this is to forget that a human, in addition to involvement in the collective biosphere, is also a developing individual, within the "Ring-Pass-Not" of his or her personality. Morever, unless the intuitions of the multitudes are only wishful thinking and not based on inner knowledge, it would seem that some form of human individuality is not restricted to time. Following its own cycles, it returns to earth many times before it can become truly free of the "wheel of rebirth," after which it determines for itself whether or not it will make use of a new body.

In the meantime, the vast array of cosmic forces is working out its own pattern. In it individuals have their own unique place, and it may be that certain karmic forces do not come into manifest operation until the "slot" in time arrives into which a person fits. It is only as the inner Self takes charge of the personal field that a gradual growth of freedom of choice and will comes into view and modifies the resultant of karmic effects, at any given moment.

We should not think of karma as a fixed quantity so much as a constantly rebalancing and moving pattern impinging on an individual at each moment of time; and, further, that it is one in which individuality plays an increasing part.

This new turn of events is known both to psychologists and to all kinds of religious teachers or gurus as a stage in individual self-realization. It starts when pupils or students come consciously in touch with what I have called the pantheon within, begin to know "how they tick," and bring the conflicting elements into harmony and order so that they work together instead of as a warring and self-negating mob.

Now, we may say, the processes of karma become reversed.

In the past, individuals have been at their mercy, a more or less passive victim of their own acts. Now, however, through what is taking place within, one becomes increasingly able to alter the effects of these past acts on the immediate situation. The gods within become harmonized and no longer virtually cancel themselves out in conflict, but like a well drilled team work in increasing unison, so that the individual personality brings from within itself a new force which plays into the external pattern of karmic effects. To put it provocatively, the active Self remakes the past from its operational point in the immediate present—something clearly unthinkable if one's mind sees life only from the angle of linear and sequential time. Yet it is not only believed but known to be so, by the mind which can effectively hold two views: causality and what, for lack of a Western word, we call Taoism or synchronistic, co-incidental science. (The word "co-incidental" designates the meaningful incidence at a given time and place of the various factors involved in any situation.)

The co-incidence of outer and inner events and situations can perhaps best be illustrated by reference to the horoscope of a newborn child. For despite what one scholar described as its "intrinsic improbability," astrology, properly used and understood, has proved to many intelligent people—including C. G. Jung—that a chart of the heavens at the time of a birth can give endless insight into the child's latent character. And, later in life, because the relation of the stars and planets have changed, it will help to indicate what concatenated "influences" are at work on and in him at any time. This does not mean that individuals are fated from birth to be the slave of their nativity, because, as I have said, the nuclear Self is not a passive onlooker in the development of a character, but plays an increasingly powerful part in the process, as one becomes self-realizing and self-actualizing.

So while it is true that, say, a "badly aspected" Saturn may lead to a frustrated, held-down personality, or Uranus may indicate the likelihood of upheavals and changes, the wise, by understanding *and accepting* themselves in a positive manner, will discover how, by cooperating with the forces in the personality—the gods both within and outside oneself —they can change their whole attitude toward life and find harmony and happiness. Saturn-bound persons, when they have performed the magic act of self-acceptance, may find the most obstinate obstacles melt away in a manner which seemed impossible so long as they feared, rejected, or tried to escape from them. Uranians may find a quiet harmony coming into their lives. It is as if the change inside the personality also changes the environment. Or, physically sick or disabled persons may find out how to live happily with their disability, "staying with it" instead of fighting it, and so halving its pain. Victor Frankl, in *Man in Search of Meaning*, points out that the inalienable freedom to *choose one's attitude of mind* persists, even in a Nazi prison camp.

How to bring about this change is an individual matter. But in general terms it comes about as a result of any kind of yoga, including that of psychological analysis of the right kind. The key to it is self-knowledge and self-understanding through deep self-examination.

Happiness is not found by trying to escape suffering but by realizing that it is something one has evoked by one's own acts. So also is pleasure: one should enjoy ("find joy in") the pleasant things in life, and avoid mortification (to mortify means to kill) from the detached central point which is Self in the deeper sense, not the reflections of that Self in the desire-field of personal ego.

Thus it would seem that the "Man of Tao," or Confucian "Superior Man," the true yogi or rishi, mystic or saint, is one who, in whatever terms, or by whatever method—whether it be meditation or psychological analysis—brings order into the house of the personality. Such persons become arbiters of their own acts. They will still, since they are human, "generate" karma; but not only will they, step by step, learn how to deal with what lies behind them in terms of time; they will find the way to resolve, at the existential instant in which it occurs, any new karma which they create. Then the backlog, if any, shrinks until it disappears altogether and they are free. They "rule their stars," not by attempting to force their will on the universe, but by learning its laws and becoming its completely obedient servant. In this way, as against that of the prekarmic, premental animal, they will now work from the center of their being as self-aware, self-understanding individuals, Perfected Humans.

To sum up on a practical level, the active, self-actualizing person needs to realize that:

(a) Karma is geared into the whole cosmic process;

(b) It represents the personal and individual impact of this process on oneself;

(c) It is selfhood which initiates the chain of cause and effect which we call karma. This selfhood may be strong or weak, depending on the degree to which one has ordered and taken control of the forces within the personal field. If it is weak, persons are carried more or less passively by the ebb and flow of the collective forces around them. If it is strong, they step-by-step take charge of their own destiny.

(d) Selfhood or self-identity is acquired, not by attempts to force matters into the shape one believes one desires, but by understanding and self-awareness. For as one not only knows but, as Teilhard puts it, learns to see oneself in the process of knowing, what has been an indirect, more or less ineffective impact of the true Self on the environment becomes more direct and cooperative with the total cosmic process we know as Nature or God.

(e) To do this well requires a mind developed sufficiently to integrate what, in one aspect, is the duality of the ordinary science of causality with that of what Jung has called synchronicity, or *Tao*.

(f) When this occurs it is as if the Self, as it were, remakes the past from the immediate *now*, insofar as it changes the immediate impact of ancient causes on the present. The result is modified by the Self at the moment that past impinges on it at any instant of time.

(g) This, clearly, from the immediate instant, influences the future: for the wise person, ideally, deals in a positive way with events as they occur and leaves no backlog of unresolved material to be carried forward. There are no new causal residues to bring out effects at a later date, and the individual becomes free in the deeper sense, ready for the great step which is known as entry into *Nirvana, Moksha,* liberation, or salvation.

(h) Such principles, even if only partially understood and practiced, have an immediate practical lesson for us in our daily lives. For they show us that karma is no accident, but that, in its exactness, we are born at a particular time and a particular place because, whether we like it or not, it is the only proper one, and so the best for us at the time. This should make us think very carefully, before we try (as so many do today) to uproot ourselves from our own culture and embrace an alien one, seeking to become Hindus or Zenists or Sufis when we are born in the West; or, in reverse, trying to turn into Europeans or Americans when born in the East. The result is rarely a success, because would-be converts are in effect fugitives from the life they "earned" karmically. They have run away from reality into what, psychologically, is fantasy, however genuine the actual religion or creed they adopt. In general (though there are a few exceptions among individuals who have not fallen into the trap which awaits most of these transvestites), the step they have taken in uprooting themselves from the culture where they belong is backward from, not forward to, Reality. Sooner or later they will have to discover that spiritual freedom is to be found at home, not in a foreign land, however seemingly romantic and "holy" it is supposed to be: to the one who has the eyes to see, London, Los Angeles, and Paris are just as spiritual and holy as Varanasi, Mecca, and Jerusalem.

There is another lesson to be learned from karma, which we would do well to introduce into our way of thinking, if not yet into our speech. It is becoming increasingly important today when men and women vie with one another for sexual equality. It is to be hoped that at the back of this there lies a profound intuition, that we are in reality neither men nor women but human monads, and as such

at once sexless and also having the qualities of both masculinity and femininity. But the "Ring-Pass-Not" of the monad
is, in each incarnation, sexed as either masculine or feminine;
and, since the incarnation represents the fruits of karmic
experience, there is a reason why the Self is, for a while,
embodied in a male or female body.

The task of would-be wise individuals is to live with
their sex, learning the deeper meaning of masculinity or
femininity, while at the same time not diminishing or
reneging on the spiritual and mental qualities of the other
sex but bringing them into play from within. This integrates
the masculine or the feminine "unconscious" with the
conscious and operative sexuality of the outer garment of
that unconsciousness. This is a fact recognized by the
better kind of depth psychologist, notably by Jung and his
colleagues, where the man's "anima" or the woman's
"animus" is taken as an important "archetypal image" in
every self-realizing student. A "man" should live like a man
while using his feminine intuitions and feelings; a "woman"
should be able to be feminine without either weakening
her masculinity or trying to become dominant and "masculine" in the wrong way.

This, of course, is a far cry from saying that we should
not study other philosophies and religions. On the contrary, the wider our scope the better, provided we add to
our mental knowledge the supraintellectual function of
understanding, and thus acquire wisdom. What is harmful
to the individual is the emotive quality of thinking that,
by becoming outwardly a Hindu swami or Buddhist monk
or Japanese Zenist, one is liberating oneself from one's
karma. At the same time, we need to discover that the liberation which the serious and realistic seeker is trying to reach
can be found anywhere, any time, when the student is inwardly ready. It is probably so near that we cannot touch
it because we reach too far, so obvious that we cannot see
it; and, moreover, it may even be that we have already
touched it but, with minds full of doctrines, mental concepts, rites and observances, we cloud over the vision our
inward eye has given us. Rituals, meditations, disciplines

and the like may help, but they do so only for a time. After that they become clogs in the wheel of progress, addictions as to any other drug. It takes courage to drop all the contents of one's mind, accumulated through aeons of time, and to proceed unfettered into the darkness, relying not even upon a nameless and faceless god, but upon one's own individual Self. Yet, I believe, such is the way in which the individual finds release and mastery over the wheel of rebirth and of karma.

Part Two

There is more to be said about karma than I have written above. For it would seem that the goal of every human being can be summarized by saying that *nirvana, moksha,* liberation, salvation can be reached only when persons are karma-free, that is, when there is no backlog of causes playing into their present state; when they are, so to speak, completely gathered up into the immediate *now.* But so long at least as they are incarnate, their very existence, their presence in the manifested universe, means that they are generating karma at every instant and by every act, physical or psychic. The difference between such persons and the rest is, however, that they have found the means to resolve this karma at the very instant it is generated, and they pass from moment to moment in time.

In principle, this means that they have learned to attune themselves absolutely to the cosmic pattern as it is at that moment, so that there is no kind of stress or conflict between what is taking place within the individual monadic field and what is happening in the universe as a whole.

Whether we look upon the universe as proceeding through time from past to future, or whether we see it as a constant dynamic state in which creation and destruction (or better, resolution) are always at work together, each fleeting moment can be seen as an integrated whole of which we are a part. Our job, then, is to bring ourselves into step with the universal rhythm and to keep pace with its forward movement. This is the whole purpose behind what we know as

religion and should be the aim of all religious creeds
and disciplines.

In other words, there is a personal and individual impact
of karma, in the greater sense of movement in the cosmos,
on our own individual monadic field. This field, as I have
suggested, centers round its own "sun" or "god," the true
Self, and it is because this Self is not yet in command of
its field that humans find themselves in trouble, out of
tune with the world in which they live. They will suffer
for this until harmony is restored, not because God punishes,
but because free will enables them to act differently from
other monads, both on their own level and at the levels
which contain them (e.g., the biosphere of the Earth, the
solar system, and so on). Erich Fromm said that the first
genuinely human act was when, in Eden, Adam and Eve
disobeyed Nature (God) and asserted themselves in such a
way that they cut across the laws of prehumanity, thus
beginning the long karmic road.

Humanity's task is thus to restore itself to a state of nature,
of harmony with the world, to return to God—without,
however, losing the precious things acquired during
"estrangement." One of these is individuality, the sense
of Selfhood, which distinguishes the human from the
prehuman animal.

This Selfhood, however, has to become something very
different from the little selfhood of the psychological ego,
which is constantly obtruding itself and interfering with
events in daily life, demanding the fulfillment of instinc-
tive desire.

The process of extracting Self from egoism is the aim of
every true religious school. Moreover, as students move
along the paths laid down by these religions, they have
step by step to find their own individual discipline and
proceed alone and unaided except from within.

It is here that the modern schools of the deepest of depth
psychology can be of immense use, because (thanks to
Freud, however much we may disagree with his interpretations) they teach us to confront ourselves, and suggest
the means of "getting at" the unknown side of ourselves

which we call the unconscious. The same could, in theory, be done by a direct study of the forces, psychic and physical, named by science but known more intimately to us as archetypal images of gods, heroes, symbols. A valuable way to begin on this way is that adumbrated by Freud in his *Psychopathology of Everyday Life*—even if we find his preoccupation with the physical body inadequate and tiresome. For he draws our attention to the meaningfulness of mistakes, slips of the tongue, and the "irrational" world of dreams and fantasies. We find meaning in these things when we learn to study them; and they will start us on the discovery of this inner field around the Self, the unconscious. One needs to go through this state; it leads on to what are really the grass roots of humanity's actual quality.

Now we begin to meet the essential Human, in the form of what Jung called the archetypal images: the gods of the pantheon within us, figures of power and charismatic value which are capable, as we allow them to operate on and in us, of carrying us from the realm of *the gods* to that of *God*, the numinous Source of all things. We are, in other words, entering the world of myth, that is, of the deeper truths about ourselves and our origins as human entities. Myth has been said by Annie Besant, as well as by Jung, to be the true history of humanity, both individual and as a species, and to represent our attempts at spiritual self-realization in the form of dramatic stories.

As we learn about myth as applied to each of us individually, we begin to take control over our destinies, i.e., of our relationship to the cosmic myth which is the universe as a whole. This is worth realizing, as it is clearly much closer to our daily experience to think in terms of myth and of gods and goddesses, of symbols and sacramental acts and objects, than to use the languages of physics and mathematics. For while they are equally valid, they are much more remote for the ordinary individual.

Each of us, as a monad, is the expression of a personal and individual myth; it is for each of us to fulfill and complete that myth in terms of the personal, subjective drama we touch in our dreams, visions, inner experiences. For as we work it out, we bring our nuclear Self into its true place as the center of our personal lives. Also, by ordering the "gods" within us, we catch up, as it were, with the cosmic situation as it moves from moment to moment in constant flow, and so find at once complete freedom, the "liberation" so often spoken of today. But, paradoxically, we do so by becoming completely obedient and at one with the world we call external to our personal monadic selves. This is to say, in another way, that we free ourselves from the law of karma by becoming part of the universal karma which is the very life of a manifested Godhead.

What it amounts to is that we cannot know God without knowing and understanding the gods: those gods which are both cosmic forces and forces within our own monadic sphere. We may know all the teachings about the universe (I use the word "teachings" rather than "fact" because most of the facts about the cosmos are quite beyond our immediate experience, and so have to be taken as unproved hypotheses), but they will have little value or significance to us unless we know our own home-self, our own domestic gods, the actors in the individual myth which is each one of us. The fact that (like the monadic principle outlined earlier in this article) this myth is based on the same blue-print (*see* comparative mythology and its exegesis in psychological and religious texts) with the same basic figures of hero, villain, demonic forces, redeemer, etc., does not detract from this principle. The pantheon is in us, but it functions in its own individual way, this way being linked with the general pattern exhibited in the universe at any moment of time.

As these gods represent karma in a cosmic sense, so do they represent karma in relation to our own individuality. Liberation and *nirvana* ("the cessation of error and of strife") come when the individual monadic pattern harmonizes with the cosmic one, and so becomes integrated with it. We are then "united with God the Father" and so become the pattern of the universal Christ or Buddha.

QUEST BOOKS
are published by
The Theosophical Society in America,
Wheaton, Illinois 60189–0270,
a branch of a world organization
dedicated to the promotion of the unity of
humanity and the encouragement of the study of
religion, philosophy, and science, to the end that
we may better understand ourselves and our place in
the universe. The Society stands for complete
freedom of individual search and belief.
In the Classics Series well-known
theosophical works are made
available in popular editions.
For more information
write or call.
1-708-668-1571

We publish books on:

Health and Healing • Eastern Mysticism
Philosophy • Reincarnation • Religion
Science • Transpersonal Psychology
Yoga and Meditation

Other books of possible interest include:

At the Feet of the Master *by "Alcyone"*
J. Krishnamurti's precepts for right living

Beyond Individualism *by Dane Rudhyar*
From ego-centeredness to higher consciousness

Cayce, Karma and Reincarnation *by I.C. Sharma*
Similarity between philosophies of Cayce and India

The Choicemaker *by E. Howes & S. Moon*
Our need to make choices as vital to our evolution

Commentaries on Living *by J. Krishnamurti*
Series 1, 2 & 3. Dialogue on many aspects of living

The Great Awakening *by Robert Powell*
Comparison of Krishnamurti and Zen philosophies

Opening of the Wisdom Eye *by The Dalai Lama*
The path of enlightenment through Buddhism

Spectrum of Consciousness *by Ken Wilber*
Psychotherapy; non-duality of spirit; value of religions

Still Forest Pool *ed. by J. Kornfield & P. Breiter*
The living philosophy of Achaan Chah, forest master

A Way to Self Discovery *by I.K. Taimni*
Way of life for serious aspirants of esoteric wisdom

Western Approach to Zen *by Christmas Humphreys*
Zen Buddhism adapted to an Occidental culture

Available from:

The Theosophical Publishing House
P.O. Box 270, Wheaton, Ilinois 60189-0270